POLITICAL CENSORSHIP OF THE ARTS AND THE PRESS IN NINETEENTH-CENTURY EUROPE

By the same author

POLITICAL REPRESSION IN MODERN AMERICA: From 1870
  to the Present
POLITICAL REPRESSION IN NINETEENTH-CENTURY
  EUROPE

Political Censorship of the Arts and the Press in Nineteenth-Century Europe

Robert Justin Goldstein
Professor of Political Science
Oakland University, Rochester, Michigan

St. Martin's Press New York

First published in the United States of America in 1989

Printed in the People's Republic of China

ISBN 0–312–02470–3

Library of Congress Cataloging-in-Publication Data
Goldstein, Robert Justin.
    Political censorship of the arts and the press in nineteenth-
    century Europe / Robert Justin Goldstein.
          p.   cm.
    Bibliography: p.
    Includes index.
    ISBN 0–312–02470–3: $35.00 (est.)
    1. Censorship—Europe—History—19th century. 2. Freedom of the
press—Europe—History—19th century. 3. Arts—Censorship—Europe—
History—19th century. 4. Europe—Politics and
government—1789–1900.   I. Title.
Z658.E85G64 1989
323.44′5—dc 19   88–23372
                                                                  CIP

In memory of my mother,
Fannie Tepper Goldstein (1901–86),
and Plato Goldstein (1969–86)

Contents

List of Plates

Plate 1: In 1898, after Prussian officials decreed a ban on the sale of the German caricature journal *Simplicissimus* in state railway stations, the magazine published this cartoon satirising the authorities' exaggerated fear of caricatures. It shows railway officials removing *Simplicissimus* from a train station. The journal is dripping blood and is so dangerous that the railway officials hold it at arm's length with a huge pair of tongs. (Photograph courtesy of Michigan State University Library, East Lansing.)

Plate 2: The Portuguese caricature journal *A Parodia* frequently was censored by the authorities during the 1900–7 period. In this illustration, which appeared on 24 December 1902, a censor is shown as finding an objectionable 'allusion' in every possible illustration proposed by *A Parodia*. As shown at the bottom, only a completely blank page pleases him. (Photograph courtesy of Library of Congress, Washington.)

Plate 3: Censors in France could approve caricatures as submitted, forbid them entirely or approve them only with changes. On 3 August 1873 the French caricature journal *L'Eclipse* appeared with the drawing on the right by André Gill of a man carrying a barrel labelled 'forgetfulness'. (Photograph courtesy of Northwestern University Library, Evanston, Illinois.) In the original drawing, on the left (published in Charles Fontane, *André Gill* [Paris, 1927]), Adolphe Thiers, the recently deposed president of France, was depicted in the barrel. With this crucial element effaced from the published caricature by the censorship, Gill's message that Thiers' service to France was being forgotten was completely destroyed.

Plate 4: In mid-nineteenth-century France, all living subjects of a caricature had to give their approval before they could be the subjects of a published drawing. On 20 February 1870, *L'Eclipse* published the caricature on the right (photograph courtesy of Northwestern University Library), with a blank face where caricaturist André Gill had originally planned to depict the reactionary journalist Louis Veuillot, as is indicated in the drawing on the left (which was published in Fontane's *André Gill*, 1927). Veuillot refused to give his authorisation, but the text accompanying the published drawing made clear who the missing man was, as it referred to the 'gloomy face which the censorship has forced us to cut' as that of an 'elegant journalist' whose name was known by *L'Univers*, Veuillot's newspaper.

Plate 5: Caricature journals which suffered from censorship developed a bitter hatred for that institution. This hatred was brilliantly expressed by the French caricature journal *Le Sifflet* on 14 November 1875, which shows censors at work. They are trying to censor *Le Sifflet* but cut off each others' heads with their huge scissors by mistake. The caricature is ironically captioned 'Terrible Accident!!!'. (Photograph courtesy of the British Newspaper Library, Colindale, London.)

Plate 6: The brief abolition of censorship of caricature in 1905 allowed Russian artists to express their disdain for repression of the press in Russia. On the left, the journal *Zhupel* ('Bugbear') depicts censorship as a horrible creature wearing a military cap subjecting an issue to the most minute scrutiny. On the right, *Zarnitzky* ('Summer Lightning') portrays a print-shop barred and padlocked by the authorities. (Photographs courtesy of University of Michigan Library, Ann Arbor.)

Plate 7: The brutal repression of the 1905 Russian Revolution by Tsar Nicholas II made him a favourite target of caricature journals throughout Europe (see Plate 15, below). On the left, the Viennese journal *Der Floh* of February 1905 portrays caricature journals such as *Simplicissimus* of Germany, *Le Rire* of France and itself as thanking the tsar for providing them with such good material. On the right, the German journal *Ulk* of 26 January 1906 satirises the continuing censorship in Russia by showing the tsar's children presenting him with a blacked-out copy of *Ulk*. The children ask him, 'What could this be?', and he responds, 'Me.' *Ulk* informed its readers that to save the tsarist authorities trouble, it had already taken the precaution of inking out the tsar's face. (Photographs courtesy of the Library of Congress.)

Plate 8: Censorship produced similar artistic protests in different countries. On the left, the French caricaturist André Gill depicts what it is like to be an artist amidst censorship: he portrays himself in

L'Eclipse of 26 November 1871, as blindfolded yet forced to avoid walking on an egg-minefield containing various subjects forbidden to him: the government, the laws, the police, Bonapartism, etc. On the right, the Portuguese journal *A Parodia* makes the same point in a caricature published on 2 March 1906, which is obviously 'borrowed' from Gill's earlier caricature. (Photographs courtesy of Northwestern University Library and the Library of Congress.)

Plate 9: French caricaturists portrayed the hated censorship in the form of 'Madame Anastasie', a horrid old woman who wreaked havoc with her huge pair of scissors. In this drawing from 26 June 1875, *Le Don Quichotte* depicts Anastasie as a sort of Don Quixote in reverse, attempting to destroy the windmill-symbol of truth and beauty. The drawing was accompanied by lengthy written attacks on censorship, including a poem advising Anastasie to 'thrust, without superfluous words, your huge scissors into your stomach. . . . You would destroy an abuse.' (Photograph courtesy of Wayne State University Library.)

Plate 10: *Simplicissimus* caricaturist Thomas Theodor Heine was sentenced to six months in jail for an 1898 drawing which mocked German Kaiser Wilhelm II's foreign policy. On the right, Heine shows himself 'the way I'll be drawing my next picture' in a caricature published in November 1898. Underneath the drawing is a caption reading, 'Life is serious, art is fun.' On the left, another Heine drawing from 1897 shows a caricaturist's worst nightmare: a journalist with Heine's features with a sign around his neck reading 'guilty of lèse majesté' is shown being led to a guillotine. (Photographs courtesy of Michigan State University Library.)

Plate 11: The 1848 German revolution freed caricature from government controls, but such freedom was short-lived. On the left, an 1848 issue of the German caricature journal *Fliegende Blatter* shows censorship, depicted as a ghostly figure whose tools, shown at the top, are scissors and black ink, buried by the 1848 revolution. However, on the right, *Leuchtkugeln*, in an 1851 issue, shows its editor on trial, shortly before the Munich-based republican caricature journal was forced to close under the weight of crushing fines. (Photographs courtesy of University of Michigan Library and the Library of Congress.)

Plate 12: The Portuguese caricature journal *A Parodia* often published drawings attacking censorship. The caricature on the left, from 24 December 1902, along with that on the right, from 23 February 1906, both protest the ban on the drawings originally scheduled to appear on the front pages. The drawing on the right, entitled 'A Despot', uses the censor's pencil as a symbol of oppression. (Photographs courtesy of the Library of Congress.)

Plate 13: The bitterly anti-clerical Roman caricature journal *L'Asino* ('The Donkey') was banned from sale in the Vatican City. In the caricature on the left, published on 7 April 1907, *L'Asino* depicts its symbol being barred from the Vatican by a Swiss Guard. The Barcelona journal *Cu-Cut!* antagonised the Spanish military by constantly ridiculing the notoriously inept army. In the caricature on the right, published on 21 September 1906, a Spanish army officer who had visited the Russian military in Manchuria during the Russo-Japanese war is shown responding to a question about what he had learned: 'What we knew already: how to lose battles.' Two months later, army troops ransacked the journal's editorial and printing offices, thereby creating a major political crisis in Spain. (Photographs courtesy of the Italian National Library, Florence, and Catalan National Library, Barcelona.)

Plate 14: The German caricature journal *Simplicissimus* frequently clashed with the authorities. Caricaturist Thomas Theodor Heine was fined for the cartoon on the left, published in May 1903, which criticised German diplomacy as too deferential to the United States by depicting a supposed secret diplomatic training school in Berlin which all ambassadors had to attend to qualify for their posts. The issue on the right, published 19 January 1904, was confiscated for 'incitement to class conflict'. It was published during a bitter textile strike at Crimmatschau and portrays a group of policemen and wealthy capitalists standing on a platform crushing emaciated workers. The caption reads, 'We need more police up here! The people are not sufficiently squashed.' (Photographs courtesy of Michigan State University Library.)

Plate 15: On a number of occasions, countries took action against caricature journals which they felt would disrupt their diplomatic relations with other countries. The *Simplicissimus* issue on the left, published in 1901, was confiscated apparently because German officials feared the impact on the British government. The caricature shows the British king, Edward VII, and a British soldier trampling tiny inhabitants of a British concentration camp established during the Boer War into a bloody pulp. The caption has the king saying, 'This blood is splashing me from head to toe. My crown is getting filthy.' The November 1905 issue of *L'Assiette au Beurre*, on the right, was banned from street sales by the French government, which clearly feared repercussions from Russia resulting from the clear suggestion of the drawing that reform would only come in Russia when Tsar Nicholas II was no longer among the living. (Photographs courtesy of Michigan State University Library, University of Michigan Library.)

Plate 16:   Editor Nikolai Shebuev of the Russian journal *Pulemet* ('Machine Gun') was sentenced to a year in jail for the 1905 drawing on the left, which suggested Tsar Nicholas II's promised reforms were a hoax by superimposing a bloody handprint over his reform manifesto. Russian illustrator Ivan Bilibin was detained for 26 hours for the 1905 drawing on the right, published in *Zhupel*, which mocked the tsar by surrounding a picture of a donkey with imperial regalia. (Photographs courtesy of the Library of Congress, University of Michigan Library.)

Preface

'The impact of works of art is so great that they can hardly be left with unlimited freedom', declared the South Korean Vice-Minister of Culture and Information, Choi Chang Yoon, in September 1987, amidst an election campaign widely viewed as presaging a liberalisation of politics in that country. 'We have our social and moral values that must be defended and upheld', he added. 'We will not allow things brought up that are detrimental to our society or our national security.'

To prevent such 'detrimental' material from being distributed in South Korea, the government there traditionally has censored the press, books, movies, plays, songs and the visual arts, compiling a list of over 600 banned books and nearly 1000 forbidden songs by the 1987 election. Among 186 songs which were released from the blacklist as part of the 1987 'liberalisation' was one entitled 'Morning Dew', an unofficial anthem of the student protest movement, which tells the story of a man who spends a painful, restless night, but then gains the courage to go on upon waking and seeing the dew. 'Morning Dew', which was widely interpreted as a call for resistance against the bleakness of life resulting from a politically repressive regime, had been banned by the government in 1975 for being 'inappropriate to the spirit of the age'. Also as part of the 1987 liberalisation, producers of films and plays no longer have to submit scripts in advance to government officials, but the final works must be screened for approval before they can be shown or performed.

Clandestinely obtained copies of hundreds of secret directives issued by the South Korean Information Ministry to newspapers in 1986 revealed that the government had directed the press to give minimal coverage to opposition leaders Kim Young Sam and Kim Dae Jung and not to publish pictures of them. The regime's especial sensitivity to pictures was also shown when a cartoonist was forced to retire from a leading newspaper after drawing a character resembling President Chun Doo Hwan, in alleged violation of a law banning caricatures which insult the head of state.[1]

Such examples reflecting the widespread censorship of the press and the arts in South Korea, and the great sensitivity of the authorities there to the power of these media could be endlessly repeated for the vast majority of countries in the Third World today, as well as for the communist regimes of Eastern Europe. Within the lifetime of many of the readers of this book, the citizens of many non-communist regimes in Europe have also endured such censorship of the press and the arts – in Nazi Germany, Fascist Italy, Spain under Franco, and Portugal under Salazar, for example. Even today, in relatively democratic societies such as the United Kingdom, such censorship is not unknown, as is shown by the 1987 _Spycatcher_ episode and the seizure of tapes from the BBC to prevent the broadcasting of programmes about the intelligence services. In nineteenth-century Europe, political censorship was pervasive throughout the continent, as this book will seek to document.

Censorship of the press and arts above all reflects the fact that, in an age of urban industrialisation, widespread literacy and rapid transportation and communications, what average citizens think matters to political leaders. Much of the political struggle therefore consists of a battle for control of the minds of the population. In feudal societies, characterised by scattered rural populations, mass illiteracy, and an overwhelmingly parochial orientation to life resulting from transportation and communications systems no more advanced than when the horse was domesticated in pre-biblical times, this was not the case. Kings, nobles, tribal leaders and religious patriarchs generally ruled with little concern for what their subjects thought, and, in an age before newspapers, television, political parties and opinion polls, they had few means of obtaining such information even if they did care.

Although rudimentary forms of censorship have existed throughout history, modern forms of rigorous, pervasive, bureaucratised and systematic censorship largely date from the French Revolution. While the French Revolution is a historical turning-point for many reasons, it was especially so in marking the emergence of mass public opinion as a factor in political life. The purpose of this book is to try to summarise how political regimes sought to fight what they viewed as this new menace by trying to control what information and opinions were transmitted by the press and the arts of nineteenth-century Europe. The book will also trace popular struggles to eliminate and evade such controls, as part of the general struggle for democracy and what is now called 'human rights'. This struggle was a central focus of nineteenth-century European politics.

As will be documented in this book, in those countries of North-western Europe where modernisation advanced relatively early and extensively, public pressure forced the elimination or drastic easing of governmental control over the press and arts as part of a general trend of democratisation by 1914, much as similar developments forced concessions in South Korea in 1987. However, where modernisation was retarded, as in most countries in South-western, Central and Eastern Europe, authoritarian rule, along with harsh controls over the press and the arts, continued. The failure of democratic traditions to take root in these countries by 1914 created the foundations for post-First World War censorship and political repression in Spain, Portugal, Italy, Austria, Germany, Hungary, the Balkans and Russia. Thus, political censorship is not only a barometer of the general political atmosphere in a country, but often a useful predictor of future political trends. A study of this subject is therefore interesting not only in its own right but also for the light that it sheds upon more general political conditions and prospects, especially because in so many ways both the methods of repression and attempts to overcome them which this book documents for nineteenth-century Europe are being repeated in Eastern Europe and all over the Third World today.

An entire book could be constructed drawing such parallels. For example, in Poland and Malaysia today, as in nineteenth-century France and Russia, clandestine presses publish and circulate what government censors will not allow to appear legally. In Taiwan today, as in Sweden in the 1830s, when the government bans a magazine by name, the same staff resume publication of the same magazine under a different name. Since it is impossible in Taiwan to urge 'independence' (i.e. official separation from mainland China), dissident publications there use the code word 'self-determination', just as in tsarist Russia newspapers could not advocate a constitution and so called for the 'crowning of the edifice'. Indonesian authorities ink out or paste over offensive material in imported publications today, just as the Russian authorities did 100 years ago. Today's South African press controls are so complicated that a 322-page *Newspapermen's Guide to the Law* has been published, just as in France in 1851 two judges published a handbook on the scores of French press laws, to aid befuddled lawyers and journalists. To protest against censorship, South African papers in the 1980s published cartoons with blank spaces in the 'speech balloons' and replaced censored text with similar blanks, just as French caricature journals in the 1870s replaced banned drawings with verbal protests about the censorship and German papers in the 1830s left white space where material had been censored out (in South Africa in 1986 as in Germany in 1834, the authorities eventually outlawed such use of blank space).

In South Africa today the authorities are especially sensitive to cartoons, just as authorities throughout Europe were in the nineteenth century; thus, in 1986 South African officials banned a cartoon showing two blindfolded whites sniffing the air, with one asking, 'What's cooking?' and the other replying, 'I don't know, but it smells revolting.' In Nicaragua in 1986, the authorities forbade publication of photographs of opposition spokesman Cardinal Miguel Obando y Bravo, just as the Russian regime banned photographs of dissident writer Leo Tolstoy in 1902. In today's Russia, South Africa and China, as in Russia and Germany in 1910, all films must be approved by censors using political criteria; thus, in March 1987 South African censors banned the film *Witness to Apartheid*, which had been nominated for an Academy Award in the United States. *The Official Story*, a 1985 Academy Award-winning movie about human-rights atrocities under the military regime in Argentina in the 1970s (which could be made only after film censorship was ended in Argentina, following the fall of the junta there), today circulates via clandestine video-cassettes in Chile, just as the manuscripts of banned plays were widely circulated in nineteenth-century Russia. All the plays of Vaclav Havel have been banned in Czechoslovakia since 1969, just as the plays of Victor Hugo were banned in France between 1852 and 1867. In Poland today, plays banned from the public stage are clandestinely performed in private homes, just as censored plays were staged at 'private clubs' 100 years ago in France, Germany and Britain.[2]

This book originated in the continuation of research undertaken for my study *Political Repression in Nineteenth-Century Europe* (1983). That book sought to summarise material which previously had been scattered in hundreds of specialised articles, books and monographs, but had never before been brought together in a general study. The essential theme of the book was that, given the traditional monarchical–aristocratic structure of Europe at the beginning of the nineteenth-century, the modernisation of the continent during the next 100 years under the twin impetuses of the industrial and French revolutions inevitably led to an enormous struggle over what we now call 'human rights' issues. Working people, who had previously been politically invisible and impotent, who had typically been illiterate and had spent their entire lives in small villages, accepting as immutable the rigid hierarchy of a feudal political and economic order, developed new ideas and new demands as the result of the spread of mass literacy and the exposure to different concepts fostered by the development of the railways, the growth of a mass press, and rapid urbanisation and industrialisation. For the first time in world history, the masses made a sustained attempt to organise and to voice demands. These demands focused on the need for social reforms and 'human rights', such as the right to vote, speak, publish and organise without restrictions. Since such reforms would have posed a threat to the power and wealth of traditional aristocratic elites, these elites, often with the support of newly emerging middle-class and business elites, typically responded with repression quite similar to that so common today under similar circumstances in the Third World.

Since my earlier book was an attempt to provide an overall survey of information related to human-rights problems in nineteenth-century Europe, it was not feasible there to devote much space to any one aspect of the problem. In the area of political censorship, I included a short discussion of repression of the press, but, primarily due to my lack of knowledge at the time, I included virtually nothing about censorship of the arts, including theatre, opera, cinema and caricature. During my subsequent research, I discovered a vast amount of additional material concerning political censorship in nineteenth-century Europe. It became evident to me from the pervasiveness of such controls and the energy, time and money devoted to enforcing them that the governments of nineteenth-century Europe attached great importance to such censorship, as they clearly saw themselves as struggling for control over the minds of their subjects. The information I uncovered concerning political censorship in nineteenth-century Europe was scattered through a vast number of specialised books and articles on particular writers and artists, particular countries and particular periods. Since the amount of material is substantial and no previous study has attempted to gather together information about political censorship for all of Europe during the nineteenth-century, a book on this subject seemed warranted, especially given the clear importance of political censorship from the standpoints of the governments involved, the artists and writers directly affected, and the general populace, whom censorship deprived of the ability to experience the unfettered expression of ideas.

The introductory chapter of this book attempts to explain the general political and social context of political censorship in nineteenth-century Europe. It is designed for the reader with no strong general background knowledge of this period of European history and can obviously only sketch the surface of conditions in an enormously diverse region. The heart of the book consists of chapters on five different media – the press, caricature, theatre, opera and cinema – which suffered from widespread political censorship in nineteenth-century Europe. In each chapter I discuss why that political mode of expression led the authorities to resort to censorship, what techniques and bureaucratic apparatuses were used to enforce censorship, what means were used to evade censorship, and what effect the censorship had upon the artists and populations involved. In a concluding chapter, I attempt to reach some generalisations about the overall nature and significance of nineteenth-century European political censorship.

It is probably no coincidence that, although this book is likely to be categorised as a work of 'history', it has been written by a political scientist. The canons of historiographical methodology would have required me to have mastered all twenty-five or so European languages and to have burrowed through the archives of all of the European countries before attempting a work such as this. Had I done so, this probably would have been a better book, but it also would never have been written. Such a task would have consumed several lifetimes, no doubt explaining why historians perhaps better qualified than I to perform it have failed to do so. Even without doing any government archival work and knowing only two European languages, English and French, the research for this book ultimately took ten years, involving the reading of several thousand books and journal articles and the examination of hundreds of volumes of nineteenth-century caricature journals (such journals were especially feared by governments because even the illiterate could understand them, a fact which I appreciated, as it enabled me to 'read' such journals in Russian, Spanish, Italian, Portuguese and German).

In order to avoid flooding the book with thousands rather than hundreds of notes, I have adopted the following measures. In the five chapters which form the heart of the book, I have given references for every significant fact, but have generally grouped such references together in one note for each paragraph of text (usually signalled at the end of the paragraph) instead of providing a note for each individual statement. For the introduction (Chapter 1), which seeks only to provide background information and makes no claim to break new ground, I have provided references only for direct quotations. In each chapter, full bibliographical information is supplied for each source on its first citation. Subsequent references to the same work in the same chapter are given in abbreviated form, cross-referenced to the note giving full details. The reader is thereby saved the trouble of searching through scores of notes to find the original citation.

Scattered portions of the text have appeared in preliminary form in several journal articles, and I am grateful for permission to republish material from the following sources: 'Freedom of the Press in Europe, 1815–1914', *Journalism Monographs*, 80 (Feb 1983); 'Political Censorship of the Theatre in Nineteenth-Century Europe', *Theatre Research International*, 12 (Fall 1987) 220–41; and 'Political Censorship of the Opera in Europe, 1815–1914', *Opera Journal* (September 1988). I am indebted to three institutions which helped make the research and writing of this book possible by providing research expenses and/or leave from my teaching duties: the Swann Foundation for Caricature and Cartoon; the National Endowment for the Humanities; and Oakland University, Rochester, Michigan. I received helpful comments and suggestions from three people who generously agreed to read portions of the manuscript: Professor Peter Stearns of Carnegie-Mellon University; Rebecca Collignon; and Deborah Szobel, editorial assistant at Oakland University. A number of libraries granted me borrowing privileges and/or access to rare and valuable nineteenth-century caricature journals and I am deeply indebted to them. They were the libraries of the University of Michigan at Ann Arbor, the University of California at Berkeley, Wayne State University, Michigan State University, and Northwestern University; the Library of Congress; the British Newspaper Library; the Bibliothèque Nationale in Paris; the Catalan National Library in Barcelona; and the Italian National Library in Florence. I am also deeply indebted to Barbara Somerville of the Oakland University Library Interlibrary Loan Department, who cheerfully helped me obtain a ridiculously large number of obscure books and journals. Although I did all of the photography for this book, I am immensely grateful to the Photographic Services Department of the University of Michigan for developing and printing the photographs from nineteenth-century caricature journals.

Finally, in the very finest tradition of last but not least, I am greatly indebted to those who handled the editing of this book. At Macmillan Press in London, this book was welcomed from the very start with great enthusiasm and handled until the very end with great professionalism by my editor, Pauline Snelson. On behalf of Macmillan Press, the copy-editing was undertaken by Longworth Editorial Services, where it was performed with extraordinary care by Graham Eyre and Valery Rose.

All of the caricature reproductions included in the plate section of this book illustrate material on censorship of caricature, which is discussed in Chapter 3. In order to reproduce the caricatures in as large a size as possible, the captions accompanying the plates are very short. More complete captions for each plate are included in the 'List of Plates' in the prefatory matter and the source of each illustration is indicated therein. Additional contextual information about the plates is included in Chapter 3, on the following pages: on p. 75 for plates 1 and 2; on p. 78 for plate 3; on p. 79 for plate 4; on p. 83 for plates 5–9; on pp. 84 and 103 for plate 10; on p. 96 for plate 11; on p. 103 for plate 12; on pp. 103 and 104 for plate 13; on p. 105 for plate 14; on pp. 105 and 107 for plate 15; and on p. 111 for plate 16.

1 The Context of Political Censorship in Nineteenth-Century Europe

THE MODERNISATION OF EUROPE DURING THE NINETEENTH CENTURY

The nineteenth century was a period of unprecedentedly great change in Europe, which drastically transformed the social, economic, political and cultural landscapes of the continent. As J. M. Roberts has written, 'A man born in 1800 who lived out the psalmist's span of three-score years and ten could have seen the world more changed in his lifetime than it had been in the previous thousand years.'[1] There were, or course, major elements of continuity as well as change between the Europe of 1815 and the Europe of 1914. But, if the continent was characterised by a mixture of the Middle Ages and of modernity in both 1815 and 1914, during the course of those 100 years there was a decisive shift in the direction of modernity. An average European of the Middle Ages transported into the Europe of 1815 would have found relatively few changes in daily life which would have confused or amazed him, but if suddenly transported into the Europe of 1914 he would have been alternately bewildered and enthralled by new inventions and social and political developments that affected the lives of everyone. He would have found his fellow Europeans wearing machine-made, store-bought clothes, moving from city to city by rail, travelling within cities by bicycles, motor cars, trams and underground railways, and reading in their homes at night, by electric light, newspapers containing information instantaneously transmitted across countries and continents by telegraph and telephone. Even Europeans who had witnessed all of these developments within their lifetime regarded the introduction between 1895 and 1914 of the motion picture, the radio and the aeroplane as something akin to magic; a European transported from the Middle Ages probably would have viewed the cinema, the wireless and aircraft as products of witchcraft.

1

Political power was monopolised almost everywhere in Europe in 1815 by monarchs and landowning aristocrats. Most European countries lacked written constitutions, and the few countries with elected national legislatures restricted the suffrage to a tiny, extremely wealthy percentage of the population. By placing all power in non-elected hands or those chosen by a small, unrepresentative segment of their citizenry, by censoring the press, by denying citizens freedom of assembly and association, and by failing to provide even primary education, virtually every European country in 1815 effectively foreclosed from the vast majority of their subjects any significant opportunity of peacefully influencing those who ruled them. In Central, South-western and Eastern Europe the nobility enjoyed social and legal privileges which placed them in a world apart from the masses, most of whom were ignorant and illiterate serfs bound to the soil and whose lives were almost totally dominated by their landlords. Although the social and economic gulf between rich and poor remained huge by 1914, many of the formal political disabilities imposed upon the masses had been eliminated or alleviated by then. Thus, on the eve of the First World War, almost every European country had granted all adult males the vote, provided free, compulsory elementary education for all citizens, and abolished all legal (if not social) privileges of the aristocracy. Serfdom had been abolished everywhere and monarchical–aristocratic power was limited to at least some degree in every country by elected legislatures, constitutional restrictions, a press freed from prior censorship and by interest groups organised by an increasingly literate and informed citizenry.

Some of the decisive changes in nineteenth-century Europe can be easily traced by examining key indexes of modernisation. In 1815, about 70 per cent of European adults were illiterate, while by 1914 over 70 per cent could read. In 1815, less than 3 per cent of the European population lived in cities of 100,000 or more inhabitants, while in 1914 almost 15 per cent did. The number of Europeans living in such large towns increased from about 20 million to about 50 million between 1870 and 1914. The foundations of modern European industry were laid in the nineteenth century, and after 1870 industry replaced agriculture as the most significant element in the European economy. Over 80 per cent of the European labour force was employed in agriculture in 1815, but by 1914 that figure had dropped to about 60 per cent; conversely the number employed in industry had jumped from about 10 per cent to about 25 per cent, and large factories, almost unknown at the beginning of the nineteenth century, dotted the landscape on the eve of the First World War. Between 1815 and 1914 the volume of industrial production registered an elevenfold increase in Great Britain and a fivefold increase in France. The European economy grew especially rapidly after 1850 as industrialisation spread well beyond its original centres in Britain, Belgium and parts of France. The volume of European exports more than tripled between 1850 and 1880, and between 1850 and 1914 industrial production increased tenfold in Germany and Russia and more than threefold in Italy, Austria and Sweden. In Germany in the 1850s, agriculture, forestry and fishing contributed 45 per cent of the net national product, while industry, transport and mining accounted for only 22 per cent; by 1910 these figures were reversed.

Although the conditions of life for the average European remained poor throughout the nineteenth century, average standards of living noticeably improved by the end of the period, with an especially marked improvement after about 1860. Perhaps the clearest indicators of improvement can be found in health and demographic statistics. In 1815, the percentage of all children born alive who did not survive their first birthday (i.e. the infant mortality rate) approached 25 per cent, and the average life expectancy for the entire population was 30–35 years, only a few years longer than in the Middle Ages and 20–25 years less than the present life expectancy in the Third World. By 1914, overall European infant mortality rates had fallen below 15 per cent, while life expectancy had increased substantially to 45–50 years. Between 1815 and 1914, the European population, which had remained relatively stagnant during the Middle Ages, more than doubled from 215 to 450 million. These figures reflected improvements in medicine, sanitation, and the amount and distribution of food supplies, the introduction of governmental social insurance pro-grammes, and an increase in mass purchasing power. Especially in North-western Europe, gains in living standards were substantial after 1860, with an estimated doubling of real per capita income by 1914. This was reflected in, for example, a 130 per cent increase in average consumption of meat in Germany. Even in the relatively backward regions of South-eastern Europe, real income increased by over 80 per cent during this period. Meanwhile, the average European's working week declined from about 84 hours in 1850 to 60 hours in 1910.

Improvements in the distribution of food supplies reflected revolu-tionary advances in transportation and communication. In 1815, the fastest forms of transportation and communication were horses on land and sailing ships on water, as they had been for thousands of years. The introduction of the telegraph, the steamship and the railway between 1825 and 1850 transformed the pace and the ease of transportation and communication. Thus, the development of rail and steamship networks (railroad track increased from 3800 to 308,000 kilometres between 1840 and 1910, while the number of passengers carried increased from 300 million in 1860 to 5234 million in 1910) reduced the time required to travel around the world from a year in 1848 to under three months in 1872. The introduction of the telegraph made communications between major European cities instantaneous; back in 1848, it had taken five days to transmit news from Paris to Vienna via the most rapid communications service, that of the Rothschild bank. By 1914, the development of the telephone, the wireless, electricity and the internal combustion engine had further revolutionised communications and transportation. The tram, the underground railway and the motor car transformed urban transportation, while electricity was literally transforming night into day, at least in urban areas.

Most of the statistics presented above are rough averages for the whole of Europe and therefore hide as much as they reveal. The pace of change varied enormously from region to region, and there remained a vast difference between the conditions of the wealthy few and those of the far-poorer many. In general, the countries of North-western Europe (Britain, France, Switzerland, the Low Countries and Scandinavia) were in the vanguard of modernisation, while those in South-western and Eastern Europe (Iberia, the Balkans, Hungary and Russia) trailed far behind, with the countries of Central Europe (Germany, Italy and Austria) coming somewhere in between. Thus, per capita income in Russia in 1913 was only one third that of the average in Western Europe (a decline from 1860, when it had been one half) and hourly wages in Italy in 1907 were only half what they were in France. In Belgium, 46 per cent of the population was employed in industry in 1910, but the figure for Romania was only 8 per cent. Over 60 per cent of the population of England and Wales lived in towns of 20,000 or more in 1910, as opposed to only 13 per cent in Hungary. In 1910, life expectancy for the average Swede was fifty-five years and 95 per cent of Danish adults were literate, but in Bulgaria only 38 per cent of adults were literate and life expectancy was forty-four years. In Norway in 1910 about 10 per cent of all children born alive died before the age of one, but in European Russia the figure was 25 per cent. Health conditions were notably worse in Southern and Eastern Europe than in the North-western part of the continent. Almost 40 per cent of Italian army conscripts were rejected for health reasons in 1881, while in Russia the rejection figure for peasant conscripts was 64 per cent in 1890 and 78 per cent during the famine year of 1891, when 400,000 Russians died of hunger, typhus and cholera. Conditions were perhaps worst of all in the Balkans. In Serbia, seven out of seventeen provinces had no doctors in the late 1860s, and in 1915 a typhus epidemic killed 150,000, including 126 of the 400 doctors who tried to serve a total populaiton of 3 million. In Bulgaria a population of 2 million was served in 1880 by only seventy-four doctors, and in 1884 44 per cent of all deaths were recorded among children under five years of age.

Everywhere in Europe, rich and poor lived in what virtually amounted to different worlds. At the beginning of the nineteenth century, ownership of land was the primary path to wealth and power, and about 5000 fabulously wealthy landed aristocrats dominated European society, politics, culture and economics. A few hundred noble families held 25 per cent of all the land in England and Wales, and the same number owned about one-third of the vast Hapsburg Empire. The Danish and Swedish nobilities, each consti-tuting less than 1 per cent of their nations' populations, owned about one-third of all the land in their countries, and similar landholding concentrations were found in Ireland, Russia, eastern Germany, Spain and the southern parts of Portugal and Italy. The richest 2300 Russian landlords owned 3 million serfs, while the wealthiest Hungarian landlord, Prince Paul Esterházy, owned about 10 million acres, on which 700,000 peasants (6.5 per cent of the Hungarian population) lived.

Although the concentration of wealth among the very richest elements of the population had diminished somewhat by 1914, it remained enormous. Thus, less than 4 per cent of the population owned more than 25 per cent of the land in Austria, Hungary, Romania, Denmark, England, Germany, France, partitioned Poland, Russia, Spain and Italy. Between 2000 and 5000 landlords owned about half the land in Romania, Hungary and the United Kingdom, while about 10,000 owned half of Spain. While landownership still was a major path to power and wealth in 1914, by then commerce and industry also provided many opportunities. Thus, in Britain, landowners accounted for 73 per cent of millionaires in 1858–79 and commercial and financial magnates for only 14 per cent, but by 1900–14 landowners made up only 27 per cent of the total, while those engaged in industry and trade accounted for 38 per cent. French nobles constituted half of the legislative assembly in that country in 1871, but contributed less than a tenth of the membership by 1902. The new paths to wealth and power did not diminish the concentration of riches. Studies of total wealth and income (as opposed to land-ownership only) suggest that in 1910 the richest 2 per cent of all Swedes and all Frenchmen owned about 60 per cent of their countries' total wealth.

While a tiny fraction of the European population enjoyed lives of ostentatious luxury, and by 1914 there was a much larger middle class in comfortable circumstances, the vast majority of the European population lived on the margins of, or just above, the level of subsistence throughout the nineteenth century. As Theodore Hamerow has written, 'the sources describe again and again the meager income, endless toil, poor diet, and wretched housing of the working population.'[2] Even in such relatively wealthy regions as England, at least one third of the population lived in dire poverty as late as 1914, and most workers had to spend over half their income on food alone (compared, however, to three quarters fifty years before). In the French town of Lille, throughout the nineteenth century the poorest 60 per cent of the population died leaving estates together worth about 1 per cent of the total worth of all estates. Throughout France in the 1860s one third of all children died before their fifth birthday, while an official survey reported that 'some persons describe as a great event the fact of having eaten meat a few times in their lives'.[3] In the poorer regions of Europe, around 1900, studies found that half or more of all working-class families living in Budapest, Helsinki, Athens, Berlin, Chemnitz, Breslau and Dresden inhabited one-room dwellings, and that, if 'overcrowding' were defined as living in dwellings in which more than two persons occupied a room, over 25 per cent of the total population of Berlin, Vienna, Moscow, St Petersburg, Budapest, Sofia, Bucharest, Breslau and Chemnitz endured such conditions. In Bucharest, 10 per cent of the population lived ten or more to a room in 1910, while in Berlin 600,000 people were housed more than five to a room in 1912. It was to escape such conditions and often equally terrible rural poverty that an astonishing 35 million Europeans departed the continent for overseas between 1870 and 1914.

The poor who stayed in Europe paid a heavy price for their economic status. In the 1840s, mortality rates in the poorest sections of Paris were twice those in the wealthiest areas; by the late nineteenth century mortality rates had dropped for poor and rich alike, but the relative price paid by the poor had actually increased, as death rates in the worst proletarian districts of Paris (and Vienna) were four times as high as in the richest areas. In Belgium around 1900, the poor could expect to live eighteen years, while the rich had a life expectancy of fifty-four. In Berlin at the turn of the century, the mortality rate for those inhabiting one-room apartments was thirty times higher than for those living in the luxury of four rooms, while infant mortality rates in the poor sections of the city were eight times higher than in posh areas. Clearly, as English rural labourers sang, 'If life was a thing that money could buy, / The rich would live and the poor might die.'[4] The poor were even distinguished by their short stature, as the average worker was at least three inches shorter than his bourgeois counterpart.

THE POLITICAL IMPLICATIONS OF MODERNISATION

Although the modernisation of nineteenth-century Europe clearly did not eliminate poverty or the daily survival problems of the poor, it did open up new horizons for the broad mass of the population. Before the spread of the egalitarian ideas of the French Revolution, before the emergence of mass education and literacy and the accompanying development of popularly oriented newspapers, before the growth of large-scale industry and urbanisation, and before the development of the railways and the telegraph, most Europeans were trapped in an isolated and localised world of ignorance and poverty. Under these conditions, which were gradually shattered during the nineteenth century under the impact of the French and industrial revolutions, most people could not conceive that economic, social or political conditions could be different, or that they had any right to demand reforms. Modernisation in nineteenth-century Europe exposed them to new ideas and surroundings and provided new opportunities for mass organisation which, especially after about 1860, led for the first time in world history to sustained mass demands for major social, economic and political change. As John Stuart Mill observed in England in 1848,

> Of the working classes . . . it may be pronounced certain, that the patriarchal or paternal system of government is one to which they will not again be subject. That question . . . was decided when

they were taught to read, and allowed access to newspapers and political tracts. . . . It was decided when they were brought together in numbers, to work socially under the same roof. It was decided when railways enabled them to shift from place to place, . . . the working classes have taken their interests into their own hands.[5]

Modernisation also led to the emergence of a small but strategically significant middle class composed of merchants, industrialists, lawyers, doctors, journalists, and the like. During the first half of the nineteenth century, it was primarily this new middle class that led the demand for reform, especially the granting of political rights such as the right to vote and freedom of the press (at least for their class). Before the revolutions which convulsed much of Europe in 1848, the aristocratic–monarchical regimes which had dominated the continent generally resisted even these middle-class demands. However, noting carefully that social tensions between the middle and lower classes helped lead to the collapse of the revolutions in 1848, the traditional ruling elements in most countries thereafter formed a tacit alliance with the upper segments of the middle classes, yielding significantly, if not totally, to their demands for social and political acceptance, as a means of creating a stronger bulkhead against the far more feared 'dark masses'. As Jerome Blum has noted,

Politically, nobles and wealthy burghers [members of the middle class] generally held the same conservative views, and shared the same suspicions of social and political reform. Marriages between scions of great noble houses and daughters of rich industrialists and bankers multiplied, especially in the last decades of the nineteenth and first years of the twentieth century. . . . The style of life and the self-assurance of the great capitalists differed hardly at all from that of the high nobility and many were themselves ennobled. In a sense there was an interpenetration of high nobility and high bourgeoisie, in which nobles became bourgeoisified and bourgeois became feudalized.[6]

If the post-1848 aristocratic-high bourgeoisie coalition satisfied many of the demands of the middle classes, it failed to stem the tide of emerging working-class demands which were the inevitable result of the broadening horizons of the poor. This emergence of the popular classes onto the political stage was a development which was widely remarked upon during the course on the nineteenth century by the ruling elements, often with considerable dread. Thus, Napoleon's police chief, Joseph Fouché, expressed concern over what he called the 'previously unknown pressure of public opinion', while a Russian public education minister in the 1830s voiced alarm over the fact that 'the taste for reading and literary activity, which earlier was confined to the upper middle classes, is now spreading even further'.[7]

At the beginning of the century, some of the most reactionary rulers, such as Emperor Francis I of Austria (who reigned from 1792 to 1835), Tsar Nicholas I of Russia (1825–55) and King Ferdinand I (1816–25) of the now-defunct Kingdom of the Two Sicilies in southern Italy, believed that progress and its accompanying discontents could simply be kept out of their lands. Thus, Francis I's philosophy was summed up in his will, which instructed his successor to 'Govern and change nothing', and was reflected in his refusal to sanction railway construction in Austria, declaring, 'No, no, I will have nothing to do with it, lest the revolution might [be imported by it and] come into the country.' Similarly, Ferdinand I refused to approve the formation of societies for improving the mulberry bush or lighting towns with gas, on the grounds that 'associations are hurtful to the state, for they enlighten the people and spread liberal ideas'. Underlying such actions and most social policies in Europe during the pre-1848 period was the sort of reasoning offered the British reformer Robert Owen by Friedrich Gentz, secretary to Klemens von Metternich (Austrian Foreign Minister from 1809 to 1848), who masterminded the reactionary Austrian policies of the pre-1848 period which dominated the Hapsburg Empire and the German and Italian states: 'We do not by any means desire the great masses to become wealthy and independent, for how could we govern them?' Tsar Nicholas's secret police chief struck a similar chord by declaring that Russia had always been 'best protected from revolutionary disasters' by the fact that 'the monarchs have always been ahead of the nation' and therefore 'one should not hasten unduly to educate the nation lest the people reach, in extent of their understanding, a level equal that of the monarchs and then attempt to weaken their power'.[8]

After 1848, most European rulers realised not only that it was hopeless to attempt to stop the spread of such developments as popular literacy and mass urbanisation and industrialisation, and with them the emergence of demands for political, economic and social reform, but also that their countries could not compete with others without accepting or even hastening such trends, which were vital for the creation of a strong modern economy and even a strong army, given the increasing sophistication of weaponry. Yet the dilemma of modernisation only intensified: modernisation was needed to build strong countries but would also inevitably lead to rising mass demands for reform. The Russian Foreign Minister Sergei Witte expressed it perfectly when he lamented, 'Education foments social revolution, but popular ignorance loses wars.' The Russian novelist Vladimir Korolenko, when chided by an English interviewer in 1905 for wanting to catch up with the West in all things at once, explained the unstoppable desire for reform in the following allegory, in which 'electricity' represents modernisation and democracy in general:

> You mustn't forget that we are now in the twentieth century, and, to make a comparison, if I want to light a new town, it would be absurd to use tallow candles first and then to replace them with lamps and then employ gas until I shall finally make use of electric light. Electric light can be generated and it is only natural that I should use it at once.

A Hungarian peasant named Albert Szilagi, testifying before a government commission investigating peasant unrest in that country in the 1890s, also explained the inevitable result of modernisation in creating growing reform demands:

> The rightful demands of the laborers increased because the people of the land study more, know more, see more. How can you blame us? We have learnt how to read and write. We would now like to wear better clothes, eat like human beings and send our children to schools.[9]

MODERNISATION AND POLITICAL CONTROLS

As the nineteenth century progressed, it became increasingly obvious to the ruling elements everywhere in Europe that the political clock could never be turned back to the days before the French Revolution, when the masses were politically impotent and invisible. The French Revolution of 1789 and subsequent uprisings in many European countries in 1819–21, 1830–2 and 1848–9 made clear that the political views and activities of the bulk of the population could no longer be ignored. Therefore, European elites began to devote enormous amounts of energy to controlling what information and political views the masses were exposed to and what opportunities they were given to exercise their newly discovered influence. In attempting to do this, the European governing classes in effect became involved in a massive struggle for people's minds, in which they sought to eliminate political and radical ideas that were seen as threatening first their ideological and eventually their actual hegemony. This struggle was the context for pervasive attempts to censor all major forms of mass dissemination of information and views. A survey of such attempts at political censorship of the press, of polemical art such as political caricature, of the theatre, the opera, and, with the dawning of a new century, a new and powerful communication medium, the cinema, forms the heart of this volume. However, such overt political censorship was only part of a wider network of attempts to exert political control over the masses in the nineteenth century, and thus can only be properly understood in the context of political repression generally: of controls on education and limits on its availability; limitation of the franchise; restrictions on freedom of assembly and association, and also on the ability to form trade unions and take strike action.

As will be seen with regard to political censorship, this broader network of political controls remained harshest and most enduring in Central and especially South-western and Eastern Europe. These regions lagged behind North-western Europe in the process of modernisation, so poverty, disorganisation and ignorance among the masses were more prolonged and pervasive there. This meant in turn that pressure for change from the lower classes remained relatively weak, and that the ruling elites' image of the masses as dark, unwashed savages remained both strong and not totally inaccurate. Further, in these regions the middle classes generally were small in size and weak in influence. This further retarded both modernisation and reform, since the middle classes tended everywhere to favour such abstract principles as constitutional government, freedom of the press and equality before the law, which they saw primarily as tools to force the traditional aristocratic–monarchical monopolies to share political power with them, but which once conceded were difficult to deny to the lower classes also.

The result was that in Central and more especially South-western and Eastern Europe many forms of political censorship and other, broader controls, such as restrictions on the franchise and on freedom of assembly, were either never relaxed before 1914 or were only formally loosened, with little change in practice. Further, the very pervasiveness and strictness of the continuing network of political repression in these regions created something of a self-fulfilling prophecy concerning the elites' image of the masses, since those opposition groups that were able to organise and survive were, in the absence of channels for legal, peaceful opposition, forced to resort to illegal and sometimes violent methods.

In Central Europe, most of the violence was far more verbal than physical. Regimes there generally allowed some openings for the expression of dissent and accompanied repressive controls with some attempts to improve working-class conditions. In Germany and Austria, social-security programmes were introduced and political controls were somewhat relaxed by 1914. Thus, in Germany in the 1880s, when the Socialist Party was banned but major social-insurance programmes were instituted, the German Chancellor, Otto von Bismarck, noted that domestic peace could not be achieved 'entirely along the path of repression of socialist excesses, but equally through positive measures for the well-being of the workers'. Such ambiguous governmental policies tended to create equally ambiguous responses from opposition groups, as German Socialist leader Karl Kautsky reflected when he declared of his organisation, 'We are a revolutionary party, but not one that makes revolutions.' However, where peaceful channels were more tightly sealed and working-class conditions almost totally ignored, as in Russia, Spain and Hungary, physical violence became endemic among opposition elements in the pre-1914 period. Thus, in 1879 a Russian revolutionary group issued a manifesto declaring that resort to force was the only possible path of action in a regime in which 'despotism and violence' reigned supreme and where 'there is no freedom of speech or freedom of the press which would allow us to act by means of persuasion'.[10] The very resort to illegality and violence among opposition groups, of course, served to justify maintenance of harsh repression in the affected regions.

Modernisation in North-western Europe proceeded at a much faster pace than elsewhere, thereby creating a larger, often better informed and better organised and, especially after 1870, far less impoverished working class. This region also developed a markedly stronger and more assertive middle class, whose support of traditional ruling elements became vital for successful government relatively early in the nineteenth century and which therefore generally succeeded before 1850 in securing constitutional government, freedom of the press, an expanded suffrage and free elections. The greater opportunities for peaceful expression in North-western Europe tended to produce working-class movements that were far more reformist than revolutionary. This development was also fostered by the success of past repression of more radical working-class movements in some countries (i.e. the suppression of lower-class rebellions in France in 1848, 1851 and 1871, and of the Chartist movement in Britain in the period 1838–48) and the marked improvements in working-class living standards after 1870. By the turn of the century, the primary desire of the lower classes in the region was to assimilate into the existing order rather than to overthrow it.

The less threatening nature of the working classes in North-western Europe fostered a growing tendency, among the region's governments, to continue policies of gradual reform and of co-optation of the working classes. Again, something of a self-fulfilling prophecy was created, as, where political controls were relaxed sufficiently to give parties appealing to working-class interests a taste of power, the result was generally further reforms and further deradicalisation of the lower classes. For example, over the period 1898–1910 there were major democratic breakthroughs in Denmark, Sweden and Norway, bringing to power governments effectively controlled by legislatures elected by universal male suffrage and significantly influenced by working-class votes. In each case, pro-grammes addressing lower-class concerns followed: tax reforms were instituted, social-security programmes introduced, and working conditions regulated, The obvious 'reward' such reforms provided for democratic participation strengthened the already-evolving moderate, democratic character of the emerging Scandinavian socialist movements. As Arthur Balfour, British Prime Minister from 1902 to 1906 noted, 'Social legislation is not merely to be distinguished from socialist legislation, but it is its most direct opposite and its most effective antidote.'[11] In short, the general emergence of relatively moderate opposition groups in North-western Europe mirrored their political environment, just as the radical and authoritarian Russian Bolsheviks reflected the reactionary and repressive regime from which they emerged. As Konrad Adenauer, first Chancellor of the German Federal Republic, observed, 'Every state gets the socialist party it deserves.'[12]

Education

Both the availability and the content of education were subjects to which European elites paid considerable attention throughout the nineteenth century. In general, before 1860 governments exerted little effort to make free or cheap education widely available to the population. Where instruction was available from government, Church or voluntary organisations, the authorities intervened to ensure that material critical of the *status quo* was excluded and that the curriculum offered to the lower classes was largely limited to religion and basic reading and writing. It was generally agreed by European elites that to attempt to provide the masses with more knowledge would be a fruitless task given their stupidity, or could only lead to the development of subversive ideas and frustration among elements of the population that were destined for menial occupations. Thus, an 1803 Prussian decree declared, 'The children of the working class are to read the catechism, Bible and Hymn Book; to fear and love God and act accordingly; to honour authority. Whoever attempts to stuff them with more than this, sets himself a useless and thankless task.' King Frederick VI of Denmark declared in 1833, 'The peasant should learn reading, and writing and arithmetic; he should learn his duty toward God, himself and others and no more. Otherwise he gets notions into his head.' Juan Bravo Murillo, Prime Minister of Spain in 1851–2, declared in response to a proposal to provide schools for the poor, 'You want me to authorize a school at which 600 working men are to attend? Not in my time. Here we don't want men who think but oxen who work.' Especially in Russia and Catholic Europe, the Church could generally be counted upon to bolster the anti-subversive orientation of formal schooling. Napoleon declared that, 'In religion I do not see the mystery of the Incarnation but the mystery of the social order.' A catechism of the Russian Orthodox Church during the reign of Nicholas I taught that 'God commands us to love and obey from the inmost recesses of the heart every authority, and particularly the Emperor', as had been demonstrated by the example of Jesus, 'who lived and died in allegiance to the Emperor of Rome, and respectfully submitted to the judgement which condemned him to death'.[13]

After about 1860, there was a massive expansion of government-supported schools. By 1914, compulsory, free elementary-school education was virtually universal in Europe, with the major exception of Russia. Although to some extent the expansion of schooling reflected altruism on the part of middle-class liberals, to a much greater extent it reflected the feeling of middle- and upper-class elites that, with the mechanisation of industry and advances in weaponry, strong countries could be built only where everyone had a basic education and a sense of discipline, such as was inculcated in schools. Thus a conservative German newspaper declared in 1875, 'We in Germany consider education to be one of the principal ways of promoting the strength of the nation and above all military strength.' Further, it was increasingly recognised that state-controlled education could inculcate patriotic and nationalistic feelings, refute subversive ideas circulating among the lower classes, and tame elements of savagery among the most deprived elements of the population. In 1833 the French Minister of Education, François Guizot, espoused the extension of primary education to the lower classes because 'the less enlightened the multitude, the more amenable it is to being misled and subverted'; he thus saw universal elementary education as 'one of the greatest guarantees of order and social stability'. The Italian Minister of Education in 1885 defined the purpose of elementary school education as 'rearing a population as instructed as possible, but principally honest, hardworking, useful to the family and devoted to the Country and to the King'. Clearly, British working-class militant William Lovett had considerable insight when he noted that as the nineteenth century had progressed many ruling-class elements had set aside past opposition to any education for the poor in favour of 'admitting a sufficient amount of mental glimmer to cause the multitude to walk quietly and contentedly in the paths their wisdom had proscribed for them'.[14]

Even after free elementary schooling was provided in most countries, the children of the lower classes remained disadvantaged, since no country provided free secondary or higher education before 1914. Therefore, the poor could not afford to attain the advanced skills necessary to obtain positions of high status, pay and power. On the eve of the First World War less than 3 per cent of European children between the ages of fourteen and eighteen were enrolled in secondary schools, and less than 1 per cent of the college-age population was attending an institution of higher education. The effect of the denial of free education to the lower classes was clearly recognised by Russian Minister of Education Ivan Delianov, who in an 1887 decree directed state-supported secondary schools to refuse to admit 'children of coachmen, menials, cooks, washerwomen, small shopkeepers and the like', since it was 'completely unwarranted for the children of such people to leave their position in life'. In France, Guizot opposed making post-primary education available to the masses, as this would divert a 'great number of young men from their natural situation' and inspire among the educated poor 'scorn for their equals and distaste for their position which . . . no longer lets them be satisfied with a laborious and obscure existence'.[15]

The authorities took as much interest in who should teach in the schools as in what should be taught in them and who could attend them. Thus, in 1819 the Prussian government called upon all German states to rid their universities of teachers guilty of 'spreading harmful theories inimical to public order and peace or destructive to existing political institutions', while Francis I of Austria told a delegation of schoolteachers in 1821 that 'Who serves me must teach what I order; who cannot do this or comes along with new ideas, can leave or I shall get rid of him.' In France under Napoleon III, professors were even forbidden to wear beards, on the grounds that these were 'symbols of anarchy'. Hundreds of European instructors were dismissed for political reasons during the nineteenth century, occasionally in massive purges: for example, in France in 1851, 1500 teachers were dismissed. Although the degree of such control over teachers tended to ease during the nineteenth century, especially in Northwestern Europe, in many countries, such as Germany and Russia, supervision over schools remained extremely tight. In 1889 the German Kaiser, Wilhelm II, ordered Prussian schoolteachers to help combat the 'spread of socialist and communist ideas' and to show pupils 'how constantly during the present century the wages and living conditions of the working classes have improved under the guiding care of the Prussian kings'.[16]

Restrictions on the suffrage

Voting restrictions that overtly discriminated on the basis of wealth, and rigged elections that guaranteed continued power for existing regimes, were among the most crucial and pervasive forms of political control directed against the lower classes in nineteenth-century Europe. However, in many European countries at the beginning of the nineteenth century, such discriminatory mechanisms were not necessary, since they were ruled by absolute monarchs and had no national elections: this was the case in Russia, the Hapsburg Empire, Denmark, Spain, Portugal, all the Italian states and the vast majority of the German states (including Prussia, Bavaria and Saxony). In the non-absolutist states – the United Kingdom, France, the United Netherlands (Belgium and the Dutch Netherlands), Switzerland, the Kingdom of Norway and Sweden (ruled by the same king although with separate parliaments) and a few German states – the right to vote was explicitly based on wealth and was limited to a tiny fraction of the population, generally not exceeding 5 per cent. For example, in France in 1817, the right to vote was earned by paying at least 300 francs annually in direct taxes. This reduced the electorate to about 90,000 (0.35 per cent) in a populaiton of about 26 million. If all adults had been able to vote, approxima⁺ely 50 per cent of the population would have been enfranchised, but, since all European countries denied the vote to women rich and poor alike, the appropriate standard for measuring suffrage discrimination against the poor is the percentage that would have been enfranchised if all adult males had been entitled to vote, which would have been about 25 per cent throughout Europe.

Little secret was made of the fact that suffrage discrimination was designed to preserve the *status quo* in general and the political power and wealth of the traditional elites in particular. This, in Britain, the liberal historian and parliamentarian Thomas Macaulay declared that expansion of the suffrage would lead the general populace to 'plunder every man in the kingdom who had a good coat on his back and a good roof over his head', while the conservative German historian Heinrich von Treitschke denounced universal suffrage as leading to 'the superiority of soldiers over their officers, of apprentices over their masters, of workers over employers'. The disenfranchised also clearly realised the stakes involved in suffrage reform. French radicals in 1850 termed universal suffrage 'more fatal to the bourgeoisie than all the cannons in all the arsenals', and declared that, 'When the elections will be democratic, all of the poor workers' taxes will be paid in our Republic by the fat cats and the big bankers.' British reformers of the 1860s proclaimed that suffrage reform was the only way to improve 'the material welfare of the great masses of the community'. Austrian socialist leader Victor Adler declared in a famous pamphlet published in 1893 that the exploitation of Austrian workers 'is being perpetuated at this very moment by legislation that benefits the upper classes alone', a state of affairs persisting 'primarily because two-thirds of the population of Austria is totally without representation in parliament'.[17]

Constitutional government and elected legislatures were eventually introduced throughout Europe before 1914, with Russia the last country to do so, in 1905. Such reforms, along with extensions of the suffrage before 1870, generally resulted from middle-class demands for a role in political affairs, and strict financial limitations continued to deny voting rights to the poor in most countries until the late nineteenth century. Thus, in 1865, less than 8 per cent of the population (i.e. less than one third of adult males) could vote in Austria, Belgium, Hungary, Italy, the Netherlands, Norway, Spain, Sweden and the United Kingdom. In Italy, for example, although the population exceeded 25 million, only 500,000 could vote, while in Spain, with a population of 16 million, a mere 400,000 were enfranchised. In both cases, less than 3 per cent of the population had the vote.

By 1914 almost all European countries had enfranchised all adult males (Hungary and Portugal were the major exceptions), largely in response to increasingly well-organised, vociferous and sometimes violent working-class strikes and demonstrations. However, this expanded suffrage was vitiated in all countries, except for some in North-western Europe, either by complicated voting schemes that kept control in the hands of a wealthy minority or by institutionalised election-rigging. In short, the complicated voting schemes used after 1850 in Belgium, Austria, Sweden, Denmark, Romania, Russia and Prussia had the effect of weighting votes by wealth, so that ballots cast by the rich simply counted more than those cast by the poor. The wealthiest 40 per cent of Belgian voters effectively controlled elections there after 1893, as did the richest 5 per cent of Romanian voters after 1866, the top 2 per cent in Austria between 1861 and 1907, the wealthiest 1 per cent of Russians after 1906, and the richest 15 per cent of the Prussian population after 1850. While such complicated schemes were not universal, in France until about 1880, and in Spain, Portugal, Italy, Hungary and the Balkans throughout the nineteenth century, systematic ballot-rigging guaranteed that expansion of the suffrage would pose no threat to the *status quo*. In reading scholarly histories of these countries, one repeatedly encounters such phrases as 'it was the government which made the election, not the election the government' and 'elections always returned an overwhelming majority for the government in power'. The science of election fraud was perhaps most highly developed in Spain, where government newspapers occasionally, as in 1886, actually published election results before ballots were cast. Gerald Brenan's classic account *The Spanish Labyrinth* remains unsurpassed for its witty analysis of Spanish election procedures, which, at least in rural Spain, remained intact until after the First World War:

Only those who could be trusted to support the official candidate were placed on the [electoral] lists, and whenever the numbers of these were insufficient, the same persons could be put down several times. Even the dead could be called upon [known in Spain as the *lazaros* technique after the man brought back to life by Jesus in the Bible]; on one occasion a whole cemetery, 700 strong, gave their vote, and it was edifying to see that though they had been illiterate in their lifetime they had all learned to write in the grave. For some time these measures were sufficient; as however, years passed and people began to show a real desire to elect their own candidates, further falsification of the ballot became necessary. The simplest way of doing this was *actas en blanco*. The members of the ballot committee would certify that they had counted the votes, but would leave the results blank for the Civil Governor to fill in as he pleased later. If for any reason this was impossible, the police would exclude voters, ballot papers would be accidentally destroyed or gangs of toughs would break the ballot-boxes.[18]

The persistence of discriminatory suffrage systems was of critical importance in ensuring that political power and policies remained firmly under the control of the upper class, or upper and middle classes, in most European countries during much or all of the period 1815–1914. If in 1815 political power throughout Europe was monopolised by absolute monarchs and landed aristocrats, by 1914, except in some countries of North-western Europe where universal suffrage and free elections had been introduced, the poor were still shut out from significant power or influence, even if the traditional ruling elements had somewhat expanded their power base to incorporate the wealthiest elements of the professional and commercial classes. Thus, in explaining the fact that the Hungarian legislature as late as 1900 (when only 6 per cent of the population had the vote) paid no attention to the wishes of the poor, Count Albert Apponyi, a prominent Hungarian conservative politician, offered considerable insight into the general nature of much of nineteenth-century European politics when he pointed out that 'Not a single member's election depended upon the ballots of workers.'[19]

The tenuous link that meaningless elections forged between the behaviour of the political classes and the needs of the popular classes was accurately captured by Spanish social and literary critic Ortega y Gasset, who described Spanish political life around 1900 as consisting of 'phantom parties that defend ghostly ideas, and, assisted by the shades of newspapers, run ministries of hallucination'. Some of the results of excluding the masses from political power were quite real, however. Governments that maintained themselves in power through restricted suffrage or rigged ballots poured money into military projects, royal palaces, monumental government buildings and state bureaucracies while grossly neglecting education and the needs of the urban and rural poor. Around 1870, Italy, Prussia and Russia all spent ten times as much on the military as on education, while Austria spent twice as much for police as for schools. In Bulgaria in 1894 the amount of money consumed by the military exceeded the total combined expenditures of the Ministries of Education, the Interior, Justice, Commerce and Agriculture.

In most countries of nineteenth-century Europe, at least until the franchise was extended to the poor, the lower classes bore overwhelmingly the largest share of the burden of taxation, which was generally heavily levied on essential consumption items such as salt and bread, and filled the ranks of the armies – in most countries until after 1870, the wealthier classes were either formally exempt from the draft or could buy a substitute if they were selected. Thus, in Spain throughout the nineteenth century, anyone who was rich enough could buy out of the draft, with the result that over 30 per cent of Spaniards drafted by lot in 1862 escaped induction. Commenting on the restricted suffrage in Italy and the resulting imbalance in state policies, reformer Sidney Sonnino declared in 1881,

> The vast majority of the people, more than 90 per cent of them, feel estranged from our institutions, they see themselves as subjects of the state, constrained to serve it with blood and money, but do not feel that they form an organic, living part of it, nor do they take any interest in its existence and development.[20]

Restrictions on freedom of assembly and association

Most European regimes severely restricted freedom of assembly and association during much or all of the nineteenth century. Although by 1880 these freedoms had been reasonably well secured in North-western Europe, elsewhere severe restrictions were maintained in law or fact until the First World War and beyond. In the more restrictive countries, socialists, radicals and organised workers, whether peaceful or not, faced severe police harassment even after conditions had greatly improved in North-western Europe.

Before 1848, severe restrictions on free assembly and association were virtually universal in Europe, with almost all organisations and gatherings required to obtain governmental authorisation. Thus, in Austria during the early nineteenth century, even dances that involved orchestras with more than two instruments required official sanction. Although between 1848 and 1914 most countries officially accepted the principal of freedom of assembly and association, in practice governments in South-western, Central and Eastern Europe imposed such severe restrictions upon these activities and/or so frequently suspended constitutional guarantees that the exercise of these rights became either highly tenuous or impossible. In these regions, to comply with government regulations organisations had to submit detailed information about their membership and plans and submit to police surveillance, and the authorities were empowered to dissolve public meetings and organisations for vague reasons such as threatening 'public security' or straying from the proposed agenda of a meeting. During periods of political tension, constitutional guarantees were often simply suspended.

In Germany, special legislation effectively outlawed socialist organisations between 1878 and 1890, and socialists endured continual harassment ever thereafter. Thus, between 1890 and 1912, when the suppression of socialism was, according to John Moses, the 'central domestic issue' of the German regime, socialist journalists, politicians and trade unionists were sentenced to a total of 1410 years in prison for their writings, speeches, and political and labour-organising activities. What Norman Stone accurately describes as the notorious 'petty-mindedness and vindictiveness' of the Prussian police even extended to recording, for decades, exactly how many visits were made to the graves of those executed for their roles in the 1848 revolution (in 1903, 10,035 people made such visits, and wreaths laid by twenty-eight of them were removed as politically offensive).[21]

In Italy, constitutional guarantees were repeatedly suspended between 1860 and 1900, making it impossible for socialists to function until just before the outbreak of the First World War. Between 1900 and 1914 hardly a year went by without martial law being imposed somewhere in Spain. Intense persecution made socialist activity virtually impossible in Hungary; party activists there endured sentences totalling 256 years in jail during the last few years before the First World War. In Russia even the principle of freedom of assembly and association was not recognised until 1906, but in practice such freedoms were either ignored or officially suspended over large regions of the country until the fall of the tsarist regime. A 'provisional decree' of 1881 authorising the declaration of states of emergency when necessary to ensure 'order and social tranquillity' was continually renewed. Even a public lecture on 'tuberculosis and its social causes' was forbidden in Russia in 1906, while in 1913 a meeting of teachers convened in Yaroslavl to discuss new tendencies in grammar and self-expression in primary schools was banned because it threatened to 'disturb public tranquillity'.[22]

The right of workers to form unions and to strike was regulated even more strictly and for longer periods in most European countries than were general associational freedoms. Thus, trade unions were illegal until about 1870 in Belgium, Germany and the Netherlands, until 1884 in France, and until 1906 in Russia. Between 1825 and 1864, over 13,000 French workers were prosecuted for illegally striking, and almost 10,000 of them were jailed for the offence. Even in the most tolerant European countries, the first reaction to labour movements was intensely hostile. In Norway, a massive union movement was destroyed in 1850 by trumped-up charges of 'crimes against the security of the state', and the first important strike in Swedish history was smashed by troops and physical evictions in 1879. Although trade unions and strikes were technically legalised almost everywhere in Europe by 1890 (with the major exception of Russia), union activities in practice continued thereafter to face severe official restrictions and harassment in some of the Northwestern European countries (notably France and Belgium) and in virtually all of the other regimes. The attitude of most governments was expressed by a Hungarian Minister of the Interior, who, despite an 1872 law legalising strikes and unions, told a delegation of workers in 1875, 'Are you industrial workers? If so, then work industriously. You do not have to bother with anything else. You need no associations and if you mix into politics I will teach you a lesson you will never forget.' In Germany, the liberal historian and social reformer Lujo Brentano observed that 'Workers have the right to combine. But if they make use of it they are punished.' Or, as German labour lawyer Philipp Lotmar put it, 'The trade union is free, as free as an outlaw.' In Russia, legalisation of trade unions in 1906 led to the establishment of almost 1000 unions with a collective membership of 300,000 within one year, but after 1907 the government dissolved hundreds of unions and membership fell by 60 per cent by

1909. Russian unions were riddled with secret police agents, who, according to one account, sometimes comprised '50 to 75 per cent of the members'.[23]

Opposition groups were sometimes able to evade the many restrictions imposed on the right to assemble, associate, form unions and strike. Thus, in Russia in the decade before 1906, when strikes were formally legalised, almost 1600 illegal strikes were recorded, and it is clear that in France hundreds of clandestine trade unions were organised before they were made legal in 1884. Clandestine unions were often able to survive by masking their activities behind legal fronts, especially so-called 'mutual-aid societies', designed to provide workers with sickness, unemployment and old-age benefits. Many governments tolerated such societies since they reduced public relief expenditures. Thus, in Toulouse, France, where in 1862 there were ninety-six mutual-aid societies, benefiting over one-third of the working population, the public prosecutor warned his superiors of 'the danger posed by working-class trade associations, which under the cover of mutual aid, have organised the trades, subjected workers to rigorously enforced clandestine regulations and often placed employers at the mercy of their workers'. Similarly, authorised supposedly 'non-political' organisations such as choral groups, scientific organisations and agricultural associations often functioned as fronts for forbidden political organisations. Thus, an agricultural society authorised in the Italian state of Sardinia soon became heavily politicised; in the words of A. J. Whyte, 'if they began with talking of cabbages, it was not long before they were talking of kings'. German socialist leader August Bebel warned the German legislature, as it was preparing to outlaw socialist activities in 1878, that such a ban could not be enforced:

They will get together in workshops and factories, in the family circle and in pubs . . . everywhere where it is impossible to exercise control. Everyone will take two or three or perhaps a dozen pamphlets along . . . they will visit their friends and acquaintances in the country and in the distant parts of the city and give them these pamphlets. And you will find it quite impossible to stop these activities.

Bebel's prophecy proved accurate. As J. L. Snell has written of the period 1878–90, when socialist organisations were outlawed in Germany,

Front organizations were created in the form of singing clubs, smoking societies, scientific study groups or gymnastic associations. As soon as one of these could be determined to be socialistic and was banned, the police complained, it would reappear as a new organization with a new name. . . . . Secret meetings were held in forests or small villages near large cities, while others were open picnics attended by hundreds of persons wearing red ribbons or carrying flowers. Funerals of party leaders became political demonstrations; the police estimated that 20,000 of the Hamburg faithful turned out in August 1879 for the most impressive one.[24]

As will be seen when political censorship is discussed in subsequent chapters, similarly clever and evasive techniques were often used to foil attempts at censorship of the press and the arts. But attempted defiance of regimes often carried with it major penalties. As noted above with regard to the jailing of strikers in France and of socialist activists in Germany, opposition activity, whether legal and illegal, peaceful or violent, risked severe sanctions. Hundreds of thousands of Europeans were jailed or fled into exile during the nineteenth century to escape reprisals for their opposition activities, and thousands were beaten or even killed for defying restrictions on peaceful opposition activities. As John Gooch has concluded, the primary role of European armies during the nineteenth century was to serve as 'effective agents of domestic repression' and many European regimes promiscuously resorted to troops when confronted with strikes and demonstrations. Charles Tilly observes that, in most instances where violence broke out during such protests, the peace was broken 'at exactly the moment when authorities intervened' and 'the great bulk of the killing and wounding in such disturbances was done by troops and police rather than by insurgents or demonstrators'. Between 1906 and 1909, French troops and police killed nineteen strikers and wounded 700; while, in Italy between 1901 and 1904, forty workers were killed and over 200 wounded. In Belgium and Germany, Peter Stearns notes, strikes were often marked by 'cavalry charges against strike meetings' and 'bloody use of sabers on the unprotected heads of strikers'.[25] By far the most repressive regime held power in Russia, where troops were called out to aid civilian authorities over 2500 times between 1890 and 1905. Soldiers in Russia shot to death over 300 people in suppressing three strikes in 1892, 1903 and 1912 alone. They also killed an estimated 15,000 people while suppressing a revolutionary outbreak in 1905, which had been sparked by the brutal

'Bloody Sunday' massacre of 9 January, 1905, during which over 100 people were murdered when troops fired on a peaceful protest requesting extension of the franchise and labour and civil-liberties reforms.

The extensive restrictions imposed by nineteenth-century European regimes upon education, voting rights, and freedom of assembly and association clearly demonstrate that political censorship was just one of many techniques used to try to control opposition activity, especially among the lower classes. While most scholarly attention has focused almost exclusively on censorship of the press, European authorities were even more fearful of the impact of the arts, since they were perceived as accessible to the illiterate and more powerful in their impact than print. The rest of this volume will focus on political censorship of both the press and the arts in nineteenth-century Europe.

2 Political Censorship of the Press

'In waging our war, we do not throw bombs', declared the socialist newspaper *Hamburger Echo* on 27 September 1910. 'Instead we throw our newspapers amongst the masses of the working people. Printing ink is our explosive.'[1]

This remark captures will the widespread belief that the press played a crucial role in the 'war' between the dominant classes and other elements of the population that was one of the major themes of nineteenth-century European history. In an age when transportation and communications were relatively primitive, and when politics was, at least at the beginning of the century, largely an aristocratic monopoly, the press was the backbone of any attempt to organise popular political opposition and one of the few means by which members of the middle and lower classes could affect governments and attain general recognition. It is not surprising, therefore, that major battles over freedom of the press were fought in many European countries during the nineteenth century, and that conservative regimes devoted much time and effort to trying to suppress opposition publications, especially those stemming from the working class or with a socialist orientation.

In general, representatives of the traditional ruling elements in Europe detested the idea of a free press. When a university professor was arrested in the reactionary Italian state of Naples in the aftermath of the failed revolution of 1848, he was told by his persecutors that 'the three worst enemies of man are pen, ink and paper'. Klemens von Metternich, the Austrian Foreign Minister who sponsored the infamous Karlsbad Decrees of 1819, which gagged the German and Austrian press for the following thirty years, termed the press a 'scourge' and 'the greatest and consequently the most urgent evil' of his time. Viscount Henry Sidmouth, Home Secretary under the reactionary ministry of Lord Liverpool in Britain (1812–22), termed the press the 'most malignant and formidable enemy to the constitution to which it owed its freedom'. King William IV of England complained that the press was the 'vehicle of everything that is false and capricious'.[2]

The press was frequently compared to a plague or a poison that threatened the health of European society, and journalists were viewed by many conservatives as members of a degraded profession. Thus Vicomte de Bonald, a leader of the reactionary elements in France in the 1820s, defended censorship as a 'sanitary precaution to protect society from the contagion of false doctrines, just like measures taken to prevent the spread of the plague'. Similarly, the editor of the conservative French journal *La Charge* wrote on 19 May 1833 that Paris was suffering from 'journalism', which he defined as 'an epidemic disease against which they have forgotten to establish sanitary precautions'. In Russia, a conservative spokesman declared in 1917 that 'bad books, like rotten provisions, are transformed from food into deadly poison'. Pope Pius IX in his *Syllabus of Errors* (1864), which listed and denounced eighty widespread beliefs of modern life, repudiated freedom of expression as likely to lead to 'corruption of manners and minds'. The Duke of Wellington, who served as British Prime Minister between 1828 and 1830, told another leading British politician in 1827, 'I hate the whole tribe of news-writers and I prefer to suffer from their falsehoods to dirtying my fingers by communicating with them.' Leopold I of Belgium, who clearly disdained the promise of press liberty contained in his country's 1830 constitution, wrote to his cousin Princess Victoria (later Queen of Great Britain) in 1836, 'If all the Editors of the papers in which liberty of the press exists were to be assembled, you should have a crew to which you would not confide a dog that you would value, still less your honor and reputation.'[3]

Conservatives blamed virtually all the ills of the world on the press. An Austrian representative told the German Confederation Diet in 1824 that the press 'brings about unspeakable evil, by denigrating all authority, questioning all principles, attempting to reconstitute all truths', while an official of the German state of Baden told the same assembly in 1832 that newspapers were seeking 'the overthrow of all that exists in Germany'. The prefect of the French Department of Corrèze informed his superior, the Interior Minister, in 1829 that newspapers 'have today the effect of fire and poison on everything that is sacred or powerful or honorable'. Shortly before Charles X of France imposed a major crackdown on the press in 1830, thereby helping to spark off the revolution that overthrew him, he received a report from his ministers claiming that the press had been by nature at all times 'only an instrument of disorder and sedition'. An agent of the Russian secret police reported to his superiors in the 1850s that the literary world 'is today the active agent of all the trouble we are witnessing in the Empire'.[4]

Among other sins they imputed to journalism, conservatives viewed the press as fundamentally irresponsible and filled with lies and incitement to unrest, because the drive to increase circulation led it to sensationalise the news and pander to a mass audience. French politician Jean Martignac told the French Chamber of Deputies in 1822 that

> The interest of the newspapers . . . is in agitation, in the succession of events, in a permanent state of inquietude and expectation; curiosity lives only from events and uncertainty, and for the newspapers the principle of existence and the elements of success lie in curiosity; the monotony of order and peace is fatal to them; the day when the reign of passions will end, when concord, so long exiled, will return to men, newspaper enterprises will no longer have nourishment or life.

Even some liberals deplored the quest of newspapers for sensationalism and the profits that resulted from increased circulations. Swiss liberal historian and journalist Jean Sismondi lamented in 1823 that the aim of the press was 'not the public good, but to get the largest number of subscribers', while John Stuart Mill, one of the leading European defenders of the principles of freedom of speech and press, wrote in a letter that English journalists were members of the 'vilest and most degrading of all trades, because more of affectation & hypocrisy, & more subservience to the baser feelings of others, are necessary for carrying it on, than for any other trade, from that of a brothelkeeper upwards'.[5]

Although conservatives viewed the press as guilty of a multitude of sins, clearly they were most distributed by what they saw as its constant criticising of governments in power, which they believed posed a real threat to the existing order. Thus Napoleon declared that 'four hostile newspapers are more to be feared than a thousand bayonets' and that, 'If I allowed a free press, I would not be in power for another three months.' Lord Grenville, a leading English politician, thundered in 1817 that 'The seditious writers of the present day, who deluge the country . . . with their wicked and blasphemous productions, did not make it a question by whom the Government was to be administered, but whether a Government should exist at all.' Metternich wrote in 1819 that all the governments of Germany had concluded that 'the press serves a party antagonistic to all existing governments'. Sometimes it was alleged that such antagonism simply reflected a desire by opposition journalists to gain power for themselves. The French royalist Alfred Nettement concluded in a book published in 1842 that press opposition to the Bourbon monarchs of 1815–30 had been directed by men who were not concerned that 'affairs were handled in this or that manner, but [rather with] ensuring that affairs were handled by themselves'.[6]

An even worse nightmare for conservatives than that press freedom would lead to a regime dominated by journalists was that it would result in lower-class rule. The press persisted in acting as though political affairs were a matter of general interest amongst the masses, whom conservatives considered manifestly incompetent to take any interest in such matters and who in most regimes in pre-1860 Europe could not vote or serve as legislators, due to the strict income requirements governing entitlements to vote and candidacy for parliament. Referring to these restrictions, the Vicomte de Bonald asked in the 1820s, 'In a government where seven or eight thousand landowners, selected from the highest levels of society, come together each year from every part of the kingdom, to meet under the eyes of the authorities and to discuss their needs, what need is there of a political press?' Conservatives clearly felt that, if the masses were given the impression they had a right to become informed about public issues, they would increasingly also demand the right to be heard on such matters and, in their ignorance and avarice, threaten the public good (which was, of course, perceived by conservatives as coinciding with their own interests). The basic conservative argument against press freedom was that articulated bluntly and clearly by Roger L'Estrange, licenser (i.e. censor) of the English press, in 1633:

A Publick Mercury [i.e. a non-government-controlled newspaper] should never have My Vote; because I think it makes the Multitude too Familiar with the Actions and Counsels of the Superiors; too Pragmaticall and Censorious, and gives them, not only an Itch, but a kind of Colourable Right and License, to be Meddling with Government.

Newspapers which especially addressed themselves to a lower-class audience were particularly feared. Lord Ellenborough, a British conservative, in defending a proposal introduced in parliament in 1819 designed to tax the radical working-class press out of existence, declared that the 'pauper press' had become an utter stranger to truth and only sent forth a continual stream of falsehoods and malignity. . . . this mischief arising from them in the deception and delusions practised upon the lowest classes by means of the grossest and most malignant falsehoods was such that it threatened the most material injuries to the best interests of the country unless some means were devised of stemming its torrent.

Unless the 'torrent' were stemmed, Lord Ellenborough warned, the inevitable result would be a complete overturning of society which would lead to having 'statesmen at the loom and politicians at the spinning jenny'.[7]

Sometimes the remedies the conservatives proposed for dealing with the press were drastic indeed. In the eighteenth century the French Enlightenment philosopher Voltaire used the device of a bogus Ottoman decree to satirise conservative hatred of the press: this proscribed completely the 'infernal invention of printing', since such 'ease in communicating thoughts tends evidently to dissipate ignorance, which is the guardian of the state well policed'. During the nineteenth century, some politicians showed that Voltaire was not fantasising. For example, General Ramon Narváez, the dictator who dominated Spanish politics for much of the mid-nineteenth century, declared, 'It is not enough to confiscate papers; to finish with bad newspapers you must kill all the journalists'; and Friedrich Gentz, Metternich's secretary, wrote in 1819, 'As a preventive measure against the abuses of the press, absolutely nothing should be printed for years. . . . With this maxim as a rule, we should in a short time get back to God and the Truth.'[8]

While conservatives feared press freedom, nineteenth-century European liberals and radicals revered the concept, which had been one of the major themes of the eighteenth-century Enlightenment. The *Encyclopédie*, the masterwork of the Enlightenment, had stated that 'any country in which a man may not think and write his thoughts must necessarily fall into stupidity, superstition and barbarism'. The British philosopher David Hume had declared that liberty of the press would allow the nation to employ 'all learning, wit and genius' to foil the plans of tyrannical monarchs, while the Russian reformer Alexander Radishchev (who was jailed for his writings by Catherine the Great) had proclaimed that press freedom would force rulers to dare not 'depart from the way of truth, lest their policies, their wickedness and their fraud be exposed'.[9]

During the nineteenth century press freedom came increasingly to be seen by many middle- and working-class people as a power which could solve all ills. This in turn fuelled demands for an end to restriction of the press. The *Edinburgh Review* in 1821 hailed the 'genuine freedom of the press as the fountain of all intellectual light, and the source of all that is great among mankind', while English Whigs (liberals) of the period frequently drank to the toast, 'The liberty of the press – 'tis like the air we breathe – while we have it we cannot die.' The French writer François Chateaubriand, who devoted much of his public life to defending press freedom, declared, 'Liberty of the press is today the entire constitution. . . . It consoles us for disgrace; it restrains oppressors through fear of the oppressed; it is the guardian of manners, the protector against injustice. Nothing is lost as long as it exists.' The Irish-born dramatist Richard Brinsley Sheridan had a similarly exalted view of the power of press freedom. 'Against venal Lords, Commons or juries,' he exclaimed, 'against despotism of any kind or in any shape – let me but array a free press and the liberties of England will stand unshaken.' The German liberal leader Karl von Rotteck likewise declared in 1820 that a free press 'assures certain victory for truth and justice, without force, solely through the divine judgment of unfettered public opinion, through the directing authority of human reason'. When the French newspaper *L'Egalité* was suppressed in 1850, its final headline proclaimed, 'Long live freedom of the press, which kills tyrants'.[10]

For the working classes, a free press was viewed as providing education and ultimately leading to a drastic change in the orientation of society. British working-class reformer Samuel Smiles argued that 'we would mainly employ that educator, the Press, to teach working men that they must be their own elevators, educators, emancipators', and a poem written in 1841 by a British striker termed the press 'that Engine to enlarge the slave', and asked, 'can it refuse when truth and justice crave?' In 1840 a French orator by the name of Cormenin told a huge crowd gathered at Strasbourg to dedicate a statue of Gutenburg, the inventor of the modern printing press, that press freedom was the salvation of the underprivileged:

> Until now the rulers have crushed the people under the weight of their cannons; now from the powerful cylinders of the press machines escape night and day millions of sheets which cross rivers, fortresses, customs controls, mountains and seas, and which assault ignorance and despotism with the intelligence projectiles of the press. Yes, ideas, like pacific armies, will advance on the fields of

battle of the future; it is by the propaganda of ideas, by liberty of the press that you will conquer!

The British journalist Frederick Knight reached a similar conclusion, arguing that, 'Where journals are numerous, the people have power, intelligence and wealth; where journals are few, the many are in reality mere slaves.' The Russian revolutionary leader Lenin viewed the development of a newspaper as the first task of socialists, since, he argued in an article written in 1901, 'The newspaper is not only a collective propagandist and a collective agitator, it is also a collective organiser.' He explained,

> The mere technical task of regularly supplying a newspaper with copy and of promoting regular distribution will necessitate a network of local agents of the united party, who will maintain constant contact with one another, know the general state of affairs, get accustomed to performing regularly their detailed functions in the all-Russian work and test their strength in the organization of various revolutionary actions.[11]

While many Europeans clearly viewed the press largely in terms of the advantages or threats it offered to their own class interest, some saw it as a quasi-magical vehicle to end class struggles and ultimately bring about a mystical unity of the entire population. British working-class advocates of complete press freedom during struggles against newspaper taxes during the 1830s declared that such liberty would bring about the 'liberation of the whole human race' and the disappearance forever of 'internal discord, commotion and strife'. Similarly, the French liberal historian Jules Michelet, who termed the press the 'holy ark' of modern times, which fulfilled a 'sacred mission', declared in 1847 that an unfettered press could bring about a 'moral union' of French society:

> Is not the press the universal intermediary? What a sight, when from the post office, one watches newspapers leave by the thousand, these representatives of diverse opinions, who will carry until the distant frontiers the traditions of the parties, the voices of polemic, harmonizing nevertheless in a certain unity of language and of ideas! . . . Who does not believe that the national soul is going to circulate now by all the means of this great mechanism?

Even Karl Marx seems to have dissolved into mystical rapture when discussing the virtues of press freedom. He wrote in 1842,

> A free press is the omnipresent open eye of the spirit of the people, the embodied confidence of a people in itself, the articulate bond that ties the individual to the state and the world, the incorporated culture which transfigures material struggles into intellectual struggles and idealizes its raw material shape. . . . It is universal, omnipresent, omniscient. It is the ideal world, which constantly gushes from the real one and streams back to it ever richer and animated anew.[12]

Demands for press freedom were one of the major rallying cries of middle-class liberals and middle- and working-class radicals throughout the nineteenth century, and played a major role in revolutionary upheavals in 1830 in France, Belgium and Germany, as well as in the revolutions which convulsed all Central Europe in 1848 and the 1905 revolution in Russia. Even where quarrels over press freedom did not lead to revolution, they often provided a key symbolic issue which focused demands for a broader democratisation and whose resolution helped pave the way for more general reforms. For example, when Frederik VI of Denmark began considering new restrictions on the press in the 1830s, almost 600 Danes, including over 100 officials and university professors quickly signed a protest petition. Frederik's reply that 'We alone know' what is good for the people furnished the opposition with what one historian has termed a ready-made 'symbol of inane autocracy' and led to the formation of the Society for the Proper Use of Freedom of the Press, which quickly attracted 5000 members. Although Frederik issued a harsh new press law in 1837, and unmercifully harassed the leading liberal paper *Fædrelandet* (it was subjected to huge fines and during one six-month period in 1843 10 per cent of its issues were confiscated), the press society became a leading focus for democraticisation in Denmark. It played a significant role in organising the public pressure which led to a series of reforms in 1845–9 which not only gave Denmark a free press but also peacefully transformed the country from one of the leading autocracies of Europe into a fledgling democracy.[13]

While struggles over freedom of the press were a major theme in the general struggle for democracy in nineteenth-century Europe, it would be misleading to suggest that the entire population was in a constant frenzy over this issue. Until late in the century the concept of press freedom had little meaning to the vast majority of the population. Most people could not afford the luxury of buying and reading newspapers, since most of their time and income was devoted to basic survival. Thus, an Italian reformer lamented in the late 1850s that to those 'wretched people who do not know how to read, who do not want to read (and I am not saying it is their fault), the government that levies the lowest tax on salt seems preferable to the government that grants the greatest freedom of the press'. Peasants in the German Rhineland in 1848 understood the slogan 'Pressfreiheit' (press freedom) to mean freedom from 'oppressive' demands by landowners. At Elberfeld, in the Rhineland, workers reportedly heckled speakers at a rally during the 1848 revolution with the cry, 'Was geht uns Pressfreiheit an? Fressfreiheit ist es, was wir verlangen!' ('What do we care about freedom of the press? Freedom to eat is what we want!').[14]

THE DEVELOPMENT OF RESTRICTIONS ON PRESS FREEDOM

The development of the modern printing press and of techniques for repression of the press were virtually simultaneous. By 1560, about 100 years after Gutenberg built the first printing press in Europe, licensing and censorship systems for printed matter existed throughout Western Europe. The attitude of many European authorities was expressed by Pope Alexander VI, who in 1501 declared that printing could be 'very harmful if it is permitted to widen the influence of pernicous works' and that 'full control over the printers' was therefore necessary. Around the same time, Archbishop Becatelli of Ragusa declared, even more forcefully, that 'the world hath already too many books, especially since printing was invented; and it is better to forbid a thousand books without cause, than permit one that deserveth prohibition'.[15]

In 1535 Francis I of France issued a decree banning all printing whatsoever on pain of death by hanging. This was quickly repealed, but more subtle and complicated methods of regulating the press were developed, consuming enormous bureaucratic energy throughout Europe during the sixteenth, seventeenth and eighteenth centuries. In Spain during this period, at least seventy-eight different decrees were issued to regulate the press, while in France an astounding 3000 edicts and ordinances were issued in the eighteenth century alone to regulate all aspects of the printing trade. Most of the press laws were extremely vague: for example, in 1529 the Spanish authorities who governed Antwerp banned the publication of 'any evil doctrines or theological error'; a French edict of 1531 forbade publication of 'false doctrine'; and in the 1780s Catherine the Great of Russia warned that 'strange philosophising' could lead to the closure of printshops and bookstores. The first index of prohibited books published by the Catholic Church was issued in 1539, and similar lists were published by governments, including the English (from 1529), the French (from 1545) and the Austrian (from 1754; until then the Church had controlled Austrian censorship). The Austrian index of 1765 ran to 184 pages in small type and listed 3000 forbidden books, including works by Hobbes, Hume, Locke, Rousseau, Voltaire, Boccaccio, Rabelais, Swift, Lessing and even King Frederick the Great of Prussia. In France, at least 1000 books were forbidden between 1700 and 1750, while the number of French censors jumped from seventy-three to 178 between 1745 and 1789.[16]

Violations of repressive press laws called forth the most severe types of punishment. Printers and journalists convicted of written sedition, heresy or treason were subject to (and actually sentenced to) the death penalty in many countries, including Spain, France, Austria, Germany, England and Switzerland. At least six English booksellers and authors were executed between 1530 and 1533. In France three booksellers and printers were burnt at the stake during the last two months of 1534, while in the Swiss canton of Zürich the authorities sentenced seventy-four writers to death between 1500 and 1700 for such offences as 'attacks on authority' and 'sneering at matrimony'. Lesser penalties such as whipping, jailing, banishment and closure of printshops and bookstores were far more widespread, with almost 900 French authors, printers, and book- and print-sellers jailed in the Bastille alone between 1600 and 1756, including Voltaire and Denis Diderot, editor of the *Encyclopédie*. David Pottinger, a historian of the eighteenth-century French book trade, concludes that during the middle decades of the century 'there were few authors prominent or obscure, who did not spend at least 24 hours in jail'. Thousands of banned works were destroyed or even publicly burned. Voltaire's *Philosophical Dictionary* (1764), published anonymously to evade censorship, was burned by authorities in Paris, Geneva, the Netherlands and the Vatican, for example. In eighteenth-century France, at least 385 separate titles were burned, often by the public hangman, while many other books were torn up and turned into waste paper. In Russia in 1793, during the 'Jacobin scare' touched off by the French Revolution, almost 19,000 books were burned.[17]

Despite the severe press controls maintained throughout Europe, there was a flourishing trade in illegal books and newspapers throughout the period leading up to the French Revolution, especially since, as Elizabeth Eisenstein writes, 'Profits were even greater when one's products were advertised throughout Europe free of charge by printed lists of prohibited books.' When Galileo's *Dialogue on Two World Systems* was listed on the Catholic Index in the early seventeenth century, even monks and priests hastened to try to obtain it, pushing up the black-market price to ten to twelve times the original cost. One leading German publishing house instructed its authors to 'write anything . . . that will be forbidden', while Louis XVI's police chief lamented that 'Parisians have more of a propensity to believe the malicious rumors and libels that circulated clandestinely than the facts printed and published by order or with the permission of the government.' To meet the demand for forbidden printed matter in France, clandestine presses sprang up throughout the country (there were an estimated 100 such presses in Paris alone in the eighteenth century) and publishers printed books with false or no imprints so that the volumes could not be traced back to them. Printers also legally established themselves just outside the French borders, especially in relatively tolerant cities in Switzerland and the Netherlands, and established elaborate smuggling networks to transport books across the frontier. The trade in banned books in France was so widespread that the chief French official in charge of censorship between 1750 and 1763 wrote in his memoirs that 'A man who had only read those books approved by the government, as prescribed by law, would have been almost a century behind his contemporaries.' Over 1000 banned volumes were ordered in two years from a single Swiss printer by one dealer in illegal books in the French backwater town of Troyes in the 1780s, while throughout Europe in the eighteenth century at least 4500 titles were published with false imprints, naming such imaginary places of publication as Alethopolis, the Antipodes, Bacchopolis and the Ile de Calipso.[18]

With the outbreak of the French Revolution, the obvious failure of existing repressive press controls led to drastic action by regimes which feared a spread of French subversion. Several European countries sought to suppress completely from their newspapers any mention of events in France, and some banned all publications originating from there. In Spain, an order dated January 1790 banned the importation, printing or circulation of all books and papers relating to the French Revolution. A year later, all privately published Spanish periodicals, except for one non-political journal, were suppressed, in order to keep out news from France. In Bavaria in the 1790s, all references to the French Revolution and the 'rights of man' were forbidden, as were all the works of Burke, Erasmus, Frederick the Great, Kant, Montesquieu, Rousseau, Schiller, Spinoza, Swift and Voltaire. In Austria, a decree of 1793 banned any favourable reference to events in France, all reading rooms and lending libraries were closed in 1798–9, and in 1801 censorship was extended to mottoes on fans, snuff boxes, musical instruments and toys. In Russia, Catherine the Great banned the importation of all objects of French origin, and forbade the printing of anything 'against God's law, government orders or common decency'. Her successor, the mad Tsar Paul I, outlawed the importation of all printed matter, including music, regardless of its origins.[19]

Clearly, when the Napoleonic Wars ended, Europe had a strong tradition of repression of the press. Of all the European countries, only Norway had a truly free press in 1815. While a few other countries, such as Britain, Sweden and the United Netherlands, had technically abolished prior censorship of the press, they employed various administrative techniques that greatly diminished the significance of that development (in France, where the Charter of 1814 instituted a constitutional ban on prior censorship, such censorship continued in fact intermittently until 1830). As can be seen from Table 1, by 1850 press freedom had been largely achieved only in the Low Countries, Scandinavia and Britain. In 1914, major restrictions on press freedom still existed in Russia, Germany, Hungary and, to a slightly lesser extent, Austria. Even in countries where the press became largely free by 1850, repression continued to occur sporadically. For example, there was a spate of prosecutions of socialist editors in Denmark and Sweden in the 1880s; and Domela Nieuwenhuis, founder of the Dutch socialist movement, served eight months in jail for writing in 1887 that King Willem III had 'made little of his job'.[20]

Where severe restrictions on press freedom existed, newspapers often were reduced to complete blandness and could not offer any adequate coverage of public affairs. A British visitor to Spain in 1820 reported that the papers there contained nothing but reports of the weather and 'accounts of miracles wrought by different Virgins, lives of holy friars and sainted nuns, romances of marvellous conversions,

TABLE 1   *Press repression in Europe, 1815–1914*

Country	Constitutional or legal ban on prior censorship	End of severe administration of post-publication censorship	End of special press taxes (where applied)
Austria	1867	Not before 1914	1899
Belgium	1830	1830	1848
Bulgaria	1879	Periodic easing before 1914	
Denmark	1849	1846	
France	1814	1881	1881
Germany (Prussia before 1870)	1848	Not before 1914	1874
Great Britain	1695	c. 1830	1861
Hungary	1867	Not before 1914	
Italy (Piedmont before 1860)	1848	c. 1900	
Netherlands	1815	1848	1869
Norway	1814	1814	
Portugal	1834	1852	
Romania	1866	1866	
Russia	1865 (partial), 1905	Not before 1914	
Serbia	1869	1903	
Spain	1837	1883	
Sweden	1809	1838	
Switzerland	1848	c. 1830	

libels against Jews, heretics and Freemasons, and histories of apparitions'. The great Czech historian Frantisek Palacký complained in 1830, 'I do not know how it will end when we cannot write about anything except cook-books and prayer-books, fairy-tales and charades', while the Saxon journalist Robert Blum complained in the 1840s, 'We must write pure nonsense or not be published at all.' A French journalist, commenting on the German press in 1841, remarked, 'If an American Indian had had the opportunity to read such a paper for the first time, he would have come to the conclusion that German life consisted of hunting and eating,' and British observer William Howitt wrote on the same subject in 1844 that German newspapers published nothing on 'all those great questions which involve the political progress and development of a people', as 'over all the heads of such journals hangs the iron pen of the censor and fills every writer with terror'.[21]

Regulation of the press was the subject of great attention and much legislation in many of the European countries throughout the nineteenth century. This was especially the case in Spain, Serbia, Austria, Germany, Russia and France. In Spain between 1810 and 1883, at least fifteen major press laws and decrees were promulgated. By 1851, the French laws had become so complicated that, as remarked earlier, two judges published a handbook on them to aid befuddled lawyers and journalists. The French press law of 1881 replaced forty-two laws (containing 325 separate clauses) which had been passed during the previous seventy-five years by ten different regimes. A prominent Russian journalist of the late nineteenth century complained that his newspaper had to hire a specialist to keep up with the over 13,000 circulars that Russian bureaucrats had issued to give the press 'guidance' on its public-affairs coverage.[22]

TECHNIQUES OF REPRESSION

The techniques used to control the press in nineteenth-century Europe can be divided into two major categories. In the first category were the direct forms of repression, designed to prevent 'undesirables' from publishing anything (licensing of printers and newspapers), to prevent particular 'undesirable' material from appearing (prior censorship), and, where prior censorship had been abolished, to punish the publishers of 'undesirable' material which did appear in print (post-publication prosecution, sometimes known as punitive censorship). In the second category were indirect forms of repression, which did not specifically outlaw or punish particular journalists or published material, but which were designed to discourage the poor from publishing or buying newspapers by imposing financial constraints upon the press. These involved such techniques as requiring deposits of large sums of money, known as security or caution bonds, before a newspaper could be established, and the imposition of special taxes on newspapers. Frequently, direct and indirect means of press regulation coexisted in the same country.

Direct repression: prior censorship and licensing

Before 1848, the greatest discontent over press regulation was focused, in most of Europe, on the systems of prior censorship and licensing. With the major exception of Britain, which had abolished such controls in 1695, and the minor exceptions of Sweden, Norway and the Netherlands, these applied throughout Europe in 1815. Licensing requirements provided that no one could publish a newspaper or other printed matter without first receiving a permit from the government, which meant that only 'reliable' individuals were allowed to publish. In some countries only publishers had to be licensed, while in others, as in England before 1695, printers had to be licensed also. Until 1695, only twenty printers were licensed to operate in the city of London. In France until just before the French Revolution, only one paper was licensed to publish political news, and strict limits were imposed on the number of printers in Paris, in order to avoid, as a 1618 edict put it, 'the abuses, disorders, and confusion which occur daily as the result of the printing of an infinite number of scandalous, libellous and defamatory books'.[23]

Licensing was usually accompanied by prior censorship. Prior censorship generally meant that material to be published could not be set in type before it had been approved by governmental authorities. Together with licensing, prior censorship was designed to ensure that only reliable persons would be publishing at all and that the particular material published would contain nothing objectionable. Naturally, obstreperous printers and publishers risked having their licences withdrawn. In most of the Catholic countries, including Spain, Portugal, Austria and Italy, and in Orthodox Russia, printed matter often had to be cleared by officials of both Church and state under medieval censorship regulations. Although clerical censorship had generally been abolished by 1789, it was occasionally revived during the nineteenth century in times of social tension when state officials felt a need to make concessions to the Church to gain clerical support in suppressing lower-class unrest. As can be seen from Table 1, prior censorship was gradually abolished throughout Europe during the nineteenth century, and by 1914 not a single European country still exercised it. In most, although not all, of the European countries, licensing systems died along with prior censorship. This was not always the case, however. Press laws passed in Prussia in 1851, in France in 1852, and in Austria in 1867 all excluded prior censorship but maintained licensing for newspaper publishers.

Perhaps the most notorious system of prior censorship in nineteenth-century Europe was that operated in Austria before 1848.

Austria was known as the 'China of Europe' for its attempt to prevent infection of its subjects by liberal western currents. During the period 1835–48, Austria had a list of 5000 forbidden books, including works by Fichte, Rousseau, Spinoza, Heine, Lessing, Goethe and Schiller. Stanley Pech has compared the list to a 'catalogue of masterpieces of European literature'. Austrian censorship extended beyond books and newspapers to maps, business signs, and inscriptions on grave-stones, badges, medals, cufflinks and tobacco boxes. In one incident, even the word 'Liberté', painted on the sides of some china boxes shipped from France, was erased, leading a furious buyer in Trieste to refuse shipment.[24]

While the Austrian system was the most notorious in Europe, prior censorship in Russia was sometimes even more restrictive, and lasted far longer, as it was not completely abolished until 1905. Russian censorship reached its zenith under Tsar Nicolas I (1825–55), when it even extended to the mottoes printed on candy-wrappers, and when at least twelve different censorship units functioned (secular, ecclesiastical, postal, military, judicial, foreign, textbook, secret police, regular police, etc.). Virtually any government department, even that administering state horse-breeding, could intervene when printed matter affected its sphere of influence, and, as Ronald Hingley has concluded, 'it really was a wonder that anything got into print at all'. A cookery book was not allowed to refer to 'free air' in the oven, as this phrase sounded too revolutionary, and a reference to poisonous mushrooms was forbidden as sacrilegious, since many peasants ate mushrooms during Lent. Tolstoy's novel *Resurrection* (1899) was passed for publication only after 500 changes had been made. A book entitled *The Feminist Movement in America* was banned in 1875 because it was judged to be 'directed toward the censure and the weakening of the bases of the family union' and in general to contain 'ideas that are not in agreement with the structure of our state and society'.[25]

One of the most notorious aspects of Russian censorship was the careful scrutiny of all imported printed matter. During the height of the reaction in Russia after the European revolutions of 1848, even Hans Christian Andersen's stories for children and a book in French entitled *Physiology and Hygiene of the Beard and Moustache* were barred. Among the authors whose work was banned at one time or another in nineteenth-century Russia were Diderot, Goethe, Byron, Heine, Hobbes, Jefferson, Stendhal, Balzac and Hugo. Bizarrely, despite the 1865 censorship decree prohibiting books which 'expound the harmful doctrines of socialism or communism', in 1872 Marx's *Das Kapital* was allowed into the country, on the grounds that it was a 'difficult, inaccessible, strictly scientific work' that was too obscure to have any impact. Between 1866 and 1904 over 12,000 titles were banned from importation into Russia, and thousands of others were allowed in only after the censors had carefully effaced all objectionable material by blacking it out with ink or gutta-percha (an exercise popularly known as 'applying caviar') or covering it up with paste and paper. Thus, the following statement by Lessing was blacked out: 'We are not created to believe blindly, we are human beings, and have the human right to think – to what end the train of thought may lead an individual is something he must settle with himself.' A British observer commented that 'With a preparation of gutta-percha and powdered glass [the censor of imported matter] will cleanse and purify *The Times* of a paragraph or *Punch* of a joke in so neat a manner that not a vestige of printer's ink shall remain.' Sigmund Freud complained to a friend in an 1897 letter about the results of such procedures: 'Have you ever seen a foreign newspaper which has passed the Russian censorship at the frontier? Words, whole clauses, and sentences are blacked out so that what is left becomes unintelligible.'[26]

Outside Austria and Russia, probably the most ferocious censorship systems in nineteenth-century Europe were those operated in Germany and Italy before 1848. In Germany in 1835, the works of the entire school of writers known as 'Young Germany', whose leaders were the literary giants Ludwig Börne and Heinrich Heine, were banned on the grounds that these writers 'openly tend to attack the Christian religion in the most insolent way, to denigrate existing social relations, and to destroy all decency and morality, in literary works accessible to all classes of people'. The last phrase, like the Russian decision to allow in *Das Kapital* because it appeared 'inaccessible', shows that the authorities were particularly sensitive to literature which was likely to be read by the lower classes. Thus in 1826 the legal adviser of Charles X of France expressed alarm over the profusion of small, cheap booklets which were easily affordable by the poor and could be easily hidden even if they were forbidden:

We see published each day books whose format and price add to their dangers. You can judge for yourself whether these publications have as their purpose, as they declare, to enlighten the government about public needs, . . . or if they do not rather tend to propagate the most pernicious doctrine in all classes of society and to give to students, children, workers and domestics the means of shielding themselves easily from the wishes of their teachers, parents and masters and from the reaches of justice.

In 1843, Friedrich Wilhelm IV of Prussia expressed a similar concern about the accessibility of printed matter to the poor, making clear that, while serious books should be dealt with tolerantly by the censors, this should only apply to books written in a style unintelligible to a mass audience:

> What I do not want is the dissolution of scholarship and literature into newspaper scribbling [and the] spread of seductive errors and corrupt theories . . . in the most transient form among a class of the population for which this form is more appealing, and newspapers more accessible, than the products of serious examination and thorough scholarship.[27]

Such attitudes were commonplace among the ruling classes in nineteenth-century Europe. In 1834, the Russian Main Censorship Department recommended to Tsar Nicholas I that he should not permit the establishment of cheap non-religious magazines aimed at a mass audience, since the very idea of common people being influenced by secular literature was incompatible, politically or otherwise, 'with our existing order'. Nicholas concurred, noting on the recommendation forwarded to him, 'Completely true. By no means allow'. The files of German censors before 1848 are filled with police warnings about the distribution of printed matter whose 'style and cheapness' made them attractive to the 'great mass of the people'; thus in 1829 the Prussian authorities decided to ban a book not only because it contained 'exaggerated complaints about oppression, injustice, bad government', but also because it was written in a style 'attractive especially to readers from the less educated social strata' and could lead 'these sections of the populace to discontent with existing conditions'.[28]

Fear of the accessibility of 'dangerous' reading matter to the poor was reflected in a number of peculiar provisions of some of the censorship laws. In the Karlsbad Decrees of 1819, which provided the basis of censorship in Germany for the following thirty years, and in the Russian censorship decree of 1865, which remained in force for forty years, lengthy books were exempted from the prior censorship to which short books were subject. Clearly it was felt that long books (aside from being a burden on the censorship) would be too expensive and too scholarly for the lower classes. There was also more overt discrimination against the poor. In both Austria and Russia censors had the option of designating a book as available only to certain educated professions or upon special application, and it sometimes happened that books that were not allowed to be sold as individual volumes were permitted as part of an expensive set of collected works. Thus, Tsar Alexander III responded favourably in 1891 to a plea by Tolstoy's wife Sonya to allow publication of his banned novel *The Kreutzer Sonata* as volume 13 of his collected works, since, as the Tsar noted, 'not everyone could afford to buy the whole set and it would not be too widely disseminated'.[29]

Direct repression: post-publication censorship

Prior-censorship and licensing systems were the particular targets of liberal opprobrium during the nineteenth century, and, of all techniques used to control the press at the time, have continued to attract the most attention. However, systems of post-publication censorship (sometimes known as 'punitive censorship') often proved just as threatening to press freedom, and usually caused far more hardship to individuals. Even after prior-censorship systems had been eliminated, every European country maintained some laws that could be used to punish what were viewed as abuses of press liberty. In Russia, Austria, Hungary and Germany post-publication censorship was so severe that it cannot really be said that there was a free press in these countries before 1914.

In some cases, post-publication controls were administered in such a way that the boundary between them and prior censorship became almost meaningless. Under the systems established in Austria in 1867, Germany in 1874, Russia in 1865 and France in 1822, copies of 'non-censored' newspapers had to be submitted to the authorities either just before or simultaneously with the distribution of the papers. This meant that the authorities could, if they spotted objectionable material, seize the press run before any significant distribution occurred. The only differences between these 'punitive censorship' systems and those of prior censorship were that under prior censorship the censors usually got the blame if something slipped through, and the publishers did not lose money by first printing something and then having it seized. Under the systems of 'punitive censorship', the publishers and journalists involved risked huge financial losses as well as administrative or judicial sanctions for transgressing press laws. Government officials under punitive-censorship systems sometimes explicitly threatened journalists with prosecutions and confiscations if they became too troublesome. For example, although the 1850 Prussian constitution and 1851 Prussian press law abolished prior censorship, post-publication prosecutions remained possible for a variety of offences, and the government sent the following instructions to provincial officials in 1858 as journalists became increasingly critical of the regime:

> You are instructed to insure that the newspapers not excite the people, or question the king's decisions. This would only shake the people's loyalty. Speak personally to the newspaper publishers about this illegal comment on politics. Otherwise do not hesitate to employ the provisions of the 1851 press law against them.

The result of such threats and the constant danger of post-publication censorship was, as the authorities no doubt intended, that journalists were forced to act as their own censors, and sometimes out of excess caution eliminated material that the authorities might have tolerated. As the Russian journalist Alexsei Suvorin pointed out, 'One's own censorship became harsher than the state's, and was a great torment'.[30]

One of the most ingenious punitive-censorship laws of nineteenth-century Europe was that introduced by Louis Napoleon Bonaparte on 17 February, 1852, shortly after his *coup d'état* which overthrew the Second French Republic. Under this decree which governed French publishing for sixteen years, all publishers of periodicals dealing in any way with 'politics or social economy' were required to obtain licences, which had to be renewed with each staff change. A long list of press offences was defined, including the publication of false news and other-than-official accounts of legislative activity. All press offences were to be tried without juries; one felony conviction or two misdemeanour convictions automatically led to suppression of the periodical concerned. A system of administrative 'warnings' was also established, allowing the government to take action when it did not like published material but could not or did not wish to prosecute in the courts. Warnings could be based on whatever criteria struck the government's fancy; after three warnings the Minister of the Interior could suspend a journal for two months, while the President of the Republic (i.e. Louis Napoleon) could at any time act to suppress a journal if the public safety was deemed to warrant such action. During the period from 1852 to 1867 when this decree was in effect, 120 newspapers received a total of 338 warnings and suffered twenty-seven suspensions, and twelve of the papers were closed down. Under this system, one French paper complained in the 1860s, 'freedom of the press only amounts to the freedom to pay fines and to go to prison or to Belgium'. A French journalist writing about this period in his memoirs recalled,

> Obstacles and pitfalls on all sides beset the newspaper and those who wrote for it. Self-censored in the first instance, re-read and corrected with meticulous care by his editor, superintended in the last resort by the printer who was responsible before the law for everything that came off his press, stifled and hamstrung, attracting the thunderbolt and yet tied to the lightning-conductor, seated on the powder-barrel and condemned to strike the tinder box, the journalist of 1860 was truly a victim tortured by the imperial regime.[31]

The Russian press rules in effect betwen 1875 and 1905 copied the French system of 1852, under which periodicals (at least those published in St Petersburg and Moscow) were freed from prior censorship but were subject to severe administrative sanctions, including possible suspension for up to six months after three warnings, as well as to post-publication prosecution in the courts. The liberal Russian censor Aleksandr Nikentko wrote in his diary that, under the warning system as against preliminary censorship, 'the sword of Damocles now hangs over the head of writers and editors' and 'this sword is in the minister's hands; he lets it fall at his own discretion and is not even obliged to justify his action'. During the forty years this system was in effect, 280 warnings were issued and sixty-four journals were suspended, some on more than one occasion. The first warning was issued to the journal *Sovremennik* in 1865, on the grounds that 'in one of its articles there is an indirect condemnation of the principles of private property as implemented by capitalists who allegedly have taken possession in an injust way of the savings of the worker class' and that 'hatred is being stirred up against the upper and propertied classes, which are pictured as being essentially immoral because of the very fact of their existence and as being detrimental to the national welfare'. The most frequent victim was *Golos*, the leading St Petersburg daily at the end of the reign of Alexander II, which received twenty warnings and was suspended for a total of nineteen months during a period of five years before it was permanently suppressed in 1883. One unique feature of the Russian system after 1865, when prior censorship had supposedly been abolished for periodicals published in the capitals, was that beginning in 1873 the government reserved the right to order all publications not to mention some subjects at all. Publications which ignored this ban were subject to suspension for up to three months. At least 570 subjects, ranging from the censorship itself to the famine of 1892 and matters that could cast aspersions on the honour of wives of Turkish sultans, were banned from discussion in the Russian press during the period (1873–1904) when this regulation was in effect. Administrative suspensions were imposed twenty-three times for violations of the rules.[32]

Numerous other instances of massive press repression in systems which had abolished prior censorship clearly demonstrate that press freedom was by no means synonymous with lack of prior censorship. In Sweden, although prior censorship was abolished in 1809, King Karl Johan (reigned 1818–1844) used his untrammelled authority to revoke newspaper licences to suppress sixty newspapers, and between 1831 and 1837 twenty-three press prosecutions were brought in a country with few newspapers. In Germany, under a formally liberal press law passed in 1874, almost 800 prosecutions were brought within its first six months and over 3800 press trials took place by 1890. The separate 'anti-socialist' law in effect from 1878 until 1890 was used to suppress the entire socialist press: 1299 different publications, including 104 newspapers and other periodicals, were banned. Even after expiration of the anti-socialist law, socialists faced hundreds of press prosecutions, usually for *lèse majesté*, or criticism of the king. Over 600 *lèse majesté* prosecutions were brought in 1894, while in the first six months of 1913 over 100 convictions of socialist journalists resulted in sentences of forty years in jail and almost 11,000 marks in fines. In France, where prior censorship was abolished in 1830, there were 520 press prosecutions in Paris alone between 1830 and 1834. Between December 1848 and December 1850, 185 republican papers faced a total of 335 prosecutions, forcing forty of them out of business. An astounding blizzard of 2500 press prosecutions ensued within seven months during a period of political crisis in 1877.[33]

In the Hapsburg Empire, where prior censorship ended in 1867, an eighteen-month period in 1868–9 brought Czech newspaper editors sentences totalling seventeen years in jail and heavy fines. There were over 2000 prosecutions and confiscations of newspapers throughout Austria between 1877 and 1880, while in the 1880s the Czech newspaper *Narodni Listy* was confiscated 330 times. In Hungary, where prior censorship ended in 1867, newspapers published by the Slovak and Romanian minorities were systematically harassed; one Slovak paper, *Narodine Noviny*, underwent thirteen separate prosecutions between 1892 and 1904. In Italy, over 100 newspapers were arbitrarily suppressed during a period of political turmoil in 1898. In Russia, where prior censorship was partially lifted in 1865 and fully abolished in 1905, a total of 4386 penalties were imposed upon periodicals between 1905 and 1910 (compared to eighty-two between 1900 and 1904); in nearly 1000 cases newspapers were suppressed. In 1907 alone, 175 Russian editors and publishers were jailed and 413 periodicals were banned. Although even revolutionary parties were allowed to publish newspapers, their periodicals faced unmerciful harassment. Between 1912 and 1914, the Bolshevik paper *Pravda* published 645 issues, of which 155 were confiscated and thirty-six others drew fines totalling 16,550 rubles. In 1914 it was suppressed, and was not published again until after the fall of the tsarist regime. The *Pravda* offices were riddled with police agents – at one point both the publisher and editor of the paper were on the police payroll – and watched by numerous spies. According to one staff member,

> So many spies and police agents used to loiter around *Pravda*'s premises that they could not even keep track of each other. They were disguised as workers, passers-by, coachmen, and so on. Once, a local police officer in uniform got into a carriage parked in front of the plant and ordered the coachman to start up. The coachman refused, announcing that the carriage was already engaged. The officer was furious and started beating him with his baton. The coachman pulled out a gun and started beating the officer. . . . It turned out that the coachman was really a police agent whose sole task was to remain in front of *Pravda*'s printing plant and report on what was taking place.[34]

Whether they lived in countries with prior or with punitive censorship systems, journalists were constantly faced with vague press laws and inconsistent enforcement, so they could never know in advance what was liable to cause them trouble with the authorities

Austrian intellectuals who protested against their country's prior-censorship system in 1845 probably spoke for most journalists when they complained, 'The situation of the press with respect to the censor is, alas, one devoid of legality. The writer is judged by norms which he does not know and is condemned without being heard and without being able to defend himself.' Sometimes the confusion and vagueness of repressive press regulations shone clearly through even the statements of government officials. Thus, Napoleon Bonaparte told his viceroy in Italy during the French occupation in the first decade of the nineteenth century, 'I want you to suppress completely the censorship of books. This country has a narrow enough mind without straitening it any more. Of course, the publication of any work contrary to the government would be stopped.' The Austrian censorship decree of 1810 declared,

> In the future no ray of light, wherever it should appear, should be disregarded and unrecognized in the monarchy. Nor should it be robbed of any useful result. But the heart and head of the immature are to be protected cautiously from the poisonous aspirations of the self-seeking seducers and from the dangerous illusions of crazed heads.[35]

Similar confusion was evident in the censors' own statements about their operating principles. The German folklorist Jacob Grimm, who served as a censor in the German state of Hesse between 1816 and 1829 (and was later dismissed from the University of Göttingen for his political views), wrote to his two fellow censors in 1822 that 'What are punishable are demagogic works that poison and insult the existing political system, but not those that bravely and necessarily uncover the failings of individual governments.' Twenty years later, another Hessian censor declared that the censorship should not 'snoop about nervously like the police' or 'inhibit the independent development of the mind, but rather promote it – not cut away every new sprout, but rather purge the poisonous fungi that are deadly to spiritual, moral and civil life'.[36]

Numerous examples could be cited of extraordinarily vague press laws, under both prior- and punitive-censorship systems. For example, the Swedish law of 1812 allowed the King to suppress any newspaper for 'imperilling the public safety', with no court hearing or appeal allowed. A British law of 1798 banned materials 'tending to excite hatred and contempt of the person of his majesty and of the constitution and government'. The 1819 Karlsbad Decrees forbade the circulation of any printed matter which was 'inimical' to the 'maintenance of peace and quiet in Germany', while an 1841 Prussian decree outlawed anything 'offensive to morality and good will'. The 1822 Spanish press law banned writings which 'spread rules or doctrines or which refer to acts dedicated to exciting to rebellion or to disturbing the public peace, even though they may be disguised as allegories of imaginary persons or countries, or of past times or as dreams or fictions, or anything similar'. Libel was defined under this law as writings which 'made vulnerable the reputation of individuals, even though they are not named, or indicated by anagrams, allegories or in any other form'. The French press law of September 1835, deemed by the French liberal poet Alphonse de Lamartine as a 'law of iron, a reign of terror for ideas', outlawed 'any attack against the principle or form' of the government, as well as 'expressing the wish, the hope or the threat of the destruction of the constitutional monarchical order'. A French law of 1849 banned the publication of 'erroneous or inaccurate facts likely to disturb the peace'. A Russian censorship decree of 1863 outlawed materials which contradicted 'the fundamental ideas of our state structure and root conditions or public order'. Censorship laws in effect in Austrian-controlled Lombardy–Venetia and in Russia in the 1820s barred writings which violated the 'purity' of language.[37]

The vagueness of censorship laws was only compounded by the vague guidelines provided to censors by their superiors. Thus, when the liberal Russian censor Nikitenko began his duties in 1833, he was told by his supervising minister,

> You must perform your duties in such a manner that you not only base your judgments on the censorship code, but also on the particular set of circumstances with which you are faced and the course of events. Also you must work in such a way that the public has no cause to conclude that the government is hounding culture.

Such vagueness was inevitable given the impossibility of defining all possible written statements which might give offence to the authorities. Metternich defined censorship as the 'right to block the manifestation of ideas that confound the social order, the peace of the state, its interests and its good order'. Not surprisingly, the censors themselves could often not determine what they should or should not allow. Partly also, no doubt, as Helen Jacobson has written, because some censors were drawn from the ranks of 'scholars and littérateurs', while others came 'mostly from the ranks of genuine ignoramuses' who were 'uncultured, stupid and frightened', material rejected by one censor was sometimes allowed by another and censors sometimes faced penalties for being too tolerant, ranging from suspension to loss of their jobs or even jail. In despair after being briefly jailed in 1842. Nikitenko pleaded with the secret-police chief to tell Tsar Nicholas 'how difficult it is to be a censor. We really do not know what is demanded of us. . . . We are never safe and can never fulfill our obligations.' A Russian historian writing in 1892 concluded that the typical censor

positively lost his head. Constantly expecting reprimands, arrest, or discharge from his position, he groped about in the darkness, without having any clear notion of what could be passed without dangerous consequences or what might unleash the unexpected fury of the authorities against him. This made him suspicious and carping to the point of totally clouding his reasoning powers. This panic also explains why censors were able to find the spirit of revolution even in cookbooks.[38]

The difficulties experienced by censors as a result of the vagueness of their task were compounded by the fact that many disliked their job. Jacob Grimm confessed to a friend that 'in a way befitting the nature of the task, I am not quite scrupulous in my handling of it', and his fellow Hessian censor Christoph von Rommel lamented that his 'professional duty is often so much at odds with personal conviction'. Nikitenko's memoirs are filled with attacks on the idiocy of the Russian censorship, which he viewed as filled with 'abuses and senselessness' and ultimately depending upon 'the interpretation of ignoramuses and malevolent individuals who are ready to see a crime in every idea'. His fellow Russian censor the poet Fedor Tiutchev wrote to his wife that his supervisors were 'bereft of any ideas and any intelligence' and that eventually until the world collapsed 'under the weight of their stupidity, they are fatally damned to live and die in the ultimate obduracy of their idiocy'. He compared the censorship to 'curing a toothache by smashing the teeth with one's fist'. Another problem for censors was often the sheer volume of their work. The three Hessian censors of the period 1815–48 were overwhelmed by their task of examining all books, journals and newspapers circulating in their state. The Russian censor and leading poet Apollon Maikov censored 223 books in four languages totalling over 100,000 pages in a period of fourteen months. One Russian censorship official wrote that 'there was no end to the writing and recopying, which reached incredible dimensions. The poor clerks got callouses on their hands from this Sisyphean labour day and night.'[39]

Indirect repression: 'caution money' and special taxation

Aside from directly controlling who could publish and what they could print through licensing and prior and post-publication censorship, a number of European countries in the nineteenth century also used indirect controls on the press, requiring publishers to pay 'caution money' and newspapers to pay special taxes. The idea of 'caution money' was to ensure that only the relatively wealthy could publish newspapers, while the purpose of the taxes on newspapers was to ensure that only the relatively wealthy could buy them. In both cases there was discrimination against the poor, but neither device directly restricted the publication of particular material.

'Caution money' requirements, also known sometimes as security-deposit or security-bond requirements, made it illegal to publish a newspaper or periodical without having first deposited a certain sum of money with government officials. The supposed purpose of this was to ensure the payment of fines in case of transgression of the press laws, but clearly the real intention was to prevent the poor from publishing papers. As the French press magnate Emile de Girardin pointed out in 1842, the effect of the security-bond require-ment was 'to create for the benefit of some great feudatories a privilege by which the exclusive exploitation of public opinion is delivered to them as a monopoly, and thus to create in the state an aristocracy the more redoutable in that it is unrecognised'. Similarly, the French liberal Catholic spokesman Robert de Lammenais declared in 1848 that the security bond meant that 'today you have to have a lot of money to enjoy the right to speak'. 'Caution money' was required for part or all of the nineteenth century in at least Austria, Hungary, Spain, Germany, Britain, France and Russia.[40]

As F. W. J. Hemmings has noted, the 'caution money' requirement in France tended to fluctuate in 'inverse ratio to the liberality of the regime and also to the degree of security it felt it enjoyed'. In 1819, when the requirement was first introduced, Paris dailies had to deposit 10,000 francs (about $2000 in 1819 money, the equivalent of well over US$20,000 today). In 1828, following liberal election victories in 1827, the sum was lowered to 6000 francs, and it was lowered once more after the 1830 July revolution in France, which was fought partly over the issue of press liberty. The succeeding 'July Monarchy' regime of Louis-Philippe was soon embroiled in a series of battles with the press. Following an assassination attempt on the King in 1835, the security bond was raised to the enormous sum of 100,000 francs for Paris dailies. After the 1848 February revolution, fought largely against the repressive nature of the July Monarchy, the security bond was abolished. It was reintroduced, however, after the 'June Days' uprising of 1848. Although under the new law the bond was set at a much lower level than in 1835, it still forced many papers out of business. Lammenais's *Le Peuple constituant* published its final issue under the headline, 'Silence to the poor'. In 1852, the press decree of Louis Napoleon more than doubled the deposit to 50,000 francs for Paris newspapers. 'Caution money' was abolished again with the collapse of the regime of Louis Napoleon in 1870, only to be reintroduced once more in July 1871 after the suppression of the Paris Commune. It was finally abolished for good in the press law of 1881. In Spain, the security-bond requirement for Madrid dailies reached, at its peak in 1857, the equivalent of US$18,000, while in Austria under a law of 1849 it ranged up to the equivalent of US$5000. The bond in Russia in 1865 was set at 5000 rubles for a newspaper.[41]

Special taxes imposed on the press were, in a number of countries, a complement or alternative to 'caution money' requirements. They were designed, as the preamble to the 1819 newspaper stamp-tax bill in Britain forthrightly explained, to 'restrain the small publications which issue from the Press in great numbers and at a low price'. The particular targets of such 'restraining' were, of course, the poor, since the effect of the taxes was to price newspapers beyond their means. As a British parliamentary committee reported in 1851, 'the newspaper stamp prohibits the existence of such newspapers as from their price and character would be suitable to the means and wants of the labouring classes'. John Bright, a leading liberal, termed the press tax 'a tax on news, . . . a tax on knowledge, . . . a tax on the progress of human affairs'. In a futile attempt to prevent the purpose of the tax from being circumvented, in 1789 parliament even passed a law forbidding the loaning or renting out of newspapers below sales price.

The poor were well aware of the purpose of the press taxes. A newspaper vendor charged with illegally selling newspapers without having paid the stamp tax told a court in 1831,

> I stands here, your worships, upon right and principle, on behalf of the poor working unedicated classes of the country. They are called ignorant, but what is the cause of their ignorance? Why the tax which prevents them from getting information. Your worships pretty well knows the reason them in power puts on the tax; it is to keep the poor from knowing their rights; for if poor working people knowed their rights, they would soon annihilate the corrupt institutions that oppress them.[42]

Usually, taxes on the press took the form of a stamp tax which had to be paid on each newspaper sold. Stamp taxes operated for part of the nineteenth century in at least the Netherlands, Belgium, Austria, France, Germany and Britain. In some cases taxes were also imposed on newspaper advertisements and on paper, and these costs too increased the purchase price of newspapers. In Britain, where all three types of tax were imposed, they had an enormous impact upon the price and circulation of newspapers. The stamp tax per newspaper reached a peak of fourpence from 1815 until 1836, making the sale price of a newspaper two to four times what it would otherwise have been. The tax was reduced to one penny in 1836, but not abolished entirely until 1855. The advertising tax was retained until 1853, and the tax on paper until 1861. The battle to abolish the 'taxes on knowledge' in Britain raged for decades. William Gladstone, who served four times as Prime Minister, described the fight as the 'severest parliamentary struggle in which I have ever been engaged'. In France in the 1820s, the stamp tax swallowed up one third of the gross income of the largest newspaper, *Le Constitutionel*, and forced the price of a year's subscription up to 72 francs, equal to about a month's wages for the average worker. In the Netherlands, crushing stamp and advertising taxes swallowed up over 50 per cent of gross newspaper revenues and increased prices by as much as 10 cents per copy until the taxes were abolished in 1869. In Germany, newspaper taxes consumed over 25 per cent of newspaper revenues before they were repealed in 1874; thus, in 1873, the large liberal urban daily *Berliner Tageblatt* paid the astronomical sum of 200,000 marks in taxes. In Austria, stamp taxes doubled the price of newspapers until their repeal in 1899.[43]

THE IMPACT OF PRESS REPRESSION

Press repression in nineteenth-century Europe was unquestionably highly effective in controlling the expression and circulation of opposition opinions in legally printed material. It clearly also reduced the amount of printed material legally allowed to appear at all. In France, for example, only a handful of newspapers were permitted during the period of licensing and censorship which preceded the 1789 revolution. In 1789, all restrictions on the press were eliminated, with the result that within four years over 400 newspapers were founded in France, including 150 in Paris alone. In 1792–4 and 1797 there were severe crackdowns on the press; in the latter year forty-four Parisian papers were suppressed and scores of journalists were exiled. By the time Napoleon took power in 1799, only seventy-two papers were left in Paris, and he soon closed all but thirteen, declaring in a decree of 1800 that 'all papers which insert articles contrary to the respect due the social pact, to the sovereignty of the people, to the glory of the army or who publish invectives against friendly or allied governments . . . will be suppressed immediately'. By 1811, Napoleon had reduced the number of Parisian newspapers to four, had closed two-thirds of all the printshops in Paris, and had introduced a licensing requirement for all printers and booksellers that would last until 1870.

Repressive press controls under the Bourbon restoration (1815–30) and July Monarchy (1830–48) held down the growth of the press after the fall of Napoleon. With the elimination of press controls during the 1848 revolution, however, over 400 new papers sprang up overnight, and the combined daily press run for all Parisian news-papers rose from 50,000 to 400,000. After 1848, press controls were reimposed with increasing harshness. After the reintroduction of licensing under Louis Napoleon's press decree of February 1852, only fourteen Parisian dailies were allowed to continue. The number of political journals in the provinces declined from 420 in 1851 to 260 by 1865. The loosening of press controls in 1868 led to an immediate upsurge in the press once more, with 140 new journals begun in Paris alone, but a period of strict controls in the 1870s held down further growth. The passage of the liberal press law of 1881 brought a massive increase in the number of newspapers. The number of provincial dailies grew from 114 in 1880 to 280 in 1885.[44]

Data for many other European countries also show a growth in publishing under liberal press regimes and a contraction with the imposition of harsh controls. In Germany, the number of book titles published annually rose from 8000 to 14,000 with the easing of censorship controls between 1832 and 1843, but the harsh crackdown after the 1848 revolution cut the annual total of new books published to under 10,000 for over twenty years. Not until after 1870 were the levels of the 1840s again reached. In the Hapsburg Empire, there was an explosion of periodicals when press controls were ended in the aftermath of the 1848 revolution. However, a subsequent crackdown against the new freedoms reduced the number of Austrian periodicals from 388 in 1848 to 128 by 1856. An easing of controls after 1856 led to a tripling of periodicals to 345 by 1862, and following a further easing of controls in the 1860s the number of periodicals jumped to over 1300 by 1882. After the abolition of security bonds and stamp taxes in the 1890s, the number of Austrian periodicals increased to 4500 by 1912.[45]

In Russia, amidst the harsh censorship controls often personally exerted by Nicholas I, the number of periodicals published and the total number of printed pages in books approved by the censorship during his reign (1825–55) remained stable. As a result of the easing of controls under his successor, Alexander II (1855–81), the number of periodicals jumped from 104 to 230 between 1855 and 1860 and the number of book titles increased from 1012 to 3366 between 1855 and 1868. The number of printing plants in Russia increased from 150 to 800 during Alexander's reign, while the number of bookstores rocketed from forty to over 1000. The number of daily newspapers published in St Petersburg increased from six in 1860 (all under governmental control or influence) to twenty-two in 1880 (mostly private), although during the repressive reign of Alexander III (1881–94) the number fell back to 1870 levels.[46]

Newspaper taxes kept down both the number of publications and their circulation in many countries. In the Netherlands, for example, the number of daily papers jumped immediately from nine to fourteen after the abolition of stamp and advertising taxes in 1869, and further increased to fifty-four by 1890. In Britain from 1815 to 1836, when the stamp tax was fourpence per newspaper, total sales increased by only 20 per cent, but during the two years after the reduction of the tax to one penny (in 1836) total annual sales doubled from 25.5 million to over 53 million. Until the final abolition of the stamp tax in June 1855, only a handful of daily newspapers were able to establish themselves outside London; after 1855 they developed in a flood, with six provincial dailies begun on a single day in July 1855 and about ninety publishing by 1870. Newspaper circulation soared after 1855, as many papers were able to lower their price to a penny. Thus, while before 1855 the largest daily newspaper circulation in Britain was the 60,000 copies sold by *The Times*, the *Daily Telegraph*, which was established as a penny daily in 1855, achieved a circulation of 142,000 by 1861.[47]

Repression had a major impact on individual journalists' lives as well as on the lives of newspapers. The threat of censorship and prosecution affected every thought and sentence that writers formulated and wrote. Author Ludwig Frankl wrote in his memoirs of the Metternich era in Austria that 'The self-assurance of those who wrote had fallen so low that they practised a self-censorship of their own and destroyed every inborn thought as Chronos [the Greek personification of time, who destroyed all that came into existence].' Another Austrian writer, Karl Postl, whose book *Austria as It Is* (1828) was published pseudonymously in Germany and created a sensation after being widely smuggled across the border to evade the censorship, lamented,

A more fettered being than an Austrian author surely never existed. A writer in Austria must not offend against any Government; nor against any minister; nor against any hierarchy, if its members be influential; nor against the aristocracy. He must not be liberal – not philosophical – nor humourous – in short, he must be nothing at all. Under the catalogue of offences, are comprehended not only satires and witticisms; – nay, he must not explain things at all, because they might lead to serious thoughts. . . . What would have become of Shakespeare had he been doomed to live or write in Austria?[48]

In France, Maxime du Camp complained that during the regime of Napoleon III 'you had to turn your pen around seven times between your fingers, since before the courts you could sin by thought, by word, by action or by omission'. In Germany, Karl Marx, whose newspaper the *Rheinische Zeitung* was suppressed in 1843 by Friedrich Wilhelm IV of Prussia for pursuing a 'tendency' alleged to 'stir up discontent', declared that in any case he was tired of having to 'fight with needles instead of clubs' and 'tired of hypocrisy, stupidity, raw authority, and our cringing, bowing, back turning and word picking'. Commenting sarcastically on the censorship dictates of the German Confederation Diet, Ludwig Börne, whose own writings fell under the axe declared, 'If chance should reveal a mathematician among the Spanish Jacobins [radicals], the federal diet would proscribe logarithms.' Börne's fellow victim of the German censorship, Heinrich Heine, remarked in a similarly ironic vein about the pervasive influence of the censorship after it was abolished during the 1848 revolution: 'How, when a person has known censorship all his life, is he to write without it? All style will be at an end, all grammar, good usage.' In a far more serious and prescient vein, Heine commented about the censorship in words now inscribed on a memorial at the Nazi concentration camp at Dachau: 'Where books are burned, there in the end will men be burned too.' Another banned German writer, Karl Gutzkow, bitterly attacked the quality of the censors:

> Censorship might still be bearable if from the outset it did not, as a branch of the administrative bureaucracy, bear the stamp of literary incompetence. An official who has perhaps studied all the commentaries on the laws of the land but who has never studied a work of a different scholarly discipline, not to mention art, an official whose ideas are all directed towards small spaces in the administrative buildings, who has only one God, namely his superior, and only heaven, namely promotion – such a man should pass judgment on your writing?[49]

In Russia, the literary critic Vissarion Belinsky complained that, under the conditions of drastic censorship that existed in his country during the reign of Nicholas I, all liberal ideas were forbidden, 'for example that two plus two equals four and that winter is cold and summer hot'. Belinsky lamented, 'Nature sentenced me to bark like a dog and howl like a jackal, but circumstances order me to mew like a cat and to swish my tail like a fox.' Many of his fellow Russians made similar complaints. Thus, Alexander Pushkin, whose masterpieces were repeatedly mutilated or banned, sometimes on the personal orders of Tsar Nicholas, moaned in a letter to his wife, 'Only the devil could have thought of having me born in Russia with a mind and talent,' while Fyodor Dostoevsky referred to 'those swine of censors' who ruined his short novel *Notes from the Underground.* Nikolai Gogol complained that by mutilating his masterpiece *Dead Souls* the censors (who later restored much that they had cut) sought 'to tear the last mouthful of bread from my hand, that mouthful earned by seven years of sacrifice', and that 'this misery has robbed me of the use of my limbs'. Ivan Turgenev recalled having his literary drafts returned by the censors 'all crossed over, deformed with red ink, as if covered with blood', and his visits to the censor when, 'after presenting useless and degrading explanations and justifications', one had to 'listen to his unappealable, frequently mocking, verdict'. Anton Chekhov recalled that when writing a magazine story 'I could not forget for one moment that I was writing for a magazine subject to censorship', and bitterly lamented that in another instance his own editors had pre-censored his work to avoid trouble and in so doing had 'cropped it so hard they cut off the head with the hair'. In general, Chekhov lamented, the censorship made it 'not much fun being a writer', since 'it's like writing with a bone in your throat'.[50]

For thousands of nineteenth-century European journalists and authors, the effects of press repression extended far beyond having their writings butchered or being forced to censor themselves, as they were imprisoned or, in the case of many Russian writers, exiled to remote regions of the country. Some of the more prominent writers jailed or forced into exile for press offences were French socialist leaders Jules Guesde and Paul Brousse, French journalist Henri Rochefort, Russian anarchist writer Prince Peter Kropotkin, Hungarian nationalist leader Louis Kossuth, Swedish socialist leaders August Palm and Hjalmar Branting (later Prime Minister), Serbian radical leader Nicolas Pašić (later Prime Minister), Austrian socialist leader Victor Adler, British journalists William Cobbett and Richard Carlisle (who served over nine years in jail), German socialist leaders Wilhelm and Karl Liebknecht and Rosa Luxemburg, and Russian writers Michael Lermontov, Maxim Gorky, Ivan Turgenev, Leo Tolstoy and Alexander Pushkin.

Press prosecutions largely shaped the biographies of two of the most famous nineteenth-century European radicals, the German socialist Karl Marx and the French anarchist philosopher Pierre-Joseph Proudhon.[51] Marx first came to public attention as editor of the mildly radical Cologne newspaper the *Rheinische Zeitung*, begun in 1842. The paper soon began to be persecuted by the Prussian censors and, following pressure from the Russian government, was suppressed in April 1843. Marx thereupon decided to go to France to collaborate on a journal with Arnold Ruge, a Saxon journalist who had been driven from Prussia and Saxony by censorship restrictions. Marx's collaboration with Ruge collapsed, however, since most copies of the first issue of their journal, the *Deutsch-französische Jahrbücher*, were confiscated by the Prussian police when it was sent into Germany. In 1845, after an article criticising the Prussian king had appeared in a socialist journal to which Marx contributed, Marx was expelled from France under Prussian pressure. He then moved on to Brussels, but was expelled in February 1848 for publishing the *Communist Manifesto*, which had been commissioned by an obscure group of German political exiles in London. Since the 1848 revolutions toppled the governments in France and Prussia, Marx was able to return to Paris and then to Cologne, where he began the *Neue Rheinische Zeitung*. With the collapse of the Prussian revolution by early 1849, however, the *Neue Rheinische Zeitung* was suppressed. Marx was expelled from Prussia in July 1849, after being acquitted of a sedition charge, and went to the refuge of last resort for European political exiles – London. There he lived out the rest of his life in severe poverty, haunting the Reading Room of the British Museum and writing, among other works, *Das Kapital*.

Proudhon, perhaps the single most influential anarchist philosopher, first ran into trouble with French authorities for his book *Warning to Proprietors*, published in 1842. He was indicted on four charges, including 'troubling the public peace by exciting hatred or mistrust of the citizens against one or more persons' and 'exciting hatred and outrage against the king's government'. Like many victims of nineteenth-century repression, Proudhon was martyred by the prosecution and as a result became a well-known figure, even though he was acquitted by a jury which could hardly understand his point of view. Proudhon's next encounter with the authorities came in July 1848, in the wake of the 'June Days', a worker insurrection in Paris. When his newspaper, *Le Représentant du peuple*, called for a moratorium on rent payments during a time of economic depression, the government suppressed the issue, although Proudhon was shielded from prosecution because he was by then a member of the French legislature. The paper, which had a circulation of 40,000, was later shut down completely by the government. In January 1849, Proudhon's new paper, *Le Peuple*, criticised newly elected President Louis Napoleon, leading the legislature to withdraw Proudhon's parliamentary immunity. Subsequently, he was sentenced to a three-year jail term. Proudhon was allowed to edit another paper, *La Voix du peuple*, from his jail cell, but it too was soon suppressed.

When Proudhon was released from jail in June 1852, he found that French publishers would no longer touch his writings and that landlords were even reluctant to rent to him. When he finally succeeded in publishing *De la justice dans la revolution et dans l'église* in 1858, it was seized by the police. Proudhon was charged with, among other things 'reproduction in bad faith of false news likely to disturb the public peace' and 'excitement of hatred between citizens'. Upon being sentenced to three years in jail and ordered to pay a large fine, Proudhon fled to Belgium, where he stayed until 1862. An amnesty allowing him to return to France was granted, however, and when he died, in January 1865, 6000 Parisians joined his funeral procession.

As is suggested by the case of Proudhon, press prosecution sometimes produced martyrs. Such martyrdom created a prime minister almost overnight in the case of the Greek politician Charilaos Tricoupis. Tricoupis had been a relatively obscure figure until he was jailed for his sensational article 'Who is to Blame?', which appeared in the Athens paper *Kairi* in July 1874. The article placed the blame for Greece's chronic political crisis upon King George I, especially upon the King's refusal to recognise the principle of parliamentary responsibility. Tricoupis was released on bail after three days in jail and subsequently acquitted to general acclaim. Shortly thereafter, Tricoupis, now the hero of liberal forces in the country, was called upon by the King to form a ministry, which he agreed to do only when the King promised to abide thereafter by the principle of parliamentary responsibility. Although Tricoupis was defeated in the 1875 elections, which on his own insistence were free from government interference (another departure from Greek tradition), he served several terms as Prime Minister between 1878 and 1895.[52]

In another case of press repression which succeeded only in creating a martyr, the editor of the Swedish newspaper *Stockholms Posten*, Captain Anders Lindeberg, was convicted of treason in 1834 for implying that King Karl Johan should be deposed. He was sentenced to death by decapitation, under a medieval treason law. When the King mitigated the sentence to three years in prison, Lindeberg decided to highlight the King's repressive press policy by insisting upon his right to be beheaded and refusing to take advantage of the government's attempts to encourage him to escape. Finally, in desperation, the King issued a general amnesty to 'all political prisoners awaiting execution', which applied only to Lindeberg. When the editor stubbornly insisted upon his right to execution, the government solved the problem by locking him out of his cell while he was walking in the prison courtyard and then refusing him re-entry.[53]

RESISTANCE TO PRESS REPRESSION

Although press repression in nineteenth-century Europe severely cramped discussion of public affairs, led to the persecution of thousands of journalists and prompted the closure of hundreds of newspapers, the best efforts of governments to control the press were never entirely effective. Throughout the century, newspapers, journalists and elements of the general public conspired, often with considerable success, to evade press regulations by legal technicalities, evasions and outright defiance. Even the most repressive regimes – Metternich's Austria and tsarist Russia – were never able to completely stop the tide of journalistic and press resistance.

Resistance to press repression took two forms: (1) legal means of resistance, including the use of 'Aesopian language' and various technical means of evading press regulations; and (2) illegal means of resistance, including clandestine publishing ('the underground press') and smuggling of forbidden materials. Among the legal methods of resistance, the use of 'Aesopian language' (*Ezopovsky yazik*, a term which gained great currency in Russia) was universal in regimes with repressive press laws. It consisted simply of making critical political remarks without ever using language direct enough to run foul of the press laws. Thus, political criticism would be disguised as literary or social comment, or points intended to relate to one political regime would be superficially disguised as comments about another. Thus, political messages that could not be expressed directly were expressed through the use of allusion.

It was virtually impossible to prevent such material from appearing in the press without entirely suppressing the printed word, and even the most repressive governments were unable to foil such techniques completely. Thus, in Russia, Prince V. F. Odoevsky, a drafter of the 1828 censorship law, conceded that strict regulations simply led the press to become increasingly clever and that 'no police can stop all the stratagems of talented writers'. Seventy years later, V. K. Plehve, the reactionary Russian Minister of the Interior who was assassinated in 1904, reportedly asked one prominent radical, 'Why do you want freedom of the press when even without it you are a master of saying between the lines all that you wish to say?' Bertram Wolfe has elaborated on the wide range of 'Aesopian language' used in tsarist Russia:

Since direct political discussion was prohibited, all literature tended to become a criticism of Russian life, and literary criticism but another form of social criticism. . . . If the censor forbade explicit statement, he was skillfully eluded by indirection – by innocent seeming tales of other lands or times, by complicated parables, animal fables, double meanings, overtones, by investing apparently trivial events with the pent-up energies possessing the writer, so that the reader becomes compelled to dwell upon them until their hidden meanings became manifest. Men found means of conveying a criticism of the regime through a statistical monograph on German agriculture, through the study of a sovereign four centuries dead, the review of a Norwegian play, the analysis of some evil in the Prussian or some virtue in the British state.[54]

One clear example of 'Aesopian language' appeared in the Russian journal *Vestnik Evropy* in February 1901. An article supposedly discussing a new education law used an overcrowded classroom as a metaphor for Russian society:

To breathe becomes ever more difficult. . . . It is necessary to open a window, fling open the doors. . . . to give space for movement, free access to fresh air. In place of this they intend to close the ventilators, to caulk up all the crevices. There remains for the multitude only to lose its breath or to leave the room in which it is assembled for important matters.

When discussion of certain ideas was banned in Russia, they would be referred to by code words. Before serfdom was abolished in 1861, this forbidden subject was referred to as the 'reasonable distribution of economic relations'. Before the establishment of a constitution in Russia in 1905, this goal was referred to as 'the crowning of the edifice', and, after 1905, Bolshevik groups disguised their calls for the nationalistion of industry and foundation of a democratic republic with references to the 'full and unfettered demands of the year 1905'. In 1859 a Russian journal demanded, 'When, my God, will it be possible, in keeping with the demands of conscience, not to use cunning, not to fabricate allegorical phrases, but to speak one's opinion directly and simply in public?' The censor who approved this article was demoted, and the journal was suppressed.[55]

One 'Aesopian' technique used in many countries was that of thinly disguising criticism of a particular regime or government official as condemnation of another country or a historical figure. Thus, the Czech journalist Karl Havliček became famous for the articles in his newspaper *Prazke Noviny* discussing British mistreatment of Ireland, which everyone in Bohemia knew were really about Austrian denial of Czech national rights. In Serbia, the satirist Radoje Domanović became celebrated for his fables, especially his tales of the mythical 'Stradija', a country renowned for its swine and tomfooleries, where government ministers played musical chairs, and the police spared voters from troubling themselves to cast votes in free elections for members of parliament. In France, no one was fooled when in 1829, during the waning days of the reign of Charles X, Prosper Merimée published a historical study of the disastrous reign of the sixteenth-century king Charles IX.[56]

The great German historian Friedrich Dahlmann (who, in a celebrated case, was dismissed for political reasons from the University of Göttingen in 1837) became well known during the period leading up to the German revolution of 1848 for his histories of the English and French revolutions, published in 1844–5. Everyone understood that, in writing about the failings of the regimes in seventeenth-century England and eighteenth-century France, Dahlmann was really writing a parable about his own country, but he avoided direct comments on Germany so that, as he wrote to his publisher, he would not have to 'take my walking stick in hand for a trip out of Germany'. The young German historian Ludwig Quidde (who received the Nobel Peace Prize in 1927) became a sensation when it was realised that his 1894 article 'Caligula: eine Studie über römischen Cäsarenwahnsinn' ('Caligula: A Study of Roman Megalomania [literally, "Caesarean Madness"]') was in reality about Kaiser (Caesar) Wilhelm II, who was depicted as suffering from delusions of grandeur, with virtually every foible attributed to Caligula also applicable to Wilhelm. In pamphlet form, Quidde's article sold over 150,000 copies, and the German government was unable to prosecute him directly for the piece, at least not without further identifying Caligula with Wilhelm. However, Quidde was subsequently sentenced to three months in jail for some critical remarks about the Kaiser made at a public meeting, and it was made clear at the trial that the Caligula affair was the real reason for the prosecution.[57]

'Aesopian' techniques were one legal means of resisting press repression; another was the employment of various technical evasions of specific regulations. For example, after prior censorship was abolished in a number of countries, including France, Russia, Germany and Denmark, press laws at various times required that newspapers name a 'responsible editor' who would be held liable for all published material that contravened press laws. It became common in such countries for newspapers to name non-essential volunteers to serve as 'responsible editors' and serve out jail terms so that the real editors could go about their business. Thus, in Denmark during a period of harassment of the socialist press in the 1880s, one house painter volunteered to serve as responsible editor of *Social-Demokraten* for 10 krone a week, plus a weekly bonus of 5 krone when imprisoned, on the understanding that no jail term should exceed thirteen weeks in length. The Russian police reported in 1913 that the 'responsible editor' of *Pravda* was usually an 'unintelligent individual who does not take part in the work of the paper' and was often 'absolutely illiterate'. There was frequently a sign posted in the *Pravda* office reading, 'No editors needed'.[58]

In some countries it was possible to evade the banning of a newspaper by simply starting up once again with the same staff but with a slightly altered name. For example, in Sweden in the 1830s, Lars Johan Hierta's opposition paper *Aftonbladet* (*The Evening Paper*) was repeatedly shut down by King Karl Johan and repeatedly resurrected, as *Nya* [*New*] *Aftonbladet*, *Tredje* [*Third*] *Aftonbladet*, *Fjärde* [*Fourth*] *Aftonbladet*, and so on. Hierta succeeded in making a laughingstock of Swedish press regulations, and the King finally gave up in 1838 after Hierta had reached the twenty-third *Aftonbladet*. In Russia, the Bolshevik newspaper *Pravda* (*Truth*) was repeatedly suppressed after 1912, but was also allowed to keep reappearing under such titles as (in translation) *Workers' Truth*, *Proletarian Truth* and *Labour Truth*. This continued until 1914, when, after its eighth reincarnation, it was shut down for the rest of the tsarist regime.[59]

A variety of other legal devices were used to evade or protest against press restrictions. In Germany, the Karlsbad Decrees of 1819 waived prior censorship of all publications of 320 pages or more so that censors would no longer have to wade through long scholarly tomes inaccessible to the poor but could concentrate their efforts in stemming the tide of cheap radical pamphlets. Ingenious printers took advantage of the waiver by using the largest possible type and smallest possible page so that even short works would exceed 320 pages. German writers such as Heinrich Heine protested against the censorship by having blank spaces or dashes inserted where the censors had struck, but this practice was forbidden in Germany in 1834. French publishers evaded an 1820 law which restricted prior censorship to periodicals (i.e. titles published at regular intervals) by printing forbidden material in irregularly published pamphlets under such titles as 'Censorship Rejects'. Similarly, in Britain, until the stamp-tax laws were tightened up in 1819, it was possible to evade the stamp tax by publishing newspapers in a format that fell outside the technical definition of a 'newspaper'. The most famous such publication, William Cobbett's *Political Register*, achieved the astonishing circulation of 50,000 copies per week by publishing as a 'pamphlet', thus avoiding the tax which forced 'newspapers' to charge three times as much. After 1819, when the loophole was closed and Cobbett was forced to pay the tax, circulation of his journal dropped almost overnight to 400 copies per week.[60]

Some regimes that had formally abolished prior censorship required sample newspapers to be submitted to the authorities immediately upon publication, so that copies of any issue deemed to contain offensive material could be seized before circulation. Even here, however, legal evasion was possible. The Russian law of 1905 required that the first three copies of any newspaper be submitted to the Committee on Press Affairs, but did not specify how long it might take to deliver them. The editors of *Pravda*, published in St Petersburg, entrusted the task of delivering the first three copies of the day's paper to a seventy-year-old plant watchman named Matvej,

> whose advanced years and slow gait guaranteed that the trip across the city to the Committee's office would indeed be a time-consuming one. Matvej left the *Pravda* plant around 3 a.m. and usually took one and one-half to two hours to reach his destination. After delivering the papers, the old man remained in the office, ostensibly to rest but really in order to keep a close watch on the inspection. . . . If, after reading *Pravda*, the inspector turned to another newspaper, Matvej returned at a leisurely pace to the plant on foot, but if the inspector phoned the Third Police District, which included *Pravda*'s plant, Matvej flew out of the station, hailed a droshky [taxi] and raced back. Watchers stationed around the plant waited for his return and when they saw him coming . . . the alarm was passed and everyone started working feverishly. . . . By the time the police arrived, most of the papers were gone. Only a few were left behind, for the sake of 'protocol'.

Usually in such cases, less than 10 per cent of the press run was confiscated.[61]

In a number of European cities, literate members of the working classes who would otherwise not have been able to afford newspapers, given stamp taxes and the like, banded together to share newspapers or subscribed to public reading rooms where for a small fee individuals could obtain access to a large variety of papers. Ironically, whereas the taxation of newspapers was designed to inhibit the growth of a working-class consciousness, it may actually, where it stimulated the use of collective subscriptions and reading rooms, have contributed to it. John Gillis writes that 'Working class people clubbing together for subscriptions and collective reading formed the very basis of the new working-class culture in places like Lyon, Berlin and Birmingham.'[62]

In Paris, the number of *cabinets de lecture*, a sort of bookstore that rented books and journals for periods ranging from one visit to a year, soared from thirty-two to 226 between 1820 and 1850 (they declined rapidly thereafter, as the price of publications declined and incomes rose). In Britain, coffee-house and ale house proprietors found that they could attract an eager clientele and greatly increase their business by providing periodicals which their customers could not otherwise afford, and they competed for working-class customers by subscribing to large numbers of periodicals and boasting of their comforts and conveniences. In London, according to one 1829 calculation, an estimated thirty people read each newspaper as a result of such group reading institutions. One Manchester reading room advertised in March 1833 that it subscribed to ninety-six newspapers, and added,

This establishment affords advantages never before offered to the Manchester public, combining economy, health, temperance and instruction, in having a wholesome and exhilarating beverage at a small expense, instead of the noxious and intoxicating stuff usually supplied at the ale-house and dram-shop, together with the privilege of perusing the most able and popular publications of the day, whether political, literary, or scientific, in comfortable and genteel apartment, in the evening brilliantly lit with gas.

William Cobbett, in his conservative days, complained bitterly in 1807,

Ask the landlord [of an ale-house] why he takes the newspaper; he'll tell you that it attracts people to his house; and in many ways its attractions are much stronger that those of the liquor there drunk, thousands and thousands of men having become sots through the attractions of these vehicles of novelty and falsehood.[63]

Legal resistance to press repression was often accompanied by illegal resistance, which usually took the form of clandestine publishing within countries where material was banned, or the smuggling of forbidden materials into such countries from foreign countries with more liberal press laws. Countries such as Belgium, Switzerland and Britain, which were known for their more tolerant attitude towards the press, became major centres for the publication of materials subsequently smuggled into less tolerant countries such as France, Germany, Austria and Russia. Thus, when the French government proposed a harsh press law in 1826, one legislator remarked that 'Printing in France is being shut down for the benefit of Belgium'. Clandestine publishing and smuggling were perhaps most widespread in Russia, which maintained prior censorship longer than any other major country in Europe and where dissidents were forced to develop ever more ingenious methods of resistance. One indication of the widespread nature of such operations in Russia was uncovered in 1849, when a police search uncovered 2581 illegal books in one St Petersburg bookstore and another 3140 in two stores in Dorpat and Riga. A top Russian censorship official, commenting on the widespread circulation of illegal material in 1858, reported, 'We know that right now Russia is flooded with these publications, that they pass from hand to hand with a great ease of circulation, and that they have already penetrated, if not the masses, who do not read, at least the lower strata of society'.[64]

Other Russian censorship officials lamented that 'everyone knows that despite the continued existence of censorship of foreign books there is not, and never has been, a banned book which was impossible to get' and that, 'Banned books do ultimately reach the public (since there are no books which you could not get in St Petersburg if you wanted them) and in this case they would have added attraction in the eyes of the readers due to their secret fame and splendour of forbidden fruit.' Such comments by Russian officials were confirmed by foreign observers such as a German historian who noted that because of the 'strict ban' on one book it had 'been disseminated everywhere; in fact, good breeding demands that one have read it'. In 1857, the Russian secret-police chief Basile Dolgorukov privately complained that 'the highest personalities of the Empire coming home from abroad clandestinely import the publications of Iskander [Russian exile Alexander Herzen, whose newspaper *Kolokel* (*The Bell*) published in London was forbidden] and even distribute them in Russia'. Even Tsar Alexander II and his wife were known to read *Kolokel* which was probably the most influential journal distributed in Russia, with an estimated illegal circulation of 2500 there during its years of publication, 1857–62. On one occasion, some Russian officials who were attacked in an article in *Kolokel* had a counterfeit copy printed for the Tsar to read, but Herzen learned about the ruse and managed to replace it with a true copy.[65]

Aside from illegal smuggling of materials into Russia, clandestine publications were increasingly published by numerous secret presses within Russia after 1860. One Bolshevik paper published clandestinely in Russia in 1901 was printed on thin rice paper so that it could be swallowed in the event of a police raid. The most sophisticated clandestine press in Russia, which was quite literally underground, printed over a million copies of periodicals and leaflets in Baku between 1900 and 1910. Bertram Wolfe has described it thus:

> The plant expanded until it covered a vast area underground and contained a cutting machine, type in several languages, presses, binders, even a casting machine for using stereotype mats. . . . In this steadily expanded plant underneath the houses of Tartar Baku, first two, then five, then seven selfless printers worked and lived together like friars in a cloister. . . . The plant was without heat or ventilation; windows leading to the street were sealed with brick and mortar. At night they took turns going up for air for three-hour periods.[66]

The smuggling of banned books and newspapers across borders was extremely common in nineteenth-century Europe and smuggling techniques were often highly sophisticated. During the French Revolution, for example, radical literature from France was smuggled into Spain in the lining of hats and in strips of paper used to wrap the parts of clocks. Fifty years later, during the regime of Napoleon III in France, opposition literature was smuggled into the country in hollowed-out lumps of coal, by carrier pigeons, in hermetically sealed boxes dropped along the coast of Brittany, and even occasionally in plaster busts of the Emperor (the last scheme collapsed when a bust broke open under customs inspection). Giuseppe Mazzini's newspaper *Giovine Italia* (*Young Italy*) was smuggled into Italy from

France in the 1830s inside barrels of pumice stone, boxes of fish and false-bottomed trunks. In Austria, thousands of copies of banned books and pamphlets were smuggled into the country during the 1840s, and the opposition newspaper *Grenzboten*, published in Leipzig, Saxony, served as a general rallying point for the liberals. One theology professor at the University of Vienna later recalled that barred publications were frequently circulated in classrooms, with *Grenzboten* 'especially read for entertainment during the tedious lecture hours'. Vladimir Jovanović's *Sloboda* (*Liberty*) was smuggled into Serbia from Geneva in ordinary envelopes after being printed on extremely thin paper, while Lenin's newspaper *Iskra* was printed in tiny characters on thin cigarette paper and smuggled into Russia from Germany and Switzerland.[67]

Probably the most sophisticated smuggling operation was developed by the banned German socialist newspaper *Sozialdemokrat* during the period 1878–90. A smuggling operation directed by business manager Julius Motteler (known as the 'red postmaster') succeeded in getting 11,000 copies a week into Germany from Switzerland, with most of the papers transported in suitcases and other bundles shipped by train and boat. An elaborate system was worked out to notify Motteler whether or not packages had reached their destination. A successful delivery would prompt a telegraphed message such as 'Anna has departed'; a partial delivery might yield, 'Uncle sick, letter follows'; while a shipment entirely lost or confiscated might be followed by 'Uncle is ill, recovery hopeless'. The Motteler operation became so renowned that in 1895 he was asked to write a report on the system for Italian socialists who were undergoing their own repressive trials.[68]

A rather rare case of open defiance of press restrictions was the public boycotting of stamp-tax laws in Britain in 1830–6. During these six years, publishers who simply refused to pay the hated taxes published an estimated 500 periodicals, which had a peak circulation of about 200,000 per week. Working-class opposition to the taxes was so intense that the illegal publications were openly advertised and sold, despite government prosecutions which sent about 800 newspaper vendors and a number of publishers to jail. In 1836, with the reduction of the stamp tax from fourpence to one penny per copy, the so-called 'war of the unstamped' ended, although it took further agitation before the tax was completely abolished, in 1855.[69]

It should be stressed that courageous journalists and publishers did not bear all of the risk and should not get all of the credit for resisting repressive press regulations in nineteenth-century Europe. All large-scale smuggling, clandestine printing and 'unstamped' publishing operations depended on support and co-operation from large numbers of individuals who risked severe sanctions even though they had far less at stake than journalists and publishers had. Publishers and booksellers who handled illegal materials were encouraged to do so by widespread public interest in banned publications, which often pushed up prices and made selling them highly profitable. Certainly the widespread circulation of 'unstamped' papers in the 1830s in Britain and of illegal materials in Austria in the 1840s and tsarist Russia throughout the nineteenth century could not have developed without widespread latent opposition which provided a supportive climate for journalists and vendors willing to defy the regimes in question.

Swiss historian and journalist Jean Sismondi noted in 1847 that booksellers in London and Paris agreed that 'the public does not want books and that they find no sales for the books they publish, except in the countries where they are prohibited'. A seller of 'unstamped' newspapers in Britain declared in 1835,

> Were I to give over selling the Unstamped, my customers declare they will get them of some other person; as they were determined to have an Untaxed Newspaper, even if they subscribed among themselves to purchase the material for printing, for cheap knowledge they would have.

Perhaps the most appropriate epitaph, then, for attempts to repress the press in nineteenth-century Europe (and, perhaps, in any other time and place) may be a rhyme penned in 1733 by a popular British dramatist, James Branston, who asked,

> Can statutes keep the British press in awe,
> When that sells best, that's most against the law?[70]

3 Political Censorship of Caricature

In 1857 the French Minister of Fine Arts, Achille Fould, told a group of young artists that 'Art is very close to being lost when it abandons the pure and lofty regions of the beautiful and the traditional paths of the great masters.' He warned against 'seeking only the servile imitation of the least poetic and least elevated of what nature has to offer'.[1] Almost fifty years later, Kaiser Wilhelm II of Germany expressed the same outlook, in characteristically far earthier tones, in a famous denunciation of what he called 'gutter art' (*Rinnsteinkunst*):

> When art, as often happens today, shows us only misery, and shows it to us even uglier than misery is anyway, then art commits a sin against the German people. The supreme task of our cultural effort is to foster our ideals. . . . if culture is to fulfill its task completely it must reach down to the lowest levels of the population. That can be done only if art holds out its hand to raise the people up, instead of descending into the gutter.[2]

As these quotations suggest, many nineteenth-century European regimes were highly sensitive to what was portrayed in the visual arts, especially, as Kaiser Wilhelm's remarks indicate, in terms of its impact on the 'lowest levels of the population'. Particularly during the period before 1850, when few members of the lower classes could read, the concern and consequent censorship exercised over the visual arts by most major European governments exceeded even the tough restrictions exercised over the printed word. From the standpoint of conservative regimes, such tighter control over the visual arts made eminent sense, precisely because the classes that they feared the most were generally illiterate, but not blind, and also because pictures were thought to have a far greater impact than the printed word.

In 1789 an observer congratulated the revolutionary authorities in France for reinstating prior censorship of designs while abolishing press censorship, because 'paintings and engravings are the most powerful means of influencing the heart of man, because of the lasting impressions they leave'. This perception was also expressed with great clarity during the debate over the notorious 'September Laws' of 1835, which subjected all designs to censorship, despite the promise of article 7 of the 1830 constitution that 'Frenchmen have the right to publish' and circulate their opinions and 'censorship can never be re-established'. In attempting to reconcile prior censorship of the visual arts with the promises of 1830, the French Attorney General declared, in successfully urging legislative passage of the proposal,

> Article 7 of the Charter proclaims that Frenchmen have the right to circulate their opinions in published form. But, when opinions are converted into actions by the circulation of drawings, it is a question of speaking to the eyes. That is something more than the expression of an opinion; it is an incitement to action not covered by article 7.

In 1852, when censorship of caricature was imposed once more in France after the 1848 revolution had brought its abolition, the Police Minister termed drawings 'one of the most dangerous' of all means used to 'shake up and destroy the sentiments of reserve and morality so essential to conserve in the bosom of a well-ordered society', because, while even the 'worst page in the worst book requires time to be read and a certain degree of intelligence to understand it', caricatures present 'in a translation understandable to everyone the most dangerous of all seductions, that of example'.[3]

Virtually every form of the visual arts, from sculpture to painting, suffered at one time or another in nineteenth-century Europe from politically motivated governmental censorship, seizure or prosecution. However, easily the main target of sustained political repression in the field of the visual arts was political caricature, which not only was the most overtly political form of pictorial art but, since it was published in newspapers and magazines and as separate prints, was far more widely circulated than more expensive and refined forms of art such as painting and sculpture. Thus, it was a spate of lithographic caricatures, bitterly hostile to the regime of King Louis-Philippe, that provoked the September Laws of 1835. Caricatures were subjected to prior censorship for all or part of the nineteenth century in every major European country except Britain. Such restrictions lasted until about 1850 or after in Italy, Austria and Germany, and until after 1880 in France and Russia, both of which maintained such regulations well after censorship was abolished for the printed word.[4]

Even where prior censorship of caricatures was abolished, those held responsible for printing political caricatures which were deemed seditious or in violation of vaguely worded laws banning attacks on the honour of government officials were generally liable to post-publication prosecution. Thus, in France, even during the brief period when prior censorship of drawings was abolished between 1830 and 1835, caricatures continued to attract post-publication reprisals if they were deemed to incite 'hatred and contempt of the king's government' or to be guilty of an 'offence against the person of the king'. Those held culpable, and liable to be imprisoned or fined, in such circumstances included the printer, publisher and editor of the publication involved, as well as the artist. Similarly, in Germany, although prior censorship of caricature was forbidden after 1874, artists still faced possible prosecution under the vaguely worded law penalising *lèse majesté*, or 'insult' to the Kaiser. In Russia, during the brief period of the 1905 revolution when prior censorship of carica- tures was abolished, artists could still be arrested for such offences as 'insulting His Imperial Majesty and audaciously offending His Supreme Authority'. Many caricaturists and their publishers – includ- ing three truly outstanding artists, the French caricaturist Honoré Daumier, the German cartoonist Thomas Theodor Heine and the Russian illustrator Ivan Bilibin – were jailed or fined for violating such laws, a clear demonstration of the fact that the absence of prior censorship by no means guaranteed 'liberty of the crayon', as freedom of caricature became known.[5]

THE DEBATE ON 'LIBERTY OF THE CRAYON', AND THE MECHANICS OF THE CENSORSHIP

The fear of caricature and the defence of the censorship

Caricaturists were subjected to harsh persecution because they were regarded by conservative elites as the purveyors of subversion and filth likely to appeal especially to the illiterate lower classes, who were particularly feared as threats to elite power and privilege. Thus, one Englishman writing in the late eighteenth century condemned caricatures as teaching lessons 'not of morality and philanthropy, but of envy, malignity and horrible disorder', and concluded that it would be 'better, better far' if there were 'no art, than thus to pervert and employ it to purposes so base, and so subversive of everything interesting to society'. In 1831 the British journal *The Athenaeum* characterised the work of caricaturists as that of someone who 'insults inferiority of mind and exposes defects of body – and who aggravates what is already hideous, and blackens what was sufficiently dark'. A French government newspaper of 1835 urged the reimposition of prior censorship of caricature on the grounds that 'the outbursts which have profaned the art of design' had cluttered the streets with the 'degrading spectacle of a mute, living revolt against the established order' which had committed the 'most gross outrages against the king, the courts and the laws' and created a 'danger for family mores'.[6]

The German democratic and anti-militarist (but not fundamentally radical) caricature journal *Simplicissimus*, founded in 1896, was, as Robin Lenman notes, endlessly denounced by the German authoritarian establishment as 'subversive, pornographic "brothel literature" which was a danger to morality, youth and national strength'. Thus in 1898 a conservative German newspaper claimed that *Simplicissimus* was characterised by a 'flood of artistic and moral poison', while a few years later the Minister of War, von Heeringen, condemned it as the 'bacillus which destroys all our ideals' and required all German officers to pledge themselves not to read it. Bavarian officials banned the sale of *Simplicissimus* from state railway stations in 1909 after the Munich police had urged such action on the grounds that 'a publication which systematically and in the most shameless manner ridicules and seeks to bring into contempt the foundations of the existing social order is not suitable for sale in public places belonging to the state'.[7] *Simplicissimus* had already been banned (in 1898) from sale at Prussian state railway stations, leading the journal to publish an extraordinarily acute caricature exposing the authorities' exaggerated fears of the danger posed by opposition art: railway officials were portrayed evicting from a train station a copy of the magazine, which dripped blood as they transported it while holding the journal at arm's length with a huge pair of tongs (see Plate 1). A similarly acute depiction of the authorities' relentless determination to suppress all possibly subversive drawings appeared in 1902 in the Portuguese magazine *A Parodia*, which was frequently the target of censorship bans. The magazine depicted a Portuguese censor expressing opposition to virtually any form of caricature on the grounds that the drawings were all political 'allusions', and expressing happiness only with a completely blank page (see Plate 2).

The impact of opposition caricatures upon the lower classes was especially feared by the authorities. Thus, in urging Friedrich Wilhelm IV, in 1843, to reverse the recent abolition of censorship of drawings, the Prussian Minister of the Interior won his case by arguing that caricatures 'prepare for the destructive influence of negative philosophies and democratic spokesmen and authors', especially since the 'uneducated classes do not pay much notice to the printed word' but do 'pay attention to caricatures and understand them'. He added that 'to refute [a caricature] is impossible; its impression is lasting and sometimes ineradicable'. Similarly, in 1823, the Paris police prefect urged a crackdown on itinerent printsellers, since such traders frequently spread dangerous ideas among the 'lowest classes of society'. In 1827 a leading publisher of popular engravings was banned from selling pictures of Napoleon on horseback because, as the Minister of the Interior put it, they were 'coarse prints destined for the lower classes of people'. Perhaps the ultimate fear that troubled conservative elites about drawings was expressed by one of the characters in Oliver Goldsmith's play *She Stoops to Conquer* (1773): when his folly is revealed, Marlow exclaims in dread, 'I shall be stuck up in caricaura [caricature] in all the print shops!' The notoriously corrupt New York City politician William 'Boss' Tweed, who felt the sting of hostile caricatures by the brilliant cartoonist Thomas Nast in the post-Civil War period, declared, 'Those damned pictures; I don't care so much what the papers write about me – my constituents can't read, but damn it they can see pictures!'[8]

Certainly it was the case that caricatures were widely distributed and aroused enormous interest among all classes of the population, as is clear from the numerous prints which depict large crowds gathered to examine displays of caricatures. Thus, an observer in Britain described the scene at a leading printshop in 1802:

> If men be fighting over there [across the Channel] for their possessions and their bodies against the Corsican robber [Napoleon], they are fighting here to be first in Ackermann's shop and see Gillray's latest caricatures. The enthusiasm is indescribable when the next drawing appears; it is a veritable madness. You have to make your way through the crowd with your fists.

The German writer Heinrich Heine reported from Paris in 1832, during the period when opposition caricaturists had made pears a ludicrous symbol of the regime of King Louis-Philippe, that the city was festooned with 'hundreds of caricatures' featuring the pear as the 'permanent standing joke of the people', that 'the pear, and always the pear, is to be seen in every caricature', and that 'the glory from [the king's] head hath passed away and all men see in it is but a pear'. Even in Russia, where backwardness and strict censorship confined most drawings to religious subjects, the clamour for prints was great, and at fairs and markets, pedlars wandered through the crowds calling, 'Who wants The Seven Deadly Sins? Who wants the future in the other world?' The popularity of caricatures is confirmed by the extremely respectable circulation figures attained by caricature journals, especially after about 1870, when lower costs made them more broadly affordable than before. Thus, in 1911 *Punch* of London printed 90,000 copies and the German socialist caricature journal *Der Wahre Jacob* had 300,000 subscribers, while in France *La Lune* and its successor *L'Eclipse* published 30,000 to 40,000 copies in the late 1860s and *L'Assiette au beurre* sold over 250,000 copies of one of its most successful issues in 1901.[9]

Mechanics of the censorship

The 'September Laws of 1835', which were implemented in France between 1835 and 1881 whenever prior authorisation of designs was required, were typical of caricature-censorship laws in nineteenth-century Europe. They stated,

> No design, no engravings, lithographs, medals and stamps, no emblem of whatever nature and kind may be published, exposed, or put on sale without preliminary authorisation of the Ministry of the Interior at Paris and of the prefects in the departments. . . . The necessary authorisation . . . will contain a summary description of the illustration . . . the applicant wishes to publish, and the title which he intends to give it. . . . the author or publisher, on receipt of the authorisation, will deposit . . . a proof for purposes of comparison; he will guarantee the conformity of this proof with those that he intends to publish.[10]

In France and elsewhere the censorship administration was literally all powerful, since it was not required to explain or defend its decisions. Further, since censorship rulings were held to be administrative in nature, entailing no criminal penalties, no appeal could be made to the courts.[11] Hundreds if not thousands of designs were completely rejected by censors. Others could be published only in highly mutilated forms which completely destroyed their intended message. For example, a caricature by the French artist André Gill published in *L'Eclipse* on 3 August 1873 was intended to complain that the contributions of former President Adolphe Thiers were being too quickly forgotten, but it was only allowed to appear in a meaningless form with Thiers removed from the drawing (see Plate 3).

While the mechanics of censorship generally followed the same pattern throughout Europe, one unique element was introduced in France by Louis Napoleon in February 1852, following his *coup d'état* that overthrew the democratic government established in the wake of the 1848 revolution. Louis Napoleon not only reinvoked the 'September Laws', thus re-establishing the prior censorship of designs which had been abolished in 1848, but also imposed the new requirement that, before a caricature could be published, any living person depicted in it must give written consent. The new regulation, which remained in effect almost without a break until 1881, created what amounted to a dual censorship of drawings, since any caricature which depicted living people would now have to be approved both by government authorities and by the subject(s) depicted.[12]

While the 'authorisation rule' (as it will henceforth be called) was supposedly intended to prevent invasion of privacy, it also was part of a general campaign aimed at making caricaturists' lives and work more difficult, since obtaining written consent from the subjects of caricature often required much time and energy, with multiple personal visits sometimes needed. Further, the rule bolstered the censorship, in its fight to prevent the introduction of subversive allusions into designs, by making sure that any member of the establishment who was caricatured would have a chance to veto publication if he felt that the drawing would subject him to ridicule or otherwise denigrate the authorities. Victor Hugo, perhaps Napoleon III's most important opponent, who spent the whole of the Second Empire in exile, offered this explanation of the regime's especial hatred of pictures as evidenced by the dual censorship: 'The government feels itself to be hideous. It wants no portraits, especially no mirrors. Like the osprey, it takes refuge in the night; if one saw it, it would die.'[13]

The authorisation rule unquestionably had a major effect on French caricature between 1852 and 1881. Thus, virtually no caricatures of Emperor Napoleon III (ruled 1852–70) or of President MacMahon (1873–9) appeared while they were in power. Sometimes the authorisation rule led to the publication of bizarre-looking caricatures with featureless faces. Thus, in 1870 Gill published in *L'Eclipse* a drawing depicting five journalists, one of whose face was blank, because he had refused to agree to be caricatured (see Plate 4). Probably the most notorious case in which a well-known personality refused to be portrayed was that of Alphonse de Lamartine, the French author and politician. Lamartine made himself an object of widespread ridicule when he authorised the publication of his explanation of his refusal:

> I cannot authorise the derision of my human form, which, even if it would not offend man, would offend nature and place humanity in mockery. . . . it would only be a false magnanimity on my part that would authorise an offence to the dignity of a creature of God. I do not wish to be an accomplice to this. . . . My personage belongs to all the world, to the sun as to the streams, but just as it is. I do not wish voluntarily to profane it, because it represents a man and is a gift of God.[14]

On the other hand, many personalities were quite happy to have their faces displayed before all France. As Charles Gilbert-Martin of *Le Don Quichotte* noted in his memoirs published in the magazine on 21 May 1887, while some refused to be caricatured at all and some demanded to see the drawing before giving approval, others responded favourably to a request without imposing conditions, and yet others 'gave their authorisation without being asked for it', as in the case of one person who wrote, 'In case you take a fancy to portraying me in your journal, you can do with my head what you want; I deliver it to you.' As it became customary in the late 1860s for caricaturists to publish their subjects' written authorisations along with the drawings, those portrayed often spent a great deal of effort and energy on composing an appropriate statement. Thus, the famous, elderly actor Frédérick Lemaître told *La Lune* that it should really 'make caricatures of the young! Time makes caricatures of the old' (16 June 1867). The Minister of Justice, Théodore Cazot, jokingly authorised *Le Don Quichotte* to publish a portrait of him 'on condition that it make me very handsome, very eloquent, very distinguished. . . . etc., etc., etc.' (28 May 1880). Gilbert-Martin responded by drawing Cazot as he really was, a rather elderly and portly man, holding in one hand the authorisation and in the other a portrait of himself as he wanted to look: young, debonair and handsome.

The praise of caricature and the attack on the censorship

While conservative elites feared and persecuted caricaturists in nineteenth-century Europe, the caricaturists and their supporters defended the profession as one that could communicate with and enlighten all elements of society, especially the uneducated. Thus, the great artist Honoré Daumier noted that 'Caricatures are good for those who cannot read', and the director of one of the leading firms publishing popular prints told one of his artists, 'Don't forget, my son, that you design for those people who cannot read.' In 1871, one French journalist praised caricature as a stronger weapon of opposition than the printed word, because

> The pamphlet addresses itself only to the mind; in order to understand and taste it, moreover, requires a certain level or instruction, or at least of attention. Caricature hits the eyes and effects that which is the most susceptible in us, the imagination. It is intelligible to everyone; it stops us in our tracks. . . . The pamphlet only leaves in the memory ideas, and others quickly come along to erase them. Caricature engraves in the memory images of form and colour which last long after it has been viewed.

Similarly, the late-nineteenth-century German journalist Maximilien Harden, a leading critic of the regime of Wilhelm II, declared, 'No other sort of publication can have such an effect on public opinion as the illustrated satirical magazine, which appeals to the most brilliant and to the simplest mind, and with its scornful challenge and raucous laughter, attracts attention everywhere.' Russian author Leo Tolstoy declared,

> For the historian of the 22nd and 23rd centuries who describes the 19th century, [the German caricature journal] *Simplicissimus* will be the most valuable source, enabling him to become familiar not only with the state of our present-day society, but also to test the credibility of all other sources.[15]

Caricatures clearly sometimes had a profound impact upon the population. Thus, one Frenchman wrote of the opposition caricatures published in the 1830s that they allowed 'us in each of those journals to retrieve our thoughts of the previous day, translated into vivid images, sculpted in relief'. Another French observer, referring to the opposition caricatures of André Gill published in the 1860s during the waning years of Napoleon III's reign, declared Gill had cleverly targeted the 'weak point in our political adversaries' and thus had served as 'one of the most useful artisans of the fall of the Empire'. The German playwright Gerhardt Hauptmann termed *Simplicissimus* the 'sharpest and most ruthless satirical force in Germany'.[16]

Caricaturists and their supporters bitterly attacked governmental restrictions on their craft, especially in countries such as France where prior censorship of drawings was retained long after the printed word was freed from similar control. Although prior press censorship had been abolished in France in 1830 and was never reintroduced, censorship of caricature remained so contentious and important an issue that every major political shift was reflected in changes in the rules regulating caricature: thus prior censorship was abolished as a result of the downfall of previous regimes in 1815, 1830, 1848 and 1870, but subsequently reimposed in 1820, 1835, 1851 and 1871. *L'Eclipse* observed on 20 September 1874, 'One could, one day, write an exact history of the liberty which we enjoy during the era that we live through by writing a history of our caricatures.'

Censorship of caricature was abolished for good in France only in 1881, leading anguished caricaturists to complain vociferously in the meantime about what they viewed as iniquitous, unjustified and arbitrary discrimination against their profession. Thus, the caricature journal *Le Grelot* demanded on 3 February 1878, 'By what right can one prevent the crayon from saying what the pen is allowed to?' It demanded the right to equal treatment, declaring that prior censorship 'under the pretext that we might commit stupidities' was the equivalent to having a citizen 'followed by two police under the claim that he could have the intention of taking off his shorts in the street'. The Bordeaux-based journal *Le Don Quichotte*, whose editor and caricaturist, Charles Gilbert-Martin, was jailed several times for violating censorship rules, also complained with growing bitterness in the 1870s about the different treatment of pen and crayon. 'Can you explain by any plausible reason why drawing cannot enjoy the same liberty as writing?' Gilbert-Martin demanded on 25 June 1875, adding that, if authors had to submit to the same controls as artists, then the 'French press would only be a vast factory of whipped cream.'

The arbitrariness of the censors' decisions and procedures was a prime focus of complaints by French caricaturists. Thus, *Le Grelot* complained on 9 September 1871 that censorship decisions were made with 'no trial, no conviction, just an order of the Minister of the Interior', and added on 10 March 1872 that it was impossible to know what the Minister would allow, since 'what is forbidden today was authorised a week ago and perhaps will be allowed tomorrow'. *Le Don Quichotte* complained on 6 June 1875 that the censor 'adjusts his glasses, raises his eyebrows, pinches his lips and that's enough to make him infallible. . . . If his new boots trouble him, if his wife has made a scene, look out for the red pencil.' Gilbert-Martin was especially angered by censorship demands that he change the elements of one of his drawings, attacking Catholic influence in education. He explained in *Le Don Quichotte* on 15 April 1876 that he was refusing to obey an order that he remove a clerical hat from an owl and change the inscription on a piece of paper held by a duck, since these changes would make his design 'colourless, inintelligible and purposeless'. Given that the censors' 'will is the only law', Gilbert-Martin lamented, next they might demand that he 'place a geranium pot in place of the owl and a meringue in place of the duck'. In July 1874 *Le Trombinoscope* complained that the censorship, nicknamed 'Madame Anastasie' in France, repeatedly acted in the most irrational way in her decisions:

> She searches out allusions in the hatchings, seditious profiles in the shapes of shadows, and ten times out of seven she finds this solution: 'I see nothing, then there must be something': she refuses the design. . . . She persecutes for the pleasure of persecuting, but without knowing why. She would be very embarrassed if she had to justify the fits and starts of her pencil and scissors.

The authorisation rule of 1852–81 also led to many bitter complaints by caricaturists. Thus, Gilbert-Martin declared in his *Don Quichotte* column on 21 May 1880 that the rule forced on caricaturists an 'unsupportable role for which I personally have neither a backbone supple enough nor a soul humble enough', as it forced artists to 'bow and scrape' before those whom they would prefer to 'flagellate'. Noting that the need to obtain the personal approval of the subjects to be caricatured often proved highly time-consuming, he added that the authorisation rules made it difficult for artists to publish drawings commenting on current events, especially since their work was, to begin with, 'less rapid' than that of writers. Thus, the net effect of the regulation, Gilbert-Martin complained, was to 'deprive the designer of the topicality which alone can pay the costs of a journal and to leave him with the possibility only of drawing dead people, such as sixteenth-century royalty like 'Henry IV putting a chicken into a pot or Mary Stuart saying her goodbyes to France.' Léon Bienvenu, editor of *Le Trombinoscope*, declared in *L'Eclipse* on 25 October 1874, that the authorisation rule was the 'favourite trick' of the censorship and that 'never could one invent anything more stupid than to subordinate a critique to the approval of the person who is the object of it'. *Le Grelot* complained on 11 October 1878 that leading republican politicians such as Adolphe Thiers and Léon Gambetta 'gave their authorisation with two hands' if 'one made an [artistic] apology to them', but 'they refused with enthusiasm each time one criticised them in a fashion too vivid and just'. *Le Titi* concluded on 7 June 1879 that, 'So long as one cannot publish a portrait of someone without having the written authorisation of that person, liberty of the pencil will only be a myth.'

Not surprisingly, caricaturists attacked their persecutors not only in writing but also with drawings. Perhaps the clearest expression of the hatred artists felt for the censorship was a drawing with the sarcastic title 'Terrible Accident!!!' published in *Le Sifflet* on 11 November 1875: its caricature showed two censors attempting to cut *Le Sifflet* to shreds but instead cutting off each other's heads with their huge scissors (Plate 5). Most caricatures attacking the censorship depicted the authorities wreaking various sorts of havoc on artists, writers and drawings. Thus, in 1851 the French journal *Charivari* depicted a government official smashing a lithographic stone with a sledgehammer. Russian journals, during a brief period when censorship controls were abolished in the wake of the 1905 revolution, depicted the censorship as a horrifying creature in a military hat who was seen subjecting a caricature journal to minute scrutiny, and portrayed a printshop boarded up and padlocked by the authorities (Plate 6). In 1906, the German caricature journal *Ulk* satirised the Russian censorship's treatment of imported journals by publishing a drawing in which Tsar Nicholas's head was already blacked out (Plate 7). The problems the censorship caused for artists and journalists were also depicted in two similar cartoons from France in the 1870s and Portugal in the 1900s, which showed the victims of artistic censorship trying to walk on eggs to avoid forbidden topics (Plate 8). French artists often represented the censorship as 'Madame Anastasie', a wretched old hag wreaking havoc with a huge pair of scissors (Plate 9). Fittingly, as the end of prior censorship of caricature approached in 1881, a cartoon published in *La Silhouette* showed the new press law as a scythe about to cut Anastasie's neck as she went about her work of destroying caricatures.

Several striking self-caricatures depicted artists imprisoned for their work. Thus, in a drawing published in *Simplicissimus* in January 1899, its leading artist, Thomas Theodor Heine, showed himself 'as I'll be doing my next drawing' – serving a six-month sentence in jail for a drawing which ridiculed Wilhelm II's diplomatic gaffes (see Plate 10). A similar drawing by French artist Aristide Delannoy published in *L'Assiette au beurre* in 1908 showed him and his editor chained up in jail after receiving one-year sentences for publishing a caricature depicting a French general as a bloody butcher. The worst fears of artists and writers were satirised in Germany by a *Simplicissimus* caricature of 1897, which depicted a journalist wearing a *'lèse majesté'* sign around his neck as he was led to the guillotine (Plate 10).

THE HISTORY OF CARICATURE CENSORSHIP IN EUROPE

The development of caricature censorship before 1815

Sensitivity to pictorial representation extends far back into European history. In ancient Greece, Plato declared that the 'purpose of art is to educate young people to become men of noble spirit and character' and urged that any artists who left the 'stamp of baseness, license, meanness, unseemliness on painting and sculpture' be banned from practising their craft. In more modern times, censorship regulations were applied to images at least as early as the sixteenth century. These early decrees were primarily an attempt to stifle the explosion of political and religious prints which followed the diffusion of the printing press and played their part in the conflicts of the Reformation in the sixteenth and seventeenth centuries. For example, Martin Luther made extensive use of caricatures in his attacks on the Catholic Church, and boasted that he had 'maddened the Pope with those pictures of mine'. In the Edict of Worms (1521), the Holy Roman Emperor, Charles V, provided for censorship of 'both printed and illustrated' material and expressly prohibited the production of satires of all kinds. In Nuremberg, the leading German centre for the publication of prints, the authorities banned all images of Martin Luther in 1524 as well as numerous other potentially subversive or heretical subjects. In Vienna, a special imperial investigation in 1558 condemned a number of printsellers for distributing, among other 'disrespectful pictures', one showing the Pope and the Holy Roman Emperor naked. In France, Charles IX issued an edict in 1561 which extended prior censorship (already in existence for the printed word) to encompass 'cards and pictures'; those who failed to submit drawings for approval were threatened with the lash for the first offence and death for repeat offences. In seventeenth-century England, King Charles I complained about 'these Madde Designs' which ridiculed him during the Civil War, while his successor, Oliver Cromwell, prescribed death for those who circulated playing cards which belittled him. In Spain, the Inquisition practised censorship of drawings until its suppression in 1820. It issued regulations against heretical drawings in 1612 and subsequently also outlawed prints criticising the secular authorities, leading to the repeated seizure of offensive prints. In Russia, political and personal caricatures were forbidden at least as early as 1720 under the terms of Peter the Great's censorship edicts, which forbade contravention of the 'law of God, the Government, morality or the personal honour of any citizen' and warned that the 'authors of satires will be subjected to the worst tortures'.[17]

The failure of these decrees to suppress completely 'subversive' drawings before 1700 is clear from that fact that such regulations were issued over and over again and required repeated enforcement. Thus, the French authorities demanded that drawings be submitted for prior censorship not only in 1561, but also in 1581 and 1685, and in 1722 the government established a special tribunal to judge 'engravers and printers who published and distributed prints' hostile to the regime. In Germany, the 1521 Edict of Worms was repeatedly restated and reinforced by imperial officials, while local authorities, especially in Nuremberg, were also forced constantly to reiterate demands for drawings to be submitted for censorship. Russian civil and religious authorities issued regulations supplementing or repeating Peter the Great's 1720 decree in 1721, 1723, 1742, 1744, 1783, 1790 and 1800. Frequently those who were convicted of violating censorship regulations were fined, imprisoned, and had their engravings and prints confiscated and destroyed. Medieval records in Nuremberg are filled with references to 'improper pictures' and the disciplining of writers, artists and booksellers. In France, two unfortunate printers were executed in 1694 for publishing an engraving which depicted Louis XIV in the guise of a statue enchained by four women who clearly represented his mistresses.[18]

These repressive actions succeeded in destroying large numbers of hostile caricatures and intimidating and jailing many artists and printsellers, especially as the reach and effectiveness of governmental authority grew. In the eighteenth century, with the chaotic period of the religious wars well past, state power became increasingly centralised, with a strong bureaucracy to administer it. This meant that, while the censorship authorities never entirely succeeded in suppressing clandestinely circulated opposition prints, by 1775, as Ralph Shikes notes, government edicts had largely 'stilled lips and paralyzed pen and burin [an engraving tool]' in most of Europe. Thus, in Germany, William Coupe concludes, most eighteenth-century political prints were 'innocuous affairs, insipid representations of the European powers engaged in card games and the like'.[19]

Among the major European countries, there were two outstanding exceptions to this general rule: Britain, where prior censorship of both drawings and the printed word had been terminated in 1695, and political prints blossomed in the eighteenth century; and France, where during the seventeenth and the eighteenth centuries significant numbers of hostile caricatures were clandestinely printed or were smuggled in from Holland and then sold 'under the counter'. Despite frequent arrests and confiscations in France, as the *ancien régime* slowly deteriorated in the eighteenth century, illicit caricatures which mocked high officials of the realm continued to circulate widely. In the words of André Blum, 'It was said that France was an absolute monarchy tempered by songs; one could add: also by caricatures.'[20]

The fears inspired throughout Europe by the French Revolution led to the imposition of harsh new restrictions on illustrations. Thus, in Spain, the production and distribution of all prints, boxes, fans and other objects relating to the French Revolution were banned in January 1790, and in 1803 Goya was forced to withdraw from public sale his masterly drawings known as 'The Caprices', owing to the threat of a trial before the Inquisition. In Russia, Catherine the Great banned the importation of all objects of French origin, including artworks. In 1808, her grandson, Alexander I, suppressed the first caricature journal ever published in Russia because its editor, Aleksei Venetsianov, made the mistake of publishing a cartoon depicting a noble asleep with his mistress while petitioners waited outside and a cat played with important letters (Alexander thoughtfully advised Venetsianov to 'direct his talents to a much better subject and use his time more advantageously to school himself in his employment [as a land surveyor]'). Even in Britain, there were occasional post-publication reprisals for caricatures during the Jacobin scare of the 1790s; thus James Gillray, the leading caricaturist of his time, was arrested for a print of 1796 ridiculing the Prince of Wales. On the other hand, once the French revolutionary wars had begun, countries in conflict with France lifted general restrictions on political caricature that *attacked* the French Revolution and Napoleon. Indeed, they actively encouraged and even subsidised such works, of which hundreds, often highly virulent, were published in Britain, Russia, Germany and elsewhere.[21]

In France, with the effective collapse of censorship controls amidst the revolutionary agitation of mid 1789, a massive wave of satirical drawings flooded the country.[22] Although the provisional government of Paris reimposed prior censorship of drawings (but not of words) on 31 July 1789, political caricatures of all persuasions were generally tolerated for about three years. However, as the revolutionary strife increased and the tide shifted towards the Jacobins, royalist and anti-Jacobin caricatures were gradually suppressed or forced underground while Paris was swamped with violently anti-monarchical and radical drawings. At the height of the Reign of Terror in 1793–4, caricature became subject to the same repression as affected all thought, and an artist named Hercy was executed for portraying Robespierre 'guillotining the executioner after having guillotined everyone else in France'. As the French historian Arsène Alexander delicately puts it, he obtained 'as payment for his work the personal knowledge that the executioner still had someone left to kill'.[23] During the rule of the Directory (1794–9), political caricature virtually disappeared, partly due to the fear of reprisals but mostly because of a general sense of political exhaustion.

What little life was left in French political caricature was almost totally annihilated during the fifteen-year rule of Napoleon Bonaparte (1799–1814).[24] One of Napoleon's first moves after seizing power in 1799 was to forbid printsellers from displaying 'anything contrary to good morals or against the principles of government', and thereafter he became almost obsessed with eradicating opposition writings and caricatures, even banning republican symbols from playing cards.[25] He was enraged by caricatures against him produced in enemy countries, even demanding that the British government forbid the publication of caricatures paid for by French exiles. However, he also commissioned the production of caricatures ridiculing his enemies – for example, directing his secret-police chief in 1805 to 'have some caricatures made' of 'an Englishman, purse in hand, begging different powers to receive his money', and noting that 'The immense attention which the English direct to gaining time by false news shows the extreme importance of this work.'[26]

Caricature censorship in Europe, 1815–48

The story of the political censorship of caricature in the major countries of Europe between 1815 and 1848 centres almost entirely on France. In Britain the political cartoon remained essentially unfettered, while in Russia, Germany, Spain, Italy and the Hapsburg Empire strict censorship made it dangerous in the extreme to circulate critical political imagery. In these countries, regimes concentrated all their energies on preventing any re-emergence of the ideas associated with the French Revolution, and, as an expert on German political cartoons delicately puts it, 'The climate of the Metternich era scarcely offered suitable condition for the development of a thriving tradition of political graphic satire.'[27] Only in France, where audacious caricaturists sought to exploit and evade ambiguous laws, was the stage set for major conflict.

In Britain, for all practical purposes, cartoonists were free of both prior and post-publication censorship by 1815. Although conservative elites still feared the power of hostile cartoonists, by 1820 prosecution of caricaturists had fallen into such disuse that the Prince Regent (later George IV), a notorious philanderer, was reduced to trying to hush cartoonists up by buying up plates and unsold prints depicting him and his various peccadillos. He even paid £100 to the leading caricaturist George Cruikshank to secure his pledge 'not to caricature His Majesty in any immoral situation', but Cruikshank quickly evaded the agreement by depicting the new king atoning for his behaviour by doing penance in church for his numerous adulteries. Another caricaturist, Lewis Marks, took advantage of the King's vulnerability by extorting money from him on at least ten separate occasions in 1820.[28]

After 1841, British political caricature was further insured against persecution by the near-monopoly of the genre maintained by the magazine *Punch*, which poked only gentle fun at the ruling elite. Ralph Shikes and Steven Heller comment that *Punch*'s comedy was 'housebroken' and 'never – well hardly ever – made its audience wince', and a contemporary British observer remarked, with reference to the bitter caricatures common in France, 'The Parisians say of our Victorian caricatures that they smile rather than laugh.' None the less, the skins of continental European rulers were so thin that issues of *Punch* were banned in both Austria and France during the 1840s.[29]

While caricature was free in Britain after 1815, it remained fettered in Russia, the Hapsburg Empire, Spain and the German and Italian states between 1815 and 1848. Historians have noted that during this period German 'political caricature was reduced to the most complete impotence' and was 'proscribed by a pitiless censorship', and that in the Hapsburg Empire (where the censorship extended to business signs, maps and tombstones) there was 'nothing until 1848 as the terrible censorship of Metternich laid a heavy hand on everything' and stifled 'any kind of criticism of political conditions or of measures taken by the authorities'.[30] In Germany, the censorship was so strict that not even the famous soprano Jenny Lind, who served as a kind of German court ornament, could be caricatured. A brief experiment was conducted in Prussia in 1842, when pictures and cartoons were exempted from prior censorship, but Friedrich Wilhelm IV reimposed restrictions after only four months when he was inundated by a tidal wave of caricatures and satires. By 1843, censorship was again so strict that a drawing showing some robbers breaking into a house while nightwatchmen slept was forbidden in Berlin on the grounds that, since nightwatchmen were public officials, the caricature constituted an insult to the state. In Bavaria, the *Fliegende Blatter*, founded in Munich in 1845, at first indulged in some discreetly veiled pictorial political criticism, but its voice was soon muffled by a censorship crackdown and especially by a widely publicised prosecution in October 1847. Conditions were even harsher in Italy, where authorities under the reactionary influence of the Papacy and Metternich blocked the emergence of politically assertive prints; and in Spain, where, even after the abolition of the Inquisition in 1820, harsh political controls remained in place.[31] Thus, in response to a request for information about political caricature in Spain, a member of the US embassy in Madrid wrote in 1875,

I have questioned many persons here in regard to Spanish caricature, but have always received the same reply, namely that pictorial caricature, political or other, has not existed in Spain til 1868 [when a revolution overthrew the monarchy of Isabel II and established a short-lived republic]. I have searched book-stores and bookstalls, and find nothing; nor have the venders been able to aid me. It is thought at our Legation there must have been caricature in Spain, from the writings of Spaniards being so full of satire and wit; but though the germ may have existed, I am inclined to think it was not developed til the dethronement of Isabel II and the proclamation of the Republic broke down the barriers to the liberty, if not license, of the printing press. . . . Until this period, I fancy the Inquisition, censorship and other causes prevented any display of a spirit of caricature which may have existed.[32]

In Russia, iron-clad censorship was maintained throughout the period and especially at times of political tension, when, Frederick Starr notes, 'the risk of repression for satirical or oppositionist art was doubtless enormous'.[33] Thus, in the 1820s a series of copper engravings depicting a clever peasant outwitting a greedy priest and a corrupt judge was forbidden, and Alexander I personally issued an edict forbidding possession of a china statuette of a monk carrying on his back a bundle of straw in which a girl was concealed. During the tyrannical reign of Nicholas I (1825–55), an illustrated *Life of Aesop* was banned in the 1830s as 'seditious' and the most famous work of the Russian artist Paul Fedotov was mutilated by the censors. His lithograph 'A Newly Decorated Knight', depicting an unkempt officer the morning after he received his first medal, was allowed only after the medal had been removed and the picture had been retitled 'The Morning after a Party'. Major new censorship crackdowns on illustrations were initiated in 1828 and in 1839, and in 1851 all hitherto uncensored woodblocks and copper engravings were ordered to be collected and destroyed. Huge numbers of copper plates were subsequently melted down by the police and turned into scrap.[34]

Censorship restrictions in continental Europe between 1815 and 1848 were never entirely successful, but they were nearly so. While it was impossible legally to publish explicitly political caricatures in Germany, artists were able to poke fun at the clothing and habits of the aristocracy and bureaucracy, especially the stylised pigtailed wigs worn by the members of these classes. As a leading historian of German caricature, John Grand-Carteret, has noted, 'Caricaturists venged themselves en bloc against those they could not attack individually, ridiculing them in their costume, the sole thing permitted by the censors.'[35] In addition to these legal caricatures, some illicit caricatures were sold, under the counter. Thus, in September 1842, police intercepted a package of 900 copies of a forbidden caricature that were destined for sale at four Berlin stores. A few anonymous, clandestinely circulated prints survive from Germany between 1815 and 1848, such as a cartoon of 1825 entitled 'The Thinkers' Club' (modelled on a virtually identical British print of 1796), which depicts a group of gagged citizens sitting around a table under a poster which proclaims the question of the day to be 'How long may we be permitted to think?'[36]

The clearest indication that strict censorship is the primary reason for the general lack of political caricature in most European countries between 1815 and 1848 is the explosion of this art form in those countries where censorship temporarily collapsed as a result of the revolutions of 1848. William Coupe notes that in Germany the caricature business developed 'from virtually nothing' to 'a minor industry in a matter of weeks', with 35 illustrated satirical journals founded in Berlin alone. The most popular German caricature journal founded in 1848, *Kladderadatsch*, sold 4000 copies of its first issue in a single day. In Italy at least eight major caricature journals sprang up in 1848. In Russia and Spain, however, which experienced no revolution (rather, increased repression) in 1848, the absence of political caricature continued.[37]

The struggle over 'freedom of the crayon' in France, 1815–48

In France, prior censorship of caricature was abolished after the downfall of Napoleon in 1814, resulting in a flood of often violently polemical drawings which lampooned both the defeated Emperor and the restored Bourbon regime of Louis XVIII. However, opposition caricatures were soon being seized after publication and becoming the target of prosecutions, and in March 1820, following the assassination of the King's nephew, a press law was passed which declared that 'no printed, engraved or lithographed design may be published, displayed, distributed or sold without advance authorisation of the government'.[38] The Minister of Foreign Affairs assured the legislature that the government had no wish to interfere with artistic masterpieces but only sought to suppress images capable of 'nourishing or reviving in the hearts of Frenchmen sentiments which should be erased'.[39]

Political caricature by no means disappeared in France after 1820, but the censorship made it impossible to publish drawings which were viewed as overtly ridiculing the monarchy, glorifying Napoleon or threatening France's diplomatic relations with other countries. The growing criticism of the influence of the Catholic Church and especially of the Jesuits upon Louis XVIII's brother and successor, Charles X (reigned 1824–30), led in the late 1820s to severe censorship of caricatures touching on this theme. Shortly before the revolution of July 1830 that overthrew Charles, an editor of the pioneering caricature journal *La Silhouette* was sentenced to six months in jail and a fine of 1000 francs for publishing a forbidden drawing which depicted the King as a Jesuit.[40] None the less, in some cases hostile designs were allowed by the censorship, apparently through a combination of tolerance and incompetence. For example, candle snuffers (which extinguished light or, in French, 'lumière', a word also meaning enlightenment) were repeatedly used by artists as symbols of reaction, as were scissors, which symbolised the censorship, and crustaceans such as crabs, lobsters and crayfish, which give the impression of 'walking backwards'.[41]

The revolution of July 1830, partly provoked by attempts by Charles X to impose new controls on the press, brought about the downfall of the Bourbon monarchy and its replacement by Louis-Philippe of the cadet Orleanist dynasty. At the same time, censorship of caricature was abolished, unleashing a flood of political designs. The authorities responded with a campaign of post-publication repression. What the French writer Charles Baudelaire later described as a 'ruthless war' in which 'men were all passion, all fire' raged between the government and political caricaturists from 1830 until passage of the 'September Laws' of 1835, when prior censorship of designs was reimposed.[42]

The leader of the caricature war against the July Monarchy was Charles Philipon, who, in his mid twenties was the founder, editor, guiding genius (and a caricaturist) of the two leading lithographic caricature journals, the weekly *La Caricature* (1830–5) and the daily *Le Charivari* (1832–93).[43] Philipon recruited and nurtured a team of caricaturists of enormous talent and audacity, of whom it has been said that they had 'knives in their brains'[44]; they included Honoré Daumier, Grandville (Jean-Ignace-Isidore Gerard), Traviès (Charles-Joseph Traviès des Villiers) and Henry Monnier. Another element in Philipon's success was his adoption of the recently developed technique of lithography to reproduce caricatures. In comparison to the older techniques of wood and copper engraving, lithography was easier and faster for the artist to execute, was cheaper for the publisher to use and capable of producing far more copies. While in the past most caricatures had been published as independent prints, with lithography it became possible to make highly topical illustrations a regular feature of periodicals. Philipon's success above all reflected his ability to capture in caricature the widespread and growing anger of many French who felt the July Monarchy of Louis-Philippe was betraying the promises of the 1830 revolution for political freedom and social reforms – symbolised by the absurdly minute expansion of the suffrage in 1831 from 0.3 per cent to 0.5 per cent of the population, and by an explosion of post-publication press prosecutions, numbering over 500 in Paris alone between 1830 and 1834 (so unpopular were these that over 60 per cent ended in jury acquittals).[45]

After an initial flurry of violent and often brilliant artistic attacks against the fallen regime of Charles X, Philipon and his crew turned to lampooning the new regime in what became known as the 'war between Philipon and [Louis-] Philippe'. The greatest contribution to this lampooning of Louis-Philippe was Philipon's invention of the pear to represent the King, whose head bore at least a passing resemblance to what soon became the 'first fruit of France'. The pear imagery was used in scores of cartoons by Philipon's artists to depict the King in all sorts of ludicrous and repressive postures and soon became a ubiquitous symbol in popular imagery, literature and graffiti. Instead of asking 'Have you seen the lastest issue [of *La Caricature*]', Parisians inquired of each other, 'Have you seen the latest pear?' In one *La Caricature* article published in 1832, entitled 'The Invasion of the Pear' ('L'Envahissement de la poire'), a journalist reported that the mayor of Auxerre, a town 100 miles from Paris, had added to the post-no-bills sign 'nor any pears'. When Daumier was in jail in 1833, a newspaper reported that the walls of his prison were covered with fruits 'that are neither apples, nor cherries, nor peaches, nor apricots'.[46]

As the director of the war of caricatures against Louis-Philippe, Philipon suffered most severely from the government's repressive reprisals. Between 1831 and 1833 he was prosecuted half-a-dozen times for press offences connected with *La Caricature*, was convicted three times, was fined over 4000 francs and served thirteen months in jail (one common joke in France was that 'the pear doesn't give pits, but rather fines').[47] *La Caricature* was seized numerous times before being forced out of business in 1835 by accumulated fines and the September Laws. Even Philipon could not keep track of the mounting repression, later writing that 'I could no longer count the seizures, the arrest warrants, the trials, the struggles, the wounds, the attacks and the harassments of all types, any more than could a [carriage] voyager count the jolts of his trip'.[48] An examination of *La Caricature* clearly confirms this statement: the issue of 14 June 1832 reports the twenty-third seizure of the paper since its founding, yet two months later the seizure of the 9 August issue was reported as the twenty-first confiscation and then subsequently *La Caricature* reported that the correct count was twenty-two seizures! A number of artists and others associated with Philipon also suffered from governmental reprisals. *La Caricature*'s publisher (Philipon's brother-in-law Gabriel Aubert) and the paper's lithographic printer were each arrested several times between 1831 and 1833, and between March 1833 and July 1835 staff members of *Le Charivari* were arrested five times, sentenced to a total of fourteen months in jail and fined 14,500 francs. Daumier spent five months in jail for 'provoking hatred and contempt against the government of the King and for offences against the person of the King' as a result of his lithograph 'Gargantua' (published by Aubert's company as a separate print), which depicted a bloated Louis-Philippe seated on a toilet–throne, consuming food and tribute being supplied by the poor people of France and excreting honours and gifts to his aristocratic supporters.

The excuse the French government was seeking in order to end political caricature altogether presented itself on 28 July 1835, when a gruesome attempt on the King's life miscarried, leaving the King only slightly bruised but forty other persons killed or wounded. Subsequently the September Laws were passed, which imposed prior censorship on all designs. With the passage of the September Laws imminent, Philipon closed *La Caricature* in August 1835. The final issue published the text of the censorship provisions in the typographical shape of a pear, while defiantly noting that 'It took a law made especially for us to break our crayons, a law which makes it materially impossible for us to continue the work which continued before despite uncounted seizures, arrests without cause, crushing fines and long jail terms.'[49] *Le Charivari* was continued, but to its masthead slogan announcing it would 'publish a new drawing every day' was added 'censorship permitting'. Shortly after the September Laws took effect, *Le Charivari* appeared with a blank page surrounded by a funeral border, with the censored drawing described in words, a device that was used several times during the next few months (*Le Charivari* reported on 18 September that it had been forbidden to publish a drawing of a monkey eating a pear).

While the September Laws made overtly hostile political caricature impossible, as in 1820–30 the imposition of prior censorship did not succeed in entirely eliminating cartoons which lampooned the regime Philipon's cartoonists, especially Daumier, turned their talents to so called 'social' caricatures which used imaginary symbolic social types to portray the corruption, hypocrisy and money-grubbing atmosphere which permeated France in 1830–48, a period of get-rich-quick entrepreneuralism and early industrialisation. These caricatures collectively painted a devastating portrait of the government which tolerated, encouraged and was intertwined with these developments. The most famous cartoon character Daumier used to drive home his 'non-political' satire, Robert Macaire, portrayed in over 100 caricatures published between 1836 and 1838, was the archetypal bourgeois swindler who appeared in various guises as the corrupt banker, the feverish speculator, the hypocritical politician, the quack doctor and the Shylock lawyer.[50] The Macaire cartoons were fantastically successful, especially since the caricatures, in the words of Edward Lucie-Smith, 'encouraged a kind of complicity as readers followed their adventures week by week'. Even Karl Marx took note of the Macaire phenomenon, writing that the regime of Louis-Philippe was 'no more than a joint stock company for the exploitation of the French national wealth' and that the King was 'a director of this company, a Robert Macaire on the throne'.[51]

The September Laws remained in force, however, and, when pictures were viewed as going too far or when, as occasionally happened, caricatures were published in defiance of the censorship, the authorities were quick to act. Thus, although in November 1835 *Le Charivari* successfully defended itself against a prosecution by demonstrating that the illustration in question had previously been published in a book by a government minister, in two prosecutions in 1837 and 1842 staff members of *Le Charivari* were sentenced to a total of almost three years in jail and 12,000 francs in fines. In this climate self-censorship and caution inevitably played a daily role, as is perhaps most clearly indicated in Philipon's own words; in announcing the formation of a new caricature journal, the *Journal pour rire* (later renamed the *Journal amusant*) in early 1848, just a few weeks before the revolution which ended the reign of Louis-Philippe and temporarily abolished prior censorship of caricature, Philipon wrote that the new journal would provide 'gaiety always, with as much spirit as possible, but politics never . . . thanks to the September Laws'.[52]

Within a month of the overthrow of Louis-Philippe in late February 1848, the provisional republican government of France annulled the September Laws and all press convictions under the prior regime and declared that all citizens had the right and the duty to make their

opinions known via the press 'or by any other means of publication'.[53]
Le Charivari proclaimed triumphantly, 'Censorship is placed on the
block.' As in previous cases when a regime had tumbled and prior
censorship of caricature had been abolished (i.e. 1814, 1830), the
result was a flood of political caricatures, including many bitter
attacks on the fallen government. However, the most notable political
caricatures of 1848–52 warned of the threat to the new French
democracy posed by Napoleon's nephew, Louis Napoleon Bonaparte,
who was elected President of France in December 1848. The most
important caricature journal of the period was the *Revue comique*,
founded in November 1848 to warn of the Bonapartist menace.
Daumier, whose drawings continued to appear in *Le Charivari*, made
his most important contribution during this period by inventing the
character of 'Ratapoil' ('Hairy Rat' or 'Ratskin'), a sleazy combination
of thug and agent provocateur, used by him and others in over 100
cartoons in 1850–1 to warn France about Louis Napoleon's plans.
When the historian Jules Michelet visited Daumier's studio and saw
the statuette upon which Daumier had based his Ratapoil cartoons,
he exclaimed, 'Ah! you have completely hit the enemy! Here is the
Bonapartist idea forever pilloried by you!'[54]

Caricature censorship in Europe, 1848–81

The rapid military restoration of the regimes briefly toppled by
revolutions in 1848 in Germany, Austria and Italy, and the overthrow
of the French Republic by Louis Napoleon's coup of December 1851,
brought a swift end to the brief era of freedom of caricature. Virtually
all the new caricature journals collapsed amidst post-revolutionary
lethargy or were crushed by governmental repression, which generally
included renewed prior censorship, which, 'armed with its eternal
scissors, made pass from life to death the caricatures hostile to the
old regime'.[55] Thus, when General Friedrich von Wrangel occupied
Berlin with 13,000 troops in November 1848 and overthrew the
revolutionary government there, among his first measures was a
complete ban on the sale of satirical caricature journals. The editors
of the leading German democratic caricature journal of 1848, *Leuchtkugeln*, were arrested during that year for instigating revolution, and
after three years of harassment their journal was finally crushed in
1851 by jail terms and fines imposed by the Bavarian government
(see Plate 11). There were so many casualties in Germany that one
of the few survivors, *Kladderadatsch*, printed a cartoon in 1849

depicting a visit to a graveyard for satirical magazines. *Kladderadatsch* itself was able to survive only by toning down its content and largely avoiding internal German politics, although none the less two of its editors served short jail terms in the Spandau prison in late 1850 for criticising the Tsar of Russia. The situation in Germany was to remain fundamentally unchanged until after 1860. The few journals which struggled to retain any critical stance were either silenced – as in the case of two caricature journals hostile to Prussia which were founded in Saxony in the 1850s and were soon suppressed as a result of Prussian pressure – or gradually learned how to censor themselves. Thus, William Coupe writes, most German caricature journals in the 1850s 'reverted to the status of innocuous joke books, more concerned with mothers-in-law and drunks than political issues'.[56]

Developments in Germany were paralleled in Austria and Italy.[57] In Austria, the caricature journals of 1848 all quickly collapsed or were suppressed, and illustrated journals were virtually non-existent for a decade until press controls were lifted somewhat in 1859. In Italy, the Roman satirical weekly *Il Don Pirlone* was suppressed in 1849 after French troops had restored the Pope to his throne. Other victims of the post-1848 reaction in Italy included *L'Arlecchino* (Naples, 1848–9), *Lo Spirito folletto* (Milan, 1848), *Il Lampione* (Forence, 1848–9), and *Sior Antonio Rioba* (Venice, 1848–9). Only in the Kingdom of Sardinia (Piedmont), where constitutional government and freedom of the press survived after 1848, were political caricature journals able to survive. Thus, the leading Piedmont caricature journal of 1848, *Il Fischietto* of Turin, whose leading artist, Francesco Redenti, was a political refugee from Austrian-controlled Lombardy, published until 1916. The Venetian patriot Daniele Manin, writing in 1855, termed *Il Fischietto* the Italian *Charivari*, noting that 'it ridicules everyone and especially the government ministers'.[58] In fact *Il Fischietto* was judged so dangerous that all the other Italian states prohibited it in the 1850s and it occasionally had difficulties even with the Piedmontese authorities.

In France, Daumier's Ratapoil cartoons and the anti-Bonapartist caricatures of the *Revue comique* reflected the rising threat to French political freedoms, clearly in evidence as the Second Republic under the presidency of Louis Napoleon took a sharp swing to the right amidst fears, stimulated by the suppressed 'June Days' uprising of 1848, of a radical lower-class revolution. Thus, in July 1849, a law was passed requiring all persons who hawked pamphlets, songs and prints dealing with political matters to have them approved by the local authorities. According to one leftist paper, by January 1850 popular prints and almanacs were everywhere being 'suspended, confiscated, ripped up, torn to shreds'. The *Review comique* was suppressed by the government in December 1849, while caricaturist Charles Vernier and editor Leopold Pannier of *Le Charivari* were both sent to jail in April 1851 for a Vernier drawing which was held to be an illegal attack on Louis Napoleon. On 17 February 1852, about ten weeks after the *coup d'état* of 2 December 1851 that overthrew the constitutional order in France, Louis Napoleon (who later in 1852 proclaimed himself Emperor Napoleon III) issued a press decree which held the printed word in thrall by a variety of harsh administrative regulations but did not subject it to prior censorship, but which effectively outlawed political caricatures by reimposing the relevant portions of the September Laws.[59]

The result of the 1852 decree and its extraordinarily harsh administration was a near-total absence of critical political caricature in France between 1852 and 1867.[60] Unlike in the 1820s and the period 1835–48, when it had been possible to engage in sharp pictorial criticism of the regime by social or symbolic satires which targeted the ruling classes, even such muted satire was lacking. After 1867, stimulated by the regime's declining popularity and by a series of marginal reforms which conceded little but greatly whetted the appetite of the republican opposition, artists increasingly attempted to subvert or defy the existing censorship restrictions. Several new illustrated satirical journals were founded, leading to a series of skirmishes over 'freedom of the crayon' somewhat reminiscent of those that had taken place in 1830–5.[61] As one journalistic observer noted, 'The rebirth of caricature announced the rebirth of the spirit.'[62]

Many of the new journals and their caricaturists concentrated on trying to slip political allusions into their work whenever possible, and in a number of cases caricatures were published without the required prior authorisation. The inevitable result was an incessant campaign of general harassment of the offending journals, and a number of them were suppressed, including *Le Philosophe* (1867–8), *Le Hanneton* (1862–8) and *La Rue* (1867–8). By far the most important journals which suffered from governmental repression during the years preceding the fall of the Second Empire were *La Lune* (1865–7) and *L'Eclipse* (1868–76), both of which were dominated by the brilliant young caricaturist André Gill. In December 1867, *La Lune*'s publisher was jailed and the journal was suppressed for publishing an unauthorised Gill caricature deemed critical of Napoleon III's foreign policy. However, since no law banned a suppressed paper from reconstituting itself under another name, the staff of *La Lune* soon re-formed the journal under the name *L'Eclipse* (i.e. *La Lune* had been eclipsed). What followed can only be described as caricaturial guerrilla war, as Gill used every opportunity to sneak hostile political allusions into his drawings. The censorship responded by forbidding both drawings which it could understand and, to be safe, those which it couldn't. According to one tally, between January 1868 and August 1870 twenty-two of Gill's caricatures were forbidden.[63]

Periodically the works of more well-established artists in France also suffered from censorship bans. In perhaps the most notorious such case in the nineteenth century, one of Edouard Manet's masterpieces, his 1869 lithograph 'The Execution of the Emperor Maximilian', was banned (it finally was published in 1884). The ban was imposed for the obvious political reason that the event Manet portrayed was an enormous embarrassment to Napoleon III, whose attempt to establish a French outpost in Mexico had ended with his humiliating abandonment of the Archduke Maximilian of Austria, his hand-picked candidate for the Mexican throne, and Maximilian's subsequent death before a firing squad in 1867. The news of the suppression of Manet's work received great attention in the press, leading *La Tribune* to comment acidly on 31 January 1869 that 'it is to be supposed that before too long the government will be led to pursue people who simply dare to maintain that Maximilian was shot'. The young writer Emile Zola added in comments published in the same paper a few days later,

> I know exactly what kind of lithograph these gentlemen would be delighted to authorize, and if M. Manet wants to have a real success in their eyes I advise him to depict Maximilian alive and well, with his happy, smiling wife at his side. Moreover, the artist would have to make it clear that Mexico has never suffered a bloodbath and that it is living and will continue to live under the blessed rule of Napoleon's III protégé. Historic truth, thus interpreted, will bring tears of joy to the censors' eyes.[64]

The overthrow of Napoleon III on 4 September 1870, as a result of disastrous defeats during the Franco-Prussian War, was followed by the installation of a government of national defence which quickly abolished the Empire's restrictions on freedom of the press and of caricature. Although the flood of caricatures which immediately engulfed Paris at first concentrated their anger on the deposed regime, artists soon began to attack the new government (based at Versailles in early 1871) for its lacklustre prosecution of the war with Prussia. In March 1871, the Versailles regime suppressed one of the leading caricature journals, *La Caricature politique*, edited by Pilotell (Georges Labadie), who earlier had been jailed for his artistic opposition to Napoleon III. This action and the general press crackdown which accompanied it were one factor which sparked a revolt in Paris on 18 March against the Versailles government. The revolt led to the brief establishment of the Paris Commune, which was brutally suppressed in a two-month civil war, during which the victorious Versailles regime restored prior censorship of caricature (on 15 April 1871) and about 25,000 Parisians were slaughtered, mostly in cold blood.[65]

After its restoration in 1871 caricature censorship remained in effect until 1881, when it was permanently abolished in France (outside war-time). The 1870s witnessed an intensified ten-year reprise of the 1867–70 struggle over 'freedom of the crayon', in which the extraordinary harshness and arbitrariness – characterised by one historian as 'extreme incoherence'[66] – with which the censorship operated reflected the confused and uncertain nature of French politics during the period. The National Assembly elected during the final stages of the Franco-Prussian War in February 1871 was dominated by monarchists, but they were split into three parties (the Bourbonists, the Orleanists and the Bonapartists), supporting three different dynasties. Although, for lack of a monarch, France had been a *de facto* republic since September 1870, a republican form of government was officially established only in January 1875, and the republicans' control over France was only consolidated as a result of their election victories in 1876 and 1879 and the resignation in 1879 of the reactionary monarchist President, Marshal MacMahon. Thus, under a formally 'republican' regime, the leading targets among the many victims of the censorship during the 1871–9 period were republican caricature journals, which often protested long and loud in print (which remained free from censorship) when their art was forbidden. Frequently journals simply described in writing what their banned drawings would have shown.

As in the 1867–70 war over caricatures, the dominant artist between 1871 and 1879 and the prime target of the censors was André Gill. Gill's caricatures for *L'Eclipse* between 1871 and 1876 and subsequently for his own journal *La Lune rousse* (1876–9) were banned by the censors on scores of occasions, sometimes on grounds that were unfathomable at the time and remain so today. Curiously, the censorship generally tolerated caricatures of itself, and some of the finest work by Gill and others during the 1870s consisted of artistic attacks on the censors.

For republican caricaturists, perhaps the bitterest development was the continuation of prior censorship even after the consolidation of republican control of France in early 1879. Although criticism of fallen dynasties was now allowed, criticism of the existing government and comments on contentious issues such as the Church–state relationship still frequently remained under ban, leading to outraged cries accusing republican ministers of having abandoned their beliefs once in power. Thus, on 30 March 1879, *Le Grelot* reported that five sketches for that one issue had been rejected, and that the only explanation for the continuation of the censorship had to be that Bonapartists had cleverly disguised themselves as republican ministers, taking their names, habits, and 'finally introducing themselves into their skins'. The republican censorship of 1879–81 struck out at the right as well as the left, showing itself no more tolerant of monarchist caricature than the monarchist censorship had been of republican designs. Thus, the most important anti-republican caricature journal, *Le Triboulet* (1878–93), was prosecuted by the government thirty-seven times (generally for publishing unauthorised designs) and fined a total of 200,000 francs between 1878 and 1881.[67]

Caricature censorship in Europe, 1881–1914

With the permanent abolition of caricature censorship in France in 1881, every major European country except for Russia had abandoned such controls. Elsewhere in Europe, as the fears engendered by 1848 faded away and representatives of the emerging middle and professional classes (traditionally committed to freedom of the press) gained increasing power, restrictions on the press in general and on political caricature in particular had begun to ease after about 1860. Thus prior censorship was ended throughout the newly united state of Italy and the Hapsburg Empire by 1870, and the 1874 press law of united Germany specifically barred prior censorship of 'any printed material or pictorial representations that have been reproduced mechanically or chemically for the purpose of public distribution'.[68] As a result, satirical caricature journals, some of them bitterly hostile to the ruling elements, gradually began to develop. As art historian Theda Shapiro notes, one reason why so many of these journals were published by radicals and anarchists was that they favoured the visual approach of caricature 'as a means of reaching a large public that newspapers scarcely touched – the still semiliterate mass of workmen, peasants and women'.[69]

Among the major new journals were, in Italy, *Pappagallo* (founded in Bologna in 1873), *L'Asino e il Popolo* (Rome, 1892) and *Guerin Meschino* (Milan, 1882). The leading Viennese journals included *Figaro* (1857), *Der Floh* (1868) and *Kikeriki* (1862). In Germany, a ban on depicting the monarch and the constant threat of post-publication prosecutions (including a twenty-day jail term for the editors of *Kladderadatsch* in 1877) somewhat tempered the verve of a new wave of caricature journals that had begun to emerge in the 1860s, but some of them, particularly *Frankfurter Latern* (1860), *Berliner Wespen* (1868), *Ulk* (1872), *Lustige Blätter* (1885) and *Der Wahre Jacob* (1883) were quite willing to forcefully criticise the real ruler of Germany, Chancellor Otto von Bismarck (prime minister, 1862–90). After German political controls eased somewhat with the expiration of the Anti-Socialist Laws of 1878–90, another group of strongly anti-regime caricature journals emerged in the 1890s, including *Simplicissimus*, *Pan* and *Jugend*. In Spain, the short-lived republic of 1868–74 witnessed an upsurge of caricature journals, of which the most celebrated was *Gil Blas, periodico satirico*. In fact, except in Russia, politically oriented caricature journals sprang up virtually everywhere in Europe after 1860: to give some examples from the smaller states, *Borrzem Janko* was founded in Budapest in 1868, the Danish journal *Kolds-Hans* was established in 1899, and the Greek journal *Romeos* commenced publication in 1883. The greatest explosion of caricature journals in late nineteenth-century Europe emerged with the abolition of censorship in France in 1881. At least forty-five new caricature journals were established there between 1881 and 1885, and another ninety-four were founded between 1900 and 1914 (many of which, such as the self-descriptive journal *Anti-Concierge*, were ephemeral and extremely narrow in their orientation).[70]

Although, in the closing years of the nineteenth century, caricature became incomparably more free in France and elsewhere than it had been, the authorities in many countries still retained some tools to curb what they viewed as excesses. Since most press laws provided plenty of leeway for post-publication prosecution, 'the sharpness of tone in the humour' remained 'proportionate to the amount of freedom the government allowed', as magazine historian Patricia Kery notes.[71] In Germany, the extraordinarily broad *lèse majesté* laws remained in force, and were used to impose over 1000 years in prison sentences on journalists and others between 1888 and 1898. Among the victims were the editor of *Kladderadatsch*, who was sentenced to two months in prison for a cartoon of 1897 ridiculing a comment made by Kaiser Wilhelm II; and three members of the staff of *Simplicissimus*, including the caricaturist Thomas Theodore Heine, who in 1898 were jailed for a cartoon (Plate 10) and poem ridiculing the Kaiser's trip to the Middle East (the French caricature journal *Le Rire* was banned from Germany for an issue of 1898 mocking the same trip, especially for a caricature depicting the Kaiser and the Turkish Sultan using Armenians for target practice). In France, laws forbidding pornography and incitement to anarchy and anti-militarism were occasionally used after 1881 in response to political caricature. Thus, in one notorious case, the artist Louis Legrand was jailed for obscenity for two months for a drawing entitled 'Prostitution' – published in *Le Courrier français* (1884–1913) on 24 June 1888 – even though the picture was clearly a commentary on the social evils of prostitution. Punitive action of more or less frequency continued to be taken against caricaturists in many other countries. Caricature remained subject to prior censorship in Portugal as late as 1906. The Lisbon journal *A Parodia* was a frequent victim of censorship, and often featured angry attacks on restrictions on press freedom (see Plate 12). In Austria, issues of *Figaro* were periodically confiscated, and staff members of the democratically oriented caricature journal *Kikeriki* were jailed on several occasions even after the easing of censorship restrictions in 1859, although by 1905 Austrian caricaturists were fairly safe from prosecution so long as they did not target Emperor Franz Joseph. In Italy too, so long as the King was not ridiculed, caricaturists enjoyed almost total freedom from the secular authorities by 1900, but the bitterly anti-clerical Roman journal *L'Asino* was banned from Vatican City (see Plate 13).[72]

A series of anti-military political cartoons published in the popular Barcelona weekly *Cu-Cut!* provoked perhaps the most spectacular act of political repression of caricature between 1881 and 1914.[73] *Cu-Cut!*, a beautifully produced and illustrated journal, was one of a number of Spanish caricature journals which were established after 1880, when the severe press controls that had been introduced in 1874, following the collapse of the Spanish republic and subsequent restoration of the monarchy, were eased. It specialised in ridiculing the notoriously inept Spanish military. Thus, in one cartoon of 1905, the Spanish Foreign Minister was depicted telling the German Kaiser of Spain's wish to 'be at peace with all nations', with the Kaiser answering, 'That's understandable, no one likes to receive a whipping' (Plate 13). Although the Spanish government prosecuted *Cu-Cut!* on several occasions, the military in Barcelona felt that the civilian government was being too lenient. On 25 November 1905, troops of the Barcelona garrison (acting without the authorisation of the Spanish government) ransacked the editorial and printing offices of *Cu-Cut!* In the subsequent uproar, demands by the Spanish military for curbs on future verbal and pictorial attacks against them and implicit threats of a *coup d'état* led to the suspension of constitutional guarantees in Barcelona, the resignation of the Prime Minister and ultimately the passage of the 1906 Law of Jurisdictions, which greatly embittered many Spaniards by giving military courts authority to try civilians accused of defaming the armed forces.

In both France and Germany, although prior censorship of carica-ture was abolished by 1881, the authorities still reserved the right to ban the sale of journals they deemed offensive from the public streets and from state-owned railway stations. Although these weapons did not prevent the publication, sale in private stores or mailing to subscribers of periodicals, they could none the less deal a serious blow to caricature journals, which were heavily dependent on kiosk sales for their revenues. Moreover, as the regulations in question were purely administrative and did not create a criminal offence, they could not be challenged in court. The Munich police understood all this when in 1909 they successfully recommended a ban on railway-station sales of *Simplicissimus* in Bavaria, similar to that already instituted in Prussia. They noted that 'Sales in stations are consider-able and a ban will therefore have a very perceptible effect on the publishers.'[74]

Simplicissimus was clearly the leading target of German repression of caricature during the two decades before the First World War broke out (for a short period after its foundation in 1896, it was also forbidden in Austria).[75] Although 'Der Simpl's' approach was more middle-class than radical, the magazine pointedly ridiculed the foibles of the Kaiser, the military and the wealthy in an essentially authoritarian political setting. Aside from the ban on railway-station sales in Prussia and Bavaria, and the jail sentences handed out to three staff members in 1898, street sales of the journal were banned, and it suffered confiscation and prosecution on numerous occasions and on diverse grounds (although after 1898 there was only one case in which a staff member was imprisoned). The clippings file of the Hamburg political police, containing material gathered from all over Germany, includes accounts of twenty-seven confiscations in the period 1903–7 alone (see Plates 14 and 15). Administrative measures such as bans on street and station sales were especially attractive to the German authorities, because press prosecutions frequently led only to jury acquittals and free publicity that fostered increased circulations for the journals involved. Thus, after the 1898 prosecution of *Simplicissimus*, one prominent staff member wrote that the affair 'had the result that our circulation rose within four or five weeks from 15,000 to, I think, 85,000'. Similarly, a Munich prosecutor advised in 1903 against prosecutions 'which could only serve as an advertisement' for *Simplicissimus*; he apparently had in mind a 'successful' prosecution which had yielded a small fine against Heine and another staff member as well as the court-ordered destruction of all confiscated copies – which totalled only 1341 out of a press run of 80,000! Even administrative sanctions sometimes backfired, since when street sales of *Simplicissimus* were banned, merchants not only typically refused to comply with police requests voluntarily to withdraw their copies from sale, but even marked them with a red band reading 'Kolportsgeverbot' ('forbidden from street sales') to increase public interest.[76]

'Der Simpl' may have staved off more severe persecution by not directly caricaturing Kaiser Wilhelm II for many years. This was consistent with the general rule of German satirical journals not to publish overt caricatures of German royalty, since, as William Coupe has noted, 'they would have immediately been prosecuted had they attempted to do so'. Instead, *Simplicissimus* resorted to 'pear-like' evasions, depicting Wilhelm in the guise of a fairy-tale prince whose true identity was revealed only by his tell-tale turned-up moustache, 'which, as a flamboyant effect laboriously created, became the true symbol of his basic weakness'. After 1905, pressure on German caricature journals eased somewhat, with the result that Wilhelm 'became an unfailing source of materials for cartoonists, who chronicled his gaffes and aberrations with varying mixtures of contempt, good humour and irritation'.[77] This easing was attributed by the editor of *Simplicissimus* to Wilhelm's decision to allow free circulation in Germany of a collection of cartoons of him published in 1905 by a well-known French student of caricature, John Grand-Carteret.

Grand-Carteret had prefaced his book with an open letter appealing for the 'free circulation of caricature' and calling on Wilhelm to stop his practice of banning foreign and domestic caricatures which lampooned him (a similar appeal to Tsar Nicholas II in the preface to a collection of drawings of the Russian ruler received no apparent response). Grand-Carteret told the Kaiser that repression only led Germans to seek out and buy banned caricatures, which 'have for them the eternal attraction of forbidden fruit', and that attempts to keep such drawings out of Germany were hopeless 'in an epoch in which the automobile, sovereign by the powers of its speed, turns borders into only an illusory separation'. What is more,

> To fear and forbid the caricature of your person and your acts will diminish you in the eyes of Europe. If you do this you will no longer be the Kaiser, the very modern Emperor of Peace. Majesty! Place your veto of good sense and reason to your political censorship. Majesty! Make the liberating gesture which the world awaits from you. Let the images pass![78]

Although harassment of caricature eased somewhat in Germany after 1905, the authorities continued sporadically to intervene against all forms of art of which they disapproved, thereby furnishing subjects for new cartoon attacks. Thus, in one cartoon lampooning the Kaiser's cultural pretensions and notorious attempts to dictate artistic standards for German society. 'Der Simpl' portrayed a bewigged, powdered prince in a rococo throne room telling himself, 'Every day the same worry – should I paint, write, or solve the social question?' Another cartoon showed Wilhelm demanding of an artist why it took German painters so long to learn to paint and receiving the reply 'The reason, your majesty, is that in art Genius is not so hereditary as it is on the throne.' These cartoons reflected the growing anger among German artists and intellectuals over a series of incidents which established for Wilhelm the reputation of a cultural autocrat. Even one of Wilhelm's prime minister, Prince Bernhard von Bülow, lamented in his memoirs in 1930, 'I think few things damaged Wilhelm more in the eyes of the cultured section of the German people than his one-sided, blind and nearly always intolerant attitudes in matters of art.' Thus, in 1898 the Kaiser exercised his royal prerogative to overrule the recommendation of an expert jury at the Berlin Art Exhibition that a gold medal should be awarded to Käthe Kollwitz for her extraordinary cycle of lithographs and etchings 'The Weavers' depicting the suffering of German workers during the Silesian revolt of the 1840s. In 1907 he vetoed a planned sixtieth birthday retrospective at the Berlin Art Academy of the work of the realist painter Max Liebermann, since such artists were 'poisoning the soul of the German nation'. In 1912 Kollwitz's poster 'For Greater Berlin', denouncing overcrowded housing and the lack of playgrounds for poor children, was forbidden on the grounds that it 'incited class hatred' and violated the general Prussian ban on political posters, which was invoked arbitrarily and inconsistently. 'Der Simpl' caricaturist Heine also ran into censorship trouble with a poster which mocked the Kaiser's fulminations about 'gutter art' by portraying a poor woman gathering fresh flowers from a gutter while a wealthy woman's flowers wilted in her hands.[79]

In France in the period preceding the First World War, the primary target of official attacks on caricature journals was *L'Assiette au beurre* (1901–12), a small weekly of unexcelled graphic quality typically consisting of twelve to sixteen pages of cartoons by a single artist on one theme.[80] Although *L'Assiette* had no coherent political programme, it brutally and incisively lampooned the pillars of the French establishment and highlighted the ignored social grievances of the poor. On about five occasions between 1901 and 1905 the authorities banned street sales of *L'Assiette*, in each case due to apparent fear of damage to French diplomatic relations (Plate 15). In one notorious incident, street sales of the issue dated 28 September 1901, which was critical of British policy in the Boer War, was allowed only after modification of a cartoon entitled 'Impudent Albion', which showed Britain in the form of a woman baring her bottom to the world and revealing the features of King Edward VII on her buttocks. This issue prompted a personal complaint from Edward to the French ambassador, who privately termed the design 'scandalous' but conceded that it was 'very well done' and bore an 'exact resemblance' to the King. The magazine was forced to cover up Edward's features in subsequent printings, but the original ban apparently only stimulated sales, which reached an unprecedented 250,000.

Although no such incidents were followed by judicial prosecutions – perhaps because *L'Assiette* was so expensive that its audience was largely middle class – and therefore no one on the staff was ever jailed for his contributions to the magazine, two of its leading contributors were jailed for cartoons published elsewhere. Thus, Aristide Delannoy, who drew eight complete issues for *L'Assiette*, was sentenced to a year in jail (as was his editor) for a drawing published in 1908 in the journal *Les Hommes du jour*, which portrayed a French general involved in the subjugation of Morocco as a bloody-handed butcher carving up corpses. *L'Assiette*'s most prolific contributor, Jules Grandjouan, who contributed almost 800 drawings and thirty-five complete issues, was prosecuted half-a-dozen times between 1907 and 1911 for anti-militarist drawings published in other outlets. He fled France in 1911 to avoid serving an eighteen-month sentence, but was able to return in 1912 following a presidential pardon.[81]

The struggle for 'freedom of caricature' in Russia after 1850

Even in Russia, under the absolutism of the tsars, censorship control eased considerably after the death of Nicholas I in 1855 and the accession to power of Alexander II. This easing led, between 1859 and 1863, to the foundation of a number of satirical journals which used caricature, such as *Spark* and *Alarm Clock*; but, since prior censorship of both the printed word and the image continued, these journals had to resort to 'Aesopian language' and fables to obtain approval and had to substitute social satire for criticism of political figures. Even with such devices, the censorship banned many cartoons, which none the less frequently acquired enormous popularity through clandestine circulation. Thus, one cartoon which was forbidden in 1862 depicted a landowner leading a peasant on a rope and asking, 'Do you feel freer now?' after letting the rope out a bit. An illustration for a children's book was banned in the 1860s because it depicted the death of the medieval tsar Ivan IV.[82]

Fear of the picture was made especially clear in the major Russian censorship reform of 1865, which eliminated prior censorship for most books and for unillustrated periodicals published in Moscow and St Petersburg, but not for 'periodicals and other publications of prints, drawings and other pictorial representations with or without texts'. These had to be submitted for censorship clearance at least three days before publication. As a result of the wave of repression which followed an attempt on Alexander II's life in 1866, most of the satirical journals were closed or harassed into shutting down by 1875. After the assassination of Alexander in 1881 censorship of the image became even harsher. Thus, the press was forbidden to publish pictures of London police dispersing a socialist demonstration in 1886, and, when a portrait of the great writer and pacifist Leo Tolstoy

1. Caricature from the German journal *Simplicissimus* (1898) satirising the authorities' fear of caricature.

2. Caricature from the Portuguese journal *A Parodia* (1902) satirising the authorities' fear
caricature.

Marchand d'oublis.

Marchand d'oublis.

3. Caricature from the French journal *L'Eclipse* published in censored form in 1873, accompanied by the image

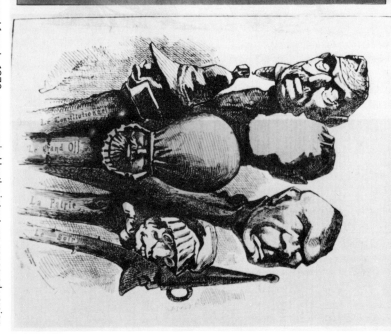

4. Caricature from the French journal *L'Eclipse* published in censored form in 1870, accompanied by the intact pre-censored version.

Caricature from the French journal *Le Sifflet* (1875) illustrating the caricaturists' hatred for censorship.

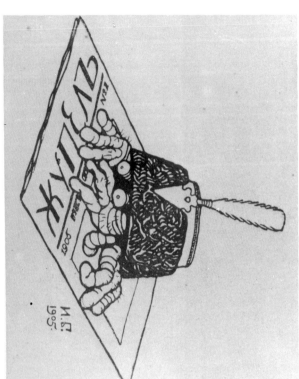

6. Caricatures from Russian journals of 1905, attacking censorship after its collapse amidst the Russian revolution of that year.

7. Caricatures from the Austrian journal *Der Floh* (1905) and the German journal *Ulk* (1906) ridiculing Russian Tsar Nicholas II and his [...] [...] policies.

8. Caricatures from the French journal *L'Éclipse* (1871) and the Portuguese journal *A Parodia* (1906) attacking censorship of caricature.

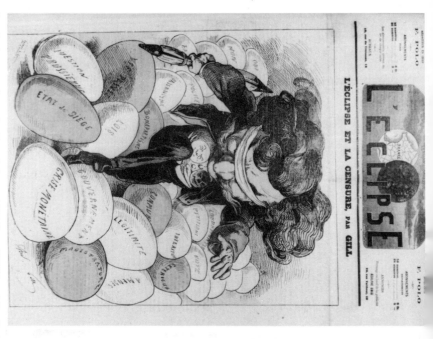

2ᵐᵉ ANNÉE.— N° 53   UN NUMÉRO : 15 CENTIMES   26 JUIN 1875.

LE DON QUICHOTTE

Rédacteur en Chef . Ch. GILBERT-MARTIN

ABONNEMENTS

UN AN.............. 10 fr.
SIX MOIS.......... 5 »

Administrateur :
A. DUMON

BUREAUX : 31, rue Delurbe.
BORDEAUX

ANNONCES

La ligne................. 1 fr.
Réclame 4 50
Faits divers.......... 6 »

BUREAUX : 31, rue Delurbe.
A BORDEAUX

VENTE EN GROS

GRABY, r. des Piliers-de-Tutelle
BORDEAUX
COSTE, rue du Croissant, 20, PARIS

UNE ÉMULE DE DON QUICHOTTE, par GILBERT-MARTIN

Caricature from the French journal *Le Don Quichotte* (1875) attacking censorship of caricature.

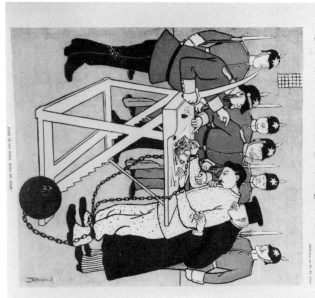

10. Caricatures from the German journal *Simplicissimus* (1897, 1898) concerning repression of the press in Germany.

11. Caricatures from the German journals *Fliegende Blätter* (1848) and *Leuchtkugeln* (1851) concerning the abolition and the re-introduction of censorship in Germany as a result of the failed revolution of 1848.

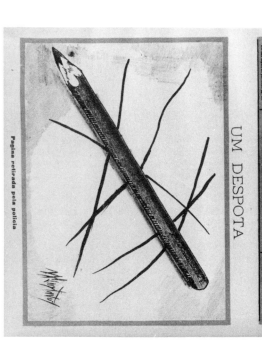

UM DESPOTA

Paginas retirada pela policia

12. Caricatures from the Portuguese journal *A Parodia* (1902, 1906) protesting against censorship of caricature.

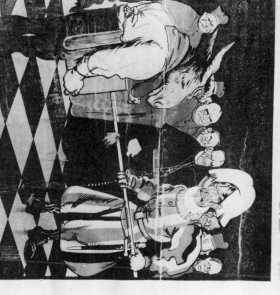

13. Caricatures from the Italian journal *L'Asino* concerning its exclusion from sale in the Vatican City (1906) attacking the Spanish ...

14. Caricatures published in the German journal *Simplicissimus* (1903, 1904) which led to prosecution and/or confiscation.

15. Caricatures published in the German journal *Simplicissimus* (1901) and the French journal *L'Assiette au Beurre* (1905), governmental reprisals intended to avoid itself.

16. Caricatures published in Russian journals in 1905 which led to prosecution and/or confiscation.

ВЫСОЧАЙШІЙ МАНИФЕСТЪ.

Божіею милостію,

МЫ, НИКОЛАЙ ВТОРЫЙ,

ИМПЕРАТОРЪ И САМОДЕРЖЕЦЪ ВСЕРОССІЙСКІЙ,

ЦАРЬ ПОЛЬСКІЙ, ВЕЛИКІЙ КНЯЗЬ ФИНЛЯНДСКІЙ,

и прочая, и прочая, и прочая.

"...НИКОЛАЙ."

Продажа нумеровъ производится въ дни выхода. Адресоваться Комиссія 14. "Пулеметъ." Фонтанка, 86.

Н. Г. Шебуевъ принимаетъ ежедневно отъ 12 до 1 часу дня. Коненскій, 14.

Типографія С.-Петербург. Тов-ва Печатн. и Издат. дѣла "Трудъ". Фонтанка 86.

become the focus of demonstrations after his excommunication by the state-controlled Russian Orthodox Church in 1901, it was ordered to be withdrawn from exhibition in St Petersburg. In 1902 the authorities directed newspapers to refrain 'for ever' from printing any portraits of Tolstoy. Harassment of the arts in Russia became so pervasive that in 1904 the Union of Russian Artists adopted a resolution which declared,

> Only free art is full of life, creative work alone brings pleasure, and if our country so rich in talent has not yet managed to leave its mark in the field of art, and to release the great artistic forces concealed within it, if our art has no real links with the Russian people, then we are firmly convinced that the main reason for this is the suffocating guardianship which not only kills arts but also suppresses all other creative activities in Russian society.[83]

In a sequence of events like that initiated by the 1848 revolutions in other European countries, the censorship dam holding back Russian caricature broke under the force of the 1905 revolution.[84] Whereas in the entire course of the nineteenth century just eighty-nine caricature journals had been published in Russia (most of them ephemeral and totally non-political), in 1905–6 at least 400 satirical periodicals blossomed, many of them displaying the most bitter hostility to the autocratic reign of Nicholas II. Most of these journals emerged after all remaining censorship had been officially abolished (in October 1905), but a few of them opened shortly after the outbreak of the revolt (in January), which was caused by the slaughter of hundreds of peaceful demonstrators in St Petersburg. In the early days of the revolution, while pictorial censorship remained in force, the new journals were forced to accept ludicrous censorship decisions and resort to ingenious evasions. Thus one cartoon of a burning candle was excised from *Zritel* (*Observer*) on the ground that it 'symbolized the extinction of the autocracy'. Another cartoon, struck from *Strekoza* (*Dragonfly*), depicted a man of bourgeois status playing solitaire, and was captioned 'For the life of me, I can't understand all this, but it's certainly very interesting.' The censor explained that the drawing could not be allowed because it was a 'tendentious illustration of the indeterminateness of the present internal situation'.[85]

To get around such restrictions the journals resorted to such techniques as separating captions from drawings after censorship approval and breaking up sequential drawings and submitting them in random order: a picture of a peasant shaking his fist, approved by the censors with the caption 'Horse-stealer Captured', would be published without the caption as an incitement to peasant revolt, and separately submitted drawings of a boy, a cat (*kot* in Russian) and a legislative (Duma) meeting, when published together, would spell out 'Boycott the State Duma.' (A similar technique was used to evade a censorship ban on a wooden toy which depicted the Tsar with a bottle in his hand sitting on a throne supported by three fat policemen: vendors simply sold the toy in separate parts, thus allowing their customers to gain the added amusement of putting it together themselves.) Since Nicholas II could not be directly depicted, 'pear-like' evasions were used: Nicholas had once been accidentally hit on the head by a Japanese policeman, so any lad portrayed with a bump on his head was universally interpreted as the Tsar, regardless of other features of his anatomy, as was the character of 'the boy with the stick' (*malchik-palchik*). Because of such devices *Zritel* was closed 'for ever' and its editor jailed in July 1905, but the magazine was resurrected following the massive strikes of October 1905, which brought about a general refusal by Russian printers to co-operate any further with the censorship. This was followed by the official end of all prior censorship on 30 October.

The end of prior censorship was immediately followed by a massive outpouring of satirical journals, with 380 officially registered with the government in November alone, and many more not even bothering to do so. While most of these journals were crude leaflets of a few pages which only lasted an issue or two (or were quickly suppressed), a significant number of them were sophisticated journals of high artistic quality. Aside from the hundreds of Russian-language satirical journals, fifty satirical journals in Yiddish and twenty in Ukrainian sprang up. One observer wrote about the explosion of satirical journals,

> They poured forth like stars on an August night. Some witty and vitriolic, some dull and vulgar, they were sold on street corners, seized by police from the hands of readers, torn up at the presses – and yet they only grew in number, deriving their energy and rage from the strikes that brought them forth.[86]

With the ending of prior censorship, a full-scale war developed between the satirical journals, which gave vent to the long-suppressed anger of the people, and the regime, whose venom far exceeded that of the French authorities in the similar struggle of 1830–5. Before it succeeded in suppressing the revolt, the regime killed over 15,000 people, wounded another 20,000 and arrested, jailed and exiled 20,000 more; it thus had no qualms about the measures it took to control a hostile press. The first issue of the journal *Payats* (*Clown*), appearing in December 1905, declared, 'Now that we have the right to laugh we're going to laugh boldly, loudly and mercilessly. Let everyone who possesses this fine sharp weapon come to us and laugh with us.' But *Clown*'s laughter was suppressed by the authorities after three issues, and the same fate beset innumerable other journals. Police smashed presses, seized copies from distribution wagons and even attacked people reading and selling journals on the streets. The journal *Pulemet* (*Machine-Gun*) was closed down after its first issue (13 November), in which one drawing showed a bloody handprint covering a decree promising greater freedoms; the printers were arrested, and the journal's editor, Nikolai Shebuev, was sentenced to a year in jail and banned from publishing for five years. The first issue of *Zhupel* (*Bugbear*), which included a stylised double-headed eagle which when turned upside-down provided a view of the Tsar's buttocks, was confiscated by the police, and the same treatment was accorded the next two issues, the second of which included a drawing of a donkey surrounded by the Tsar's heraldic emblems (Plate 16). As a result of this issue, *Zhupel* was closed and its editor, Zionvii Gzhevin, and the artist responsible for the donkey caricature, Isaac Bilibin, were arrested. Other casualties included *Zhupel*'s successor, *Adskaia Pochta* (*Mail from Hell*), suppressed after four issues; *Strely* (*Arrows*), closed after six issues in January 1906 (and its staff jailed); *Signal* and its successor *Signals*; *Stormwood* and its successors *Storm* and *Stormwind*; *Sting*, *Bombs*, *Woodpecker*, *Octopus* and *Woodgoblin*. The journal *Vampire*, which was closed after nine issues, summarised the reality of Russian civil liberties in early 1906 by noting, 'The press can publish what it wants and the police can ban what they want. Freedom of Association: Anyone is allowed to join a union, apart from two categories of people, those in government service and those not in government service.'[87]

In April 1906, prior censorship of pictures was effectively reimposed through a new press regulation which required all illustrated periodicals to be submitted to the authorities at least one day before distribution. This decree, in combination with the general atmosphere of raging government terror, effectively put an end to the sharp-

toothed satirical journals of the previous months. Although a few
moderate journals were able to start up after 1906, few sophisticated
works of political satire could appear. The leading journal, *Satirikon*
(St Petersburg, 1908–13), modelled on *Simplicissimus* and dedicated
to a struggle against 'all illegality, falsehood and banality', had to
abide censorship limits which were strict if ambiguous, as the journal
Bagpipe discovered when censors refused to permit any of its four
issues to appear. Indeed, one observer noted that between 1908 and
1914 the censorship regulations were so complicated and confusing
that

> On the one hand, it would seem that everything is permitted, and
> yet on the other, as if everything were forbidden. . . . What we
> are supposed to see as black today, we have to regard as white
> tomorrow. And these commands aren't posted up anywhere. They
> just spring up like mushrooms after the rain.[88]

For all practical purposes, the flowering of Russian caricature in
1905–6 had been buried along with the revolution itself.

4 Political Censorship of the Theatre

Censorship of the stage, like censorship of the printed word, was a widespread and well-established European tradition by 1815. However, while prior censorship of the press was eliminated throughout Europe by 1914, European countries almost universally retained prior censorship of the stage until (and sometimes well after) the First World War. Thus, in 1695 Britain became the first major European country to abolish censorship of the press, yet forty years later, in 1737, parliament systematised a formerly haphazard theatre censorship, and controls were not finally abolished until 1968. Most other European countries did not eliminate press censorship until about the middle of the nineteenth century, while maintaining theatre censorship throughout the century. Furthermore, they typically exercised much harsher controls over the stage than had been exercised over the printed word. Thus, the 1822 drama-censorship rules of the Italian state of Tuscany declared,

> The general rules for the censorship of [printed] works in which are disseminated religious principles or principles that are politically subversive, or of works based on a malicious plan threatening to weaken or destroy veneration for Religion or for the Throne and which awaken in people's minds emotions hostile to either of these, will be applied more strictly to theatrical performances.[1]

Such harsher restrictions on the theatre were by no means unique to nineteenth-century Europe. As theatre historian John Allen has noted, 'It is an interesting comment on the potential effectiveness of the stage that in many times and places the drama has been subject to far greater censorship than any other form of literature or art', reflecting bureaucratic fears that 'the theatre, with its power of affecting an audience with possibly subversive emotions and ideas, is more to be feared'.[2] These fears were especially evident in nineteenth-century Europe, because, in an age before the development of radio, television and the cinema, and in which, for much of the period in most countries, political assembly and association were forbidden or strictly controlled, the theatre provided not only the most important form of mass entertainment but also the only arena aside from the church in which regular mass gatherings were possible. In fact, since before about 1870 most Europeans were illiterate and compulsory education was in its formative stages, the theatre was widely regarded as the single most significant source of information, at least in urban areas, for a large percentage of the population. Thus, instructions given in 1852 to French theatre inspectors charged them to subject to special scrutiny those theatres in which 'the most coarse classes of people assemble', since such places 'have become the sole school in which the inferior class of society go to take lessons'.[3] Given the enormous perceived importance of the theatre, even many dissidents supported strict government supervision of the stage. Thus, French socialist politician Louis Blanc wrote in the 1840s that

> To permit a private person to act at the direction of his own caprice upon the assembled audience by the seduction of the set, the interest of the drama, the beauty of the women, the talent of the artists, the enchantment of the decoration and the lighting, that is to deliver the souls of the people as fodder to the first corrupter who comes along; that is to abandon to him the right to poison the sources of human intelligence. In such a country, in which the government would not be worthy of the name, the state could not renounce the moral direction of society by the theatre without abdicating.[4]

The persistence and rigour of controls on the theatre in nineteenth-century Europe reflected fears that over the long term it could 'poison the sources of human intelligence', as suggested by Blanc, and that in the short term it might spark off outbreaks of violence and criminality. Both of these perceived dangers, which were especially felt by conservatives throughout Europe, were summed up by the ruling of a Berlin court in the late nineteenth century which upheld the power of the police to ban a play for political reasons:

> The police are empowered to forbid the performance of a play if the effect of the performance is considered to be likely to create a danger to public peace, security and order. This does not merely apply to disturbances of order on the part of the spectators through rowdyism or other excesses, but applies also to the consideration that the audience may be inwardly misled to views that endanger

public well-being and order. This includes for instance the distur-
bance caused by the thought that the existing political order does
not grant the individual citizen his rights. In particular, the
undermining of confidence in the administration of law is a reason
to ban a dramatic work.[5]

The fear of outbreaks of 'rowdyism or other excesses' was certainly
not without foundation, since theatre audiences before the twentieth
century were considerably less docile than they are today. Thus, the
Spanish writer Cervantes (1547–1616) boasted, 'I have written 20 or
30 plays, and they were all received without cucumbers or anything
else that can be thrown.' In the nineteenth century, the disturbances
that greeted the opening nights in Paris of Victor Hugo's *Hernani* in
1830 and Alfred Jarry's *Ubu roi* in 1896 are just two of the most
well-known instances when near- or actual riots broke out in response
to plays. French conservatives frequently claimed that lax theatre
censorship, in allowing opposition dramas to be staged, helped create
the climate of dissent which led to the revolutions of 1848 and 1870.
In the 1840s, several plays by opposition writers such as Félix Pyat
and Eugène Sue provoked audience demonstrations against the
theatre censorship and the regime or incited anti-government feelings;
the conservative French drama censor Victor Hallys-Dabot later
wrote that for the audiences they 'amounted to a sort of dress
rehearsal' for the 1848 revolution. European officials particularly
remembered a performance of the opera *La Muette de Portici* in
Brussels in 1830, which was generally credited with sparking off the
Belgian revolution of that year against Dutch rule. This incident,
which is discussed in detail in Chapter 5, was still regularly referred
to in France by proponents of theatre censorship seventy-five years
later. Some conservatives even blamed the theatre for immediately
converting its audience into criminals. Thus, one French prison
director declared, 'When they put on a bad new drama, a number of
young new criminals soon arrive at my prison.'[6]

THE CONSERVATIVES' FEARS OF THE THEATRE

There were three basic reasons why conservatives feared the theatre
and argued for censorship of its productions. First, given the high
rate of illiteracy in nineteenth-century Europe, the theatre, like
caricature, was more accessible to a lower-class audience than was

the printed word, and precisely this element of the population was viewed as both most threatening in general and most easily swayed by seditious drama. Reflecting these fears, in France politically sensitive plays were often only authorised for performance at theatres known to have a middle- or upper-class clientele. A Berlin court decision of 1893 which overturned a police ban on Gerhart Hauptmann's play about a workers' revolt, *The Weavers*, similarly reflected the concern felt over the spread of unorthodox ideas among the lower classes: it allowed the play on the grounds that the playhouse presenting it 'is visited primarily by members of those circles of society who do not tend towards acts of violence and other disturbances of public order'. *The Times*, too, in an editorial of 1907 supporting the ban on a drama which dealt with abortion, was particularly concerned about the theatre's influence on the unwashed masses. It declared that, although the play provided 'probably the most authentic presentation we have yet had on the English stage of great social and political questions', its 'subject matter' together with the 'sincere realism with which it is treated, makes it in our judgment wholly unfit for performance, under ordinary conditions, before a miscellaneous public of various ages, moods and standards of intelligence'.[7]

A second reason why conservatives especially feared the stage was that, while printed works, including caricatures, were typically 'consumed' by either solitary individuals or small groups of people, the theatre gathered together large crowds, thus posing an immediate potential threat to public order if seditious material were presented on stage. For example, the Governor-General of Moscow, explaining in 1805 why he was prohibiting a play based on a tolerated book, reasoned that 'the average person reads to himself alone, while a theatrical performance is attended by the masses', who might be swayed by occasional 'daring expressions and thought against the government and rulers'. Similarly, a supporter of stage censorship in Britain told a parliamentary inquiry in 1909 that 'the intellectual pitch of the crowd is lowered and its emotional pitch is raised', thus making theatre audiences likely to be 'irrational, excitable, lacking in self-control'.[8]

A third reason put forth to justify regulation of the stage was that the impact of the spoken word was far more inflammatory than the impact of the same material in print. As one theatre historian points out, the stage has always been especially feared by the authorities because of the 'acute proximity of the audience to the actors and the convention of direct address'. In successfully urging passage of a law

of 1835 which reimposed theatre censorship despite the provisions of
the 1830 French constitution, which guaranteed the right to publish
opinions and declared that censorship could 'never' be restored, a
French official argued that plays could not be considered in the same
category as mere expressions of opinion because of the greater impact
of the spoken word:

> Let an author be contented with printing his plays, he will be
> subjected to no preventive measures . . . but when opinions are
> converted into acts by the presentation of a play . . . it is no longer
> the manifestation of an opinion, it is an action, with which the
> constitution is not occupied and which it confides to the high
> direction of the established power.[9]

The combined dangers presented by a mass audience and the
impact of the spoken word were frequently cited as posing an
especially severe threat to public order and 'proper thinking'. Thus
in a letter of 1820 supporting theatre censorship, the Austrian actor
and writer F. J. W. Ziegler wrote,

> Woe betide the German audience, which has not yet recognized
> the spoken play as a potent political force throughout the whole
> of Germany; and in its creeping ways, that force, working slowly,
> but even more surely against religion, law and monarchy, has done
> more damage than all the political pamphlets could do, since the
> enthusiasm from the spoken word heard by thousands goes deeper
> than the coldness of political texts read by few.

A British supporter of theatre censorship argued similarly in telling
a British parliamentary committee in 1832 that the theatre needed to
be restrained because 'it is presented to the eyes and ears in the most
attractive manner' and 'instead of being offered to one reader, as in
the case of a book, is presented to hundreds or perhaps thousands
of persons at once'. In a book published in 1862, the French theatre
censor Hallys-Dabot made the same point at great length:

> An electric current runs through the playhouse, passing from actor
> to spectator, inflaming them both with a sudden ardour and giving
> them an unexpected audacity. The public is like a group of children.
> Each of them by themselves is sweet, innocuous, sometimes fearful;
> but bring them together, and you are faced with a group that is

bold and noisy, often wicked. The courage or rather the cowardice of anonymity is such a powerful force! . . . Social theories of the most false and daring nature excite an audience who, in the emotion of the drama, cannot discern the lies from the portrayals and speeches which are presented to them. When thousands of spectators, swept along by the intoxication of the drama, are subjected to a fatal influence, when the reverberations of the scandal will create a disturbed public, what safeguard could society find in the slow and methodical march of the laws [i.e. post-production prosecution of a play]?[10]

Although much theatre censorship in the nineteenth century was ostensibly directed against obscenity and blasphemy, censors were primarily concerned with material that was viewed as threatening the existing socio-political order (and even allegedly obscene and blasphemous material was often viewed as a threat largely because it challenged the official standards of the ruling elements). Thus, in France between 1835 and 1847, over 48 per cent of all material rejected by the censorship was forbidden for overtly political reasons, while only 19 per cent was banned on religious grounds and 32 per cent was deemed morally offensive. Odile Krakovitch, a leading historian of theatre censorship in nineteenth-century France, draws conclusions that apply equally well to other countries: although the French censorship varied from time to time in its exact application, 'whether the censors based their actions on political, religious or moral grounds, they always acted on one and the same principle: the defence of the social class in power' and 'respect for the established order'. The result was that, until late in the century, the European stage was characterised, as theatre histories by Vera Roberts and Robert Boyer have noted, by 'glitter and tinsel, with impossibly noble heroes, ideally sweet heroines, romantic love stories, happy endings and lavish productions' which 'had only the remotest connection with real life' and 'not a modicum of thought'; such drama supplied the theatre patron with a 'mindless, amnesiac experience' that invited him to 'check his intelligence, along with his coat, at the playhouse door'.[11]

Serious criticism of the established order was generally blue-pencilled (when playwrights and theatre managers were courageous enough to submit such dramas to the censors), and even historical plays that seemed to imply criticism of the *status quo* were frequently banned. Thus it was forbidden in Prussia to depict any member o the ruling Hohenzollern dynasty, living or dead, in a way which might 'undermine popular loyalty toward the royal family'. In Britain all stage representations of living persons were forbidden, as were historical dramas viewed as containing implicit criticisms of the monarchy or the reigning monarch. For example, virtually all presentations dealing with the deposed and executed king Charles I (ruled 1625–49) were banned from the British stage between 1825 and 1852 as 'insulting to monarchy'. Similarly, in France, Victor Hugo's 1829 play *Marion de Lorme* was banned because it unfavourably depicted Charles X's long-dead ancestor Louis XIII. Alfred de Musset's *Lorenzaccio*, a play about Renaissance Italy, was banned in France in 1861 on the grounds, as the censor put it, that 'The discussion of the right to assassinate a sovereign whose crimes and iniquities, even including the murder of the prince by his parents, cry out for vengeance, . . . is a dangerous spectacle to present to the public.' In Austria, Schiller's *William Tell*, about a medieval Swiss democratic-nationalist revolt against Hapsburg rule, could only be presented after, as a report to the theatre director noted, the play had been 'adapted' so that 'Austria and her former relations to Switzerland are not mentioned, and the democratic tendency, which one might ascribe to the original, disappears in favour of a merely domestic and generally human interest'. Even trivially critical comments about ruling elites were often barred. Thus, the French dramatist Emile Augier had to strike from his play *La Pierre de touche* (c. 1850) the comments of one character that 'society was ill ordered', while the British censor struck from a play of 1829 the remark that 'honest men at court don't take up much room'. The Austrian playwright Johann Nestroy had to delete from his play *Der Talisman* the comment that 'So many true good fellows walk around in torn jackets', since this was viewed as too sympathetic to proletarians, while German censors in late nineteenth-century Bavaria refused to allow even the most feeble jokes about the state legislature.[12]

Serious treatments of social problems, especially those depicting lower-class protests, generally ran into a wall of censorship disapproval. Among the plays banned near the end of the century (when political censorship had generally eased somewhat) were four dramas sympathetically depicting strikes: Hauptmann's *The Weavers*, forbidden in the 1890s in many German cities (until allowed by the German courts) for portraying the Silesian weavers' revolt of 1844; Emile Zola's *Germinal*, temporarily banned in France in 1885 for, as the official decree put it, the play's 'socialist tendency' and especially for depicting 'troops firing at striking miners in revolt'; Maxim Gorky's 1907 play *The Enemies*, forbidden in Russia for its portrayal of a clash between textile workers and their employers; and a British play entitled *Lords and Labourers*, forbidden in 1874 on the grounds that relations between employees and their supervisors was a subject 'not fit for representation on the stage at any time'.[13]

While an unregulated and politicised theatre was seen by European elites as posing a threat of subversion, a controlled and frothy stage was perceived as potentially shoring up the establishment by diverting the minds of the potentially discontented middle and lower classes to non-political matters. Thus, in 1775 a French official declared that

spectacles [i.e. the theatre and other public entertainments] in large cities are necessary in order to divert the man of affairs, in order to amuse upstanding people and well-to-do persons and finally to occupy the people who, when not attached to any spectacle, can be induced to factionalism. You know that the populace is stirred up, thrown into confusion, flighty; it is necessary then to stabilize it; well, one cannot do it except by spectacles. . . . For that reason, legislators have established different ones in every age, and I dare to suggest that it is sound politics to continue them and even to increase them. . . . The days of the Virgin and the solemn fêtes that the church dedicates to the grandeur of religion, in which our theatres are closed out of respect for it, there is committed in the capital more evil on these days of every kind, whether debaucheries, drunkenness, libertinage, thefts and even assassination.

In Austria in 1806, during the Napoleonic wars, when price increases were about to be announced and economic problems had led the authorities to consider closing the theatres, the police sent the Emperor a similar report urging that the theatres should remain open, because

In times like the present, when such manifold sufferings depress the character of the people, the police must co-operate more than ever before in distracting the citizens in every moral way. The most dangerous hours of the day are the evening hours. They cannot be filled less harmfully than in the theatre. . . . Prudence demands . . . since entertainment and distraction of the people have always been a state maxim . . . that an entertainment familiar for years should not be closed down just at such a moment.

The Austrian police continued to stress the same points during the 1820s, declaring that theatres should be provided for the lower classes 'because lacking moral entertainment they could easily be misled'. 'Respectable cheap entertainment' such as theatre-going, the police reported, leads people, 'especially the lower classes', away from the 'more expensive, often unsalubrious pubs, coffeehouses and gambling houses to better amusements, with some influence on education and morals, and keeps theatregoers under public observation and order for the duration of the performance'. Government support of the theatre, the police stressed, tended to 'restrain those activities endangering morality and public order' while bringing 'variety to daily conversation and supplying for the latter material that is as abundant as it is harmless'.[14]

If by the nineteenth century few conservatives advocated closing the theatres altogether (as many had before then), the authorities took great pains to ensure that the stage did in fact divert people's minds from politics. Thus, Napoleon reportedly declared with regard to public entertainments. 'Let the people amuse themselves, let them dance, so long as they keep their noses out of government affairs.' In more elegant phrases, French officials in the 1850s directed the censors to eliminate 'completely from the theatres all scenes imprinted with a revolutionary spirit as well as all forms of factionalism, based on the principle that the theatre must be a place of repose and of distraction and not an overt arena of political passions'. In Russia, Tsar Nicholas I overrode the opposition of his secret police in allowing the production of sensational 'blood and thunder' dramas, which he considered 'a sort of emotional lightning conductor which grounded the energy of social protest'.[15]

Certainly in Vienna and some of the German cities, where the theatre functioned as the major focus of social gatherings, the authorities were successful in their aim of using the stage to divert public attention away from politics. In Vienna, Eda Segarra notes, the theatre was 'the center of public life' under Metternich, 'a substitute it was aptly said for [the lack of a] parliament'. An Austrian observer, in a book published anonymously (to evade the censorship) in London in 1828, noted that, as the Metternich regime had taken 'every care' to debar the Viennese from 'serious or intellectual occupation, the Prater [an amusement park], the Glacis [a major city park], the coffee houses, the Leopoldstadt theatre are the only objects of their thoughts and desires'. The German author Karl Gutzkow, whose writings were banned in Germany and Austria, offered the following description of the Austrian stage in 1845: 'The lightly frivolous, the drolly suggestive is most willingly tolerated, but any serious attempt to solve some social problem is viewed with suspicion. History, politics, religion, are completely closed subjects.'[16]

THE DEFENCE OF THEATRICAL FREEDOM

While a controlled theatre was thus viewed by the ruling elements as supportive of the *status quo*, as least some European liberals and radicals viewed the theatre as potentially an enormously useful tool for education and propaganda among the lower classes. Thus, the French dramatist Guilbert de Pixérécourt declared, 'I write for those who cannot read.' The Russian author Nikolai Gogol, whose troubles with the censorship caused him enormous mental grief, wrote to one of his friends,

> The theatre is by no means a trifle, nor a petty thing, if you take into consideration that it can accommodate a crowd of five or six thousand persons all at once, and that this multitude, whose members taken singly have nothing in common, can suddenly be shaken by the same shock, sob with the same tears, and laugh with the same general laughter. It is a kind of pulpit from which much good can be spoken to the world.

The great Russian director Konstantin Stanislavsky, in inaugurating the daringly experimental Moscow Art Theatre in 1898, told his company,

> What we are undertaking is not a simple private affair but a social task. Never forget that we are striving to brighten the dark existence of the poor classes, to give them minutes of happiness and aesthetic uplift to relieve the murk which envelops them. Our aim is to create the first intelligent, moral, open theatre and to this end we are dedicating our lives.

In Germany in 1890, the founders of the socialist-oriented Freie Volksbühne had a similar vision of the benefits of the theatre for the lower classes, declaring that the stage 'should be a source of high artistic gratification, moral uplift and a powerful stimulus to thinking about the great topics of the day'. They saw the theatre as potentially a source of 'emancipation and social regeneration' – unlike the existing theatre, which was 'subjugated to capitalism' and corrupted mass tastes by presenting plays on the level of 'society small talk . . . the circus and comic papers'. A proponent of the 'social theatre' in Belgium called for dramas which celebrated working-class virtues, by describing 'all the devotion, all the self-abnegation, all the sacrifices and all the heroism of the proletariat'.[17]

Other proponents of the educational role of the theatre argued that drama could instruct and invigorate the middle classes or prove the salvation of entire societies. Thus, the German liberal newspaper *Grenzboten*, hailing the foundation of the Leipzig Stadttheater in 1868, declared that the stage produced 'an immeasurable effect on the thought and sensitivity of the people' and termed the theatre the 'conscience of the nation, the integration-point of middle-class desires and hopes, the seat of self-identity of middle class society.' Jules Michelet, the great French republican historian, who was twice dismissed from university professorships for his political views, declared that the 'theatre, the true theatre, will revive the world', and that 'an immensely popular theatre . . . circulating in even the tiniest villages' would in the future 'unquestionably be the most powerful means of education, . . . the best hope perhaps of a national renovation'. Victor Hugo, one of his country's leading opponents of theatre censorship, termed the theatre 'a crucible of civilisation . . . which forms the public soul' and which, if subsidised and uncensored by the state, could reconcile class differences in France:

> The rich and poor, the happy and unhappy, the Parisian and the provincial, the French and the foreigners will meet each other every night, mix their soul fraternally and share in the contemplation of great works of the human spirit. From that will result popular and universal improvement.[18]

THE DEVELOPMENT OF THEATRE CENSORSHIP

Censorship of the stage in nineteenth-century Europe reflected a long-held view, dating back to Roman times, that the theatre was a den of sexual immorality, religious heresy and political sedition. Although in Greece actors were so venerated and drama was so influential that Plato referred to his country as a 'theatrocracy', by Roman times the theatre had become increasingly bawdy and disorderly. Cicero wrote that Romans 'considered the dramatic art and the theatre in general disgraceful', a perception borne out by the fact that under the Roman Empire actors were forbidden to vote or hold public office and were regarded as so contaminated that neither they nor their children were allowed to engage in any other profession. The disrepute of and discrimination against the profession were only increased by the tendency of some actors to engage in sexual excess and to use the stage to make critical political comments and parody the sacraments of the emerging Christian religion. Thus, during the first century AD the Emperor Nero banished from Italy one actor who referred to Nero's murder of his parents, and the Emperor Caligula had one actor burned alive for mocking him and executed another who had become his wife's lover. Early Christian theologians such as Tertullian, Caesarius and Augustine responded to the licentious and sacrilegious character of much of the later Roman stage by referring to theatres as the 'shrine of Venus', 'celebrations of the devil' and 'dens of iniquity'.[19]

For centuries after the sack of Rome in AD 410, the Church forbade actors to practise their craft on pain of excommunication, and, in 568 and 692 respectively, authorities in the Western and Eastern Roman Empires, acting under Church pressure, banned all theatrical spectacles. Although the theatre slowly revived later in the Middle Ages – often in the form of liturgical dramas, passion plays or other religiously inspired spectacles – distrust and suspicion of the secular stage continued and was frequently expressed by a wide spectrum of observers. Thus, in 1662 Cardinal Carlo Borromeo of Milan termed the theatre 'the source and base of nearly all evils and all crimes', while in an article published in 1666 French writer Pierre Nicole termed playwrights 'public poisoners'. Aside from the usual attacks on the theatre for sacrilege, sedition and licentiousness, a number of critics attacked it for fostering idleness and disrespect among the lower classes. Thus, a French writer complained in 1588 that the theatre was leading to the 'ruin of families of poor artisans, who fill the cheap seats two hours before the performance, passing their time in lewd ways, playing cards and dice, publicly eating and drinking in a manner which leads to fights and quarrels'. A British writer declared in 1730 that the theatre was unfit for the lower classes because

It brings them too much acquainted with that kind of Life, those Ways of acting, which are above their Sphere, and therefore improper for their Knowledge; not only as it gives them Notions of Greatness and Pleasure, unfit for their Employments and Stations, in the World, or as it may occasion great Injuries to their Health; but also that it is a Diversion that interferes with their Work, and breaks in upon their Hours of Labour.[20]

Such hostile attitudes towards the theatre were periodically reflected in haphazard regulation, persecution, and in some cases total suppression of the stage. Thus, in England between 1642 and 1660 the theatres were shut down completely under a law which declared 'all Stage-Players' to be 'Rogues' and denounced the stage as a place of 'Spectacles of pleasure, too commonly expressing lascivious Mirth and Levitie'. Short-lived closures were also imposed in Spain in 1598 and again in 1646, when the reason was given as the 'disorder and looseness' of the stage. The sixteenth-century ban on the theatre in Geneva imposed by Calvin to guard against the 'dissipation and libertinism which the actor troops disseminate among the youth' still remained in effect there 200 years later, and gained the vigorous support of Rousseau in a famous eighteenth-century controversy over freedom of the theatre. In 1738 Christian VI of Denmark decreed that 'no play actors, rope dancers, conjurers, or those who run so-called games of chance shall be found in Denmark or Norway [then under Danish rule], nor shall their plays and routines anywhere be performed or exercised'.[21]

More typical than complete suppression of the stage were attempts to regulate the theatre, usually through administrative decrees that tended to be enforced in a somewhat haphazard manner. Thus, in England in 1559, Queen Elizabeth barred the presentation of all unapproved plays and forbade all works on political and religious subjects (making local officials responsible for enforcing this decree). In 1581, restrictions on the English stage were centralised and standardised by giving the Master of Revels, an official of the royal household, the power to license 'showes, plaies, plaiers and play-makers, together with their playing places, to order and reforme, auctorise and put downe'. Attempts to regulate theatrical performances in France date back to 1398, with the first of a series of sporadic attempts to impose prior censorship on all dramatic presentations. In another such attempt, in 1641, Louis XII forbade representations of 'all dishonest actions, all lascivious words and double entendres which could affect the honest public'. However, systematic theatre censorship in France began only under Louis XIV, who in 1701 directed that all plays be submitted in advance to the Paris police to ensure that all characters conformed to standards of 'the highest purity', or, as theatre historian Glynne Wickham has put it, to make sure that 'any public utterance thought to be critical of the monarchy or suspect to the Church' would be stifled. Subsequently, Beaumarchais had to battle for over two years to secure permission to stage his play *The Marriage of Figaro* (first performed in 1775). No doubt part of the difficulty stemmed from one of Figaro's remarks:

> They all tell me that if in my writings I mention neither the government, nor public worship, nor politics, nor morals, nor people in office, nor influential corporations, nor the opera, nor the other theatres, nor any one who has ought to do with anything, I may print anything freely, subject to the approval of two or three censors.[22]

In Spain, theatre censorship began in the seventeenth century, while in Austria, where similar restrictions dated from the mid eighteenth century, Emperor Joseph II made clear in the instructions to actors he issued in 1770 that no deviation from approved scripts would be tolerated:

> No one is allowed deliberately to add or alter anything in his part or to employ unseemly gestures; everyone, on the contrary, should keep exclusively to the terms prescribed by the author and authorized by the imperial and royal theatre censorship; in case of infraction, the offender is fined one-eighth of his monthly salary.

In a number of countries, theatre censorship was drastically tightened in response to the ideological threat posed by the French Revolution. Thus, in the German state of Bavaria, 'all plays bearing on our country's history' were banned in the 1790s. As the above-quoted decree of Austrian Emperor Joseph II suggests, those who violated stage rules concerning licensing and censorship faced reprisals. In a number of instances actors and playwrights were fined, jailed or deported for their infractions. Thus, the illustrious English playwright Ben Jonson was twice briefly jailed for his dramatic indiscretions, although towards the end of his career Jonson aspired to be a censor himself.[23]

THE MECHANISMS OF THEATRE CENSORSHIP

Much early theatre censorship had a haphazard character to it, with enormous variations in enforcement from locality to locality and year to year, and with much legislation rarely effectively enforced at all. The eighteenth century and early nineteenth century witnessed in many countries an attempt to tighten and centralise regulation of the theatre (reflecting a general trend towards expansion and centralisation of state powers), as in the directions of Louis XIV and Joseph II noted above and in the formal imposition of theatre censorship in Russia in 1804. In Britain, this trend was clearly manifested in the first major parliamentary statute regulating the stage, the Licensing Act of 1737, which was largely a response by the Prime Minister, Robert Walpole, to a series of political satires directed against him by Henry Fielding and other dramatists. The Licensing Act contained two major provisions which generally became standard throughout much of Europe by the nineteenth century: (1) only licensed theatres could present 'legitimate' theatre (i.e. dramas consisting of words only – separate rules were applied if music was involved); and (2) no 'new' play could be performed for 'gain, hire or reward' without the prior approval of the Lord Chamberlain, who functioned as head of the royal household and thus replaced the Master of Revels as chief theatre censor (the Chamberlain soon delegated most of his theatre responsibilities to a member of his staff who was known as the Examiner of Plays).[24]

These twin provisions – the establishment of the so-called 'theatre monopoly' and of prior censorship – paralleled provisions which had been adopted much earlier throughout Europe to control the printed word. By the early eighteenth century no European printer could function without a licence from the government and no particular material could be printed without censorship clearance (except in Britain, where, as noted earlier, such restrictions on the press had ended in 1695). The general adoption by about 1800 of parallel provisions for regulation of the stage gave the ruling classes effective tools which on the whole succeeded in controlling the theatre and eliminating serious social and political criticism from the stage during most of the nineteenth century, particularly during the period before 1860 when political repression was especially severe throughout most of Europe. Thus, as early as 1781 the French drama critic Thomas Rousseau bitterly attacked the censorship for destroying all serious theatre:

If one surrenders his production to their censure, they cut, prune, trim, mutilate, and dissect it to the extent that there does not even remain for the poor child the shadow of its first form. After this blow, they return it to its father. Reduced to this state of languor, or even more, annihilation, this shapeless skeleton can only revolt; he makes such a heavy fall that it appears he will never be revived; he appears, falls, dies, is buried, and everything is finished.[25]

The theatre-monopoly provisions implemented in most European countries greatly restricted the number of 'legitimate' theatres and, of course, ensured that only 'reliable' theatre managers and companies would be licensed. In London after 1737, only two legitimate theatres, Drury Lane and Covent Garden, were tolerated (the Haymarket Theatre could also put on legitimate drama, but only in the summer), with actors performing illegally at other theatres deemed 'rogues and vagabonds' subject to imprisonment. Abolition of the monopoly in 1843 quickly led to the establishment of twenty-five more theatres in the London area. In France, licensing officials were more tolerant, with the number of approved theatres in Paris allowed to increase from eight in 1814 to twenty-three in 1850, but the licensing require-ment was not ended entirely until 1864, when Napoleon III decreed that henceforth anyone could build or operate a theatre and 'dramatic works of all types . . . can be represented in all the theatres'. By 1905, the number of Parisian theatres had increased to forty-three. In Germany and Italy, most of the individual states gave exclusive rights to one or two theatres, typically under strong court control, but the monopolies gradually faded away between the 1848 revolu-tions and the achievement of national unity in these countries in 1870. In Italy, the Reale Sarda company had the exclusive right to present prose drama in Turin until 1848, and the Fiorentini company had a similar monopoly in Naples until 1860. In Germany, the number of both theatres and theatre employees tripled during the twenty-five years after the theatre monopoly was abolished upon unification of the country in 1870. In Russia, the theatre monopoly in Moscow and St Petersburg, which formally began in 1827, was maintained until 1882. Until then only two or three imperial theatres under rigid governmental control could legally present legitimate drama in the two capitals, while in the next thirty years hundreds of stage groups blossomed.[26]

While the theatre monopoly was one major tool used by governments to control the stage, the censorship was far more critical and, with the major exception of France, which ended prior censorship of the stage in 1906, also far longer lasting. The theatre censorship continued in Britain until 1968, in Denmark until 1953, in Austria until 1926, and until revolutions overthrew the regimes in Russia in 1917 and in Germany in 1918 (although the later Bolshevik and Nazi regimes restored it).[27] Typically, theatre managers had to submit a copy of all scripts to the censorship at least a week or two before opening night. The censors were empowered to approve the script as submitted, ban the play entirely or approve only with deletions. In some countries, such as France, changes could sometimes be negotiated in meetings with the playwright or theatre manager. According to censor Hallys-Dabot, at such meetings the censors 'explained sincerely their objections and the others defended their thoughts!'[28]

Many details of the legal basis and administration of theatre censorship varied somewhat from state to state. For example, in Britain after 1737 and in France after 1835 stage censorship was always based on statutory law, but in Russia (where there was no elected parliament before 1905) it was based solely on imperial decree. In Germany the censorship was mostly based on royal decree before 1850 and a mixture of decree and law thereafter, while in Denmark censorship had no legal authority at all but was simply exercised by the government on the basis of its traditional role in licensing theatres. In Britain the Examiner of Plays, attached to the Lord Chamberlain, head of the royal household, functioned as chief censor for the whole country. In Denmark between 1853 and 1893 a different censor supervised each theatre, but after 1893 a single censor appointed by the Justice Minister supervised all theatres. In Russia, theatre censorship was handled by the notorious Third Section (the secret political police) under Nicholas I (1825–55) and by the Press Affairs Administration under Alexander II (1855–81). In France, the Parisian theatre was controlled by a board of censors under the jurisdiction of the Bureau of Theatres, which was attached at various times to the Ministries of State, the Interior, Fine Arts and Education; in the départements, censorship decisions were made by the prefects, who could ban in the départements plays approved for Paris, but who after 1880 could not approve for the départements drama forbidden in the capital. In Germany, each state and in some cases each city had its own theatre-censorship administration, which was generally in the hands of the *Theatersicherheitspolizei* ('Police responsible for theatre security'), a special branch of the *Sittenpolizei*

('Moral police'). Likewise, in Italy (after 1889), in the Netherlands (after 1851) and in Spain stage censorship was controlled by local or provincial officials.

As previously noted, France abolished its theatre censorship in 1906, and a handful of minor European countries also were functioning without such controls by 1910. In Belgium after 1831, local authorities had the legal right to censor the theatre but in fact did not exercise it, while in Sweden no formal approval was required for theatrical performances although managers did have to notify the local police of their intentions and supply any requested information. While the most important German states, such as Prussia, Bavaria and Saxony, all enforced strict drama-censorship rules, some of the other states, including Württemberg, Baden, Brunswick and Hamburg, operated with uncensored stages. Portugal by 1910 had a unique system under which theatre managers could either submit scripts in advance to the police, on the understanding that any approved play could be performed without interference, or proceed without prior censorship at the risk of having the performance stopped by the police and of facing criminal prosecution.

In most countries an appeal against a negative censorship decision could only be taken to another level of the bureaucracy. Thus, in Italy after 1889, an appeal against an adverse decision by the provincial governor could only be addressed to the Minister of the Interior, and, in France and the German state of Bavaria, appeals against censors' decisions had likewise to be taken to the supervising minister. However, in some of the German states, notably Prussia and Saxony, it was possible to appeal to the courts, which quite frequently overturned censors' decisions. This happened in at least six cases between 1892 and 1896. However, the decentralised nature of the German theatre censorship meant that a court decision overturning a ban in one city did not guarantee that censors would permit the play elsewhere. The most notorious such case concerns Gerhart Hauptmann's *The Weavers*, which was banned by officials in Berlin who saw it as an *Umsturzdrama* ('subversion drama'), but allowed to be performed following a court decision in 1893. Subsequently, however, it was banned by police in seventeen other German cities and repeatedly had to be rescued by the courts. Kaiser Wilhelm II bitterly resented the Berlin court decision and continued to fight the play with various forms of harassment: by cancelling his imperial box at the Deutsches Theater (the first theatre in Berlin to stage the play), he deprived the management of 4000 marks a year

in rent; he publicly humiliated the offending judge and forced him
to retire; and he twice (in 1896 and 1899) exercised his veto to stop
Hauptmann from receiving the Schiller Prize (though he could do
nothing to prevent him from being awarded the Nobel Prize for
Literature in 1912).[29]

Aside from variations in administrative procedures, European
countries (and, in the case of Germany and other decentralised
systems, the various states and cities) varied greatly in the intensity
with which they administered theatre censorship. While the British
censorship completely rejected less than 1 per cent of all plays
submitted between 1852 and 1912, in France between 1835 and 1847
about 2.5 per cent of plays submitted were banned, and in Russia in
1866–7 about 10 per cent of plays were rejected completely and
another 13 per cent were allowed subject to changes. Italy was
divided into about ten highly repressive states before 1860, each with
its own censorship system and each fearing national unification as a
threat to its continued existence. Stendhal wrote in his diary while
visiting Naples in 1817 that a friend had informed him that 'only
three of Alfieri's tragedies are permitted here; four in Rome; five in
Bologna; seven in Milan; none in Turin'. Strindberg's *The Father*
was censored in Berlin but allowed without cuts in Copenhagen,
while his *Miss Julie* was banned in the Danish capital yet allowed in
the German. Within the German state of Bavaria, the theatre
censorship of Munich was quite strict while that in Nuremberg was
relatively lax.[30]

Although particular censorship decisions often defy explanation,
'censors at all times and places being notoriously unpredictable',[31] in
general the relative harshness of the censorship reflected the general
state of political repression in each country. Thus the repressive
regimes in Russia under Tsar Nicholas I (1825–55) and in Austria
and most of the Italian and German states before 1860 tended to
have the strictest controls on the stage. In Austria, where the censors
decreed that King Lear and Romeo and Juliet could not die in
performances of Shakespeare's plays about them, even the notoriously
reactionary Emperor Francis I (ruled 1792–1835) complained about
his own censorship. He termed it 'really stupid' and once declared,
'I must go to the theatre today. Any time now the censorship might
find a hair in the milk and forbid the play and I won't get to see it!'
Even in such regions, however, a dedicated and determined director
could create a respectable, if not thought-provoking, theatre. Such
was the case with Josef Schreyvogel, director of the Vienna

Burgtheater, who was able to develop a fine ensemble which produced superb productions in the face of one of the harshest censorships in Europe.[32]

CAPRICIOUSNESS OF THE CENSORSHIP

Theatre censorship in nineteenth-century Europe was characterised by capriciousness and inconsistency. Not only were plays banned in some countries but not others, but many plays were first approved and then banned or first banned and then allowed a few years later by the same regime. In one of the most spectacular cases of such capriciousness, Alexander Ostrovsky's play *Kozma Zakharich Minim, Sukhoruk* (named after its hero) was approved for publication in 1862 and so pleased Tsar Alexander II that he sent the author a ring worth 500 rubles; yet the play was banned from the stage the following year. In another reversal, performance was permitted by 1866.[33]

Many censorship decisions produced ludicrous results. In Austria, the censorship changed a father into an uncle in one of Schiller's play because his attitude to his son was deemed unworthy of a father; as a result, at one point the son was forced to declaim, 'There is a region in my heart whither the word uncle never penetrated.' In Britain, the phrase 'Bring my grey hairs in sorrow to my grave' was struck from one play on the grounds it was profane. The Russian dramatist Lermontov was forced to change virtually the entire plot of his play *Masquerade*, because, among other things, the censorship was scandalised by his 'indecent criticism of costume balls' among the aristocracy and 'impertinences against ladies belonging to the fashionable social sets'. Such offences were viewed as 'more than horrible: there is no name for it'. In France, censors in the 1820s refused to approve a play that had the son of a count marrying the daughter of a shopkeeper; the daughter of a great businessman was suggested as an acceptable alternative. In the 1850s, the French censors rejected a play which showed a postman who neglected his official duties, and insisted that a customs official who was mocked be changed into a winetaster – in both cases, apparently to avoid lowering public esteem for government officials. They also struck out of George Sand's play *Molière* (1851) a passage in which the hero toasted 'the poor people of France, who pay the fiddlers for all the festivals and the trumpets for all the wars'; refused to allow, in a play of 1853, the comment that 'the rich, in the design of God, are only the treasurers of the poor'; and banned from Victor Séjour's play *Les Aventuriers* (1860) the comment that, 'if a rich man wants to go hunting or dancing, they roll out a carpet for him on the way lest he weary his feet'.[34]

The noted Italian actress Adelaide Ristori wrote in her memoirs that in Turin, capital of the independent state of Sardinia before 1860, all religious references, including all mention of angels and devils, were banned, as were the words 'Italy' and 'fatherland'. Thus, in one play 'Beautiful sky of Italy' was changed to 'Beautiful sky of the world', and in another a stage direction reading 'Here the actor must express the joy which he experiences in beholding his fatherland' had 'native land' substituted for the forbidden word to avoid any apparent expression of patriotism in pantomime. After the suppression of the 1848 revolution in Rome, the authorities forbade the appearance of the Italian national colours of red, white and green together. One actor recalled that, in a play where an actress had white and green in her dress, 'another who wore a red ribbon must not come near her', and that one night he was fined 'for wearing a blue uniform with red facings and white ornaments, for the excellent reason that the blue looked green by artificial light'.[35]

There were three major reasons for the inconsistency and capriciousness of the censorship: (1) the vagueness of the laws and decrees prescribing what could or could not be allowed on stage (a vagueness that was probably inevitable given the nature of the censor's task); (2) the personalities of individual censors; and (3), perhaps most important of all, the general political situation at any given time.

Although some censorship rules, such as the British ban on all representations of living individuals and all dramas based on the Bible, and a French decree of 1840 banning all reference to Napoleon, were clearly defined, most of the laws and decrees authorising theatre censorship did not even try to lay down any clear guidelines. Among the drama-censorship rules of 1822 in the Italian state of Tuscany was a ban on 'performances of any kind which could in any way offend the conscience and the principles of modern times'. The British Theatre Regulation Act of 1843 simply authorised the Lord Chamberlain to suppress plays where he felt it 'fitting for the Preservation of good Manners, Decorum, or of the Public Peace'. A French ministerial circular of 1850 directed the provincial prefects to be certain that no play 'made with an injurious or exaggerated political sentiment or attacking morals and religion is presented in the theatres of your département'. The Bavarian police code of 1871 authorised censorship of the stage for the purpose of protecting 'morality, propriety or public peace'. In Russia, Tsar Alexander II's 1865 decree regulating theatres gave no criteria whatsoever for censorship, although it was typically replete with details on the procedures involved (plays must be presented in two copies of 'neatly and legibly written manuscripts'; censors must mark passages to be deleted in 'red ink'; and a theatre manager who staged a play which had been 'entered in the register of forbidden plays is liable to a fine not exceeding 500 rubles and to detention of not more than three months').[36]

When questioned, theatre censors could generally shed little light on their operating principles. One British Examiner of Plays said he tried to strike anything which 'may make a bad impression on the people at large' and another told a parliamentary inquiry in 1909, 'There are no principles that can be defined. I follow precedent.' When the Austrian dramatist Franz Grillparzer met the censor who was responsible for banning his 1823 play *King Ottokar* and asked him what was objectionable, the censor replied, 'Nothing at all, but I thought to myself, "One can never tell!"' When Berlin theatre manager Oscar Blumenthal asked the Berlin police president to explain the ban on a Hermann Sudermann play around 1900, he was told that the police had so acted because 'it just suits us', not because of any particular scenes or language. A French theatre censor testified at an 1849 hearing on stage censorship that in making decisions

> We have no other guide than our conscience. In seeing a scabrous passage, we would ask ourselves: 'Would we take our wife and daughters to a theatre to hear such things?' That was for us a criterion. In seeing passages with a political or social significance we asked ourselves, 'Does that aim at causing the different classes to rise up against each other, to excite the poor against the rich, to excite to disorder?' We asked ourselves in principle if it was possible to allow ridicule on the stage of the institutions of the country, and especially those who maintain order most effectively; if it was right to disarm the latter [e.g. the police and militia] in advance and expose them to the laughter and mockery of the crowd. We had no trouble in answering no.[37]

The personalities of individual censors played a major role in determining policies. Although a number of theatre censors, such as Francesco Ruffa (1792–1851) in Naples, Jean-Louis Laya (1761–1833) in France, and John Kemble (1807–57) in Britain, were well-known authors and scholars, many censors once in office seem to have let their power and idiosyncrasies get the better of them. Thus, Giuseppe Belli, a well-regarded poet who wrote over 2000 witty and realistic sonnets about plebeian Roman society, was known for unparalleled pedantry as a censor in Rome, leading one observer to comment that, if his principles were strictly observed, 'all that could be recited in the theatre would be the rosary'. George Colman, who served as Examiner of Plays in Britain between 1824 and 1836, was also notorious for his odd decisions, which extended to striking the word 'thighs' as indecent, and banning a reference to members of the royal family as 'all stout gentlemen'. One critic declared of Colman, 'An inordinate fear of the devil, working on a mind reduced to the last gasp of imbecility, could alone originate such a ludicrous, yet injurious abuse of paltry power.' Another Examiner, E. F. Smyth Pigott, who banned Ibsen's *Ghosts*, declared, 'I have studied Ibsen's plays pretty carefully and all the characters in Ibsen's plays appear to me morally deranged.' When Smyth Piggott died in 1895, George Bernard Shaw wrote a savage obituary, terming his reign as censor

> one long folly and panic, in which the only thing definitely discernible in a welter of intellectual confusion was his conception of the English people rushing towards an abyss of national degradation in morals and manners, and only held back on the edge of the precipice by the grasp of his strong hand.[38]

In France, Alexander Dumas's play *La Dame aux camélias*, the story of a courtesan, was banned in 1849 as offensive to public morality, yet was approved soon afterwards when Dumas's friend the Duc de Morny was named Minister of the Interior, the head of theatre censorship. At the same time Morny banned a play, approved by his predecessor, that satirised speculators. His reasoning, as one historian has paraphrased it, was that financiers, 'who render the state no small service, have a right to be shielded from the darts of impertinent satirists; whereas no offence is given to any influential segment of the community by revealing that young men about town habitually frequent the houses of loose women'.[39]

Such reversals of previous decisions were quite common, although usually they took much longer to happen and came about through a change in the political climate rather than as a result of the mere whim of censors (or the use of personal influence, which was quite frequent and often effective among the well-connected, and which in

France led to rumours that censors were being offered monetary bribes or even the sexual favours of actresses). Thus, in Russia, Pushkin's play *Boris Godunov* (1825) was permitted to be staged in 1870 after being banned for forty-five years; Alexander Griboyedov's masterpiece *Woe from Wit* (1825), originally banned and then allowed in 1831 in such mutilated form that, as one observer noted, it had 'nothing left but woe', was finally performed uncut in 1869; and Turgenev's *A Month in the Country*, banned in 1850, was eventually permitted in 1872. These reversals largely resulted from changed political conditions, which, in Russia as in other countries, were reflected in theatre-censorship policies. Thus, the reign of Tsar Nicholas I (1825–55), during which all of the above plays were banned, was one of unrelieved reaction. Nicholas insisted on the deletion of any passage which might 'evoke applause for its independent views by the "non-privileged" classes', and, panicked by the revolutions of 1848, not only headed a secret censorship committee but also personally stamped 'performance forbidden' on rejected scripts. However, conditions eased considerably under his successor, Alexander II (1855–81), who even allowed dramas depicting a former tsar, Ivan the Terrible, as the mass murderer that he was.[40]

Although drama censorship in Russia had eased considerably by 1900, periods of political tension continued to have their impact on the stage. A good illustration of this is provided by Stanislavsky in his description of the atmosphere at a performance of Ibsen's *An Enemy of the People* in the Moscow Art Theatre in 1901. The performance took place on the day after police had violently dispersed a peaceful mass demonstration for political reform.

> The hall was aroused to the limit, and grasped at the slightest hints of freedom and responded to every word of protest by Stockmann [the hero of the play]. That is why explosions of tendentious applause burst out at the most unexpected places in the action. . . . The atmosphere in the theatre was such that we expected arrests at any minute and a stop to the performance. Censors, who sat at all performances of *An Enemy of the People* and saw to it that I, who played Dr Stockman, should use only the censored text, and raised trouble over every syllable that was not admitted by the censorship, were on this evening even more watchful than on any other occasion. I had to be doubly careful. When the text of a role is cut and recut many times, it is hard not to make a mistake and say too much or too little.[41]

A year later, when the Moscow Art Theatre produced a new play by Maxim Gorky (which had at first been banned by the censorship and then was allowed in mutilated form), the authorities only allowed holders of season tickets to attend (in order to weed out the poor) and insisted that the police should check all tickets. After complaints by the theatre management that the sight of uniformed police was frightening the patrons, the police dressed as ushers, and 'one glance at policemen in frock coats was the comedy sensation of the time'.[42]

The impact of changing political conditions upon theatre censorship is especially clear in the case of France.[43] The systematic censorship established under Louis XIV was abolished in 1791 as part of the general movement towards freedom of speech characteristic of the first years of the French Revolution. However, in 1794, as the Revolution became more radical and tyrannical, censorship was reimposed and was administered in an extremely harsh fashion (in one three-month period, out of 151 plays submitted thirty-three were rejected and twenty-five others were mutilated). Napoleon continued a rigid theatre censorship when he came to power in 1799. He reduced the number of theatres permitted in Paris from thirty-three to eight in 1807, personally supervised the censors and completely banned all references to the overthrown Bourbon dynasty as well as to such other threatening topics as punishment of tyrants and (when he decided to divorce Josephine) divorce. Censorship was continued during the Bourbon restoration (1815–30), but now it was Napoleon, and the sites of his great victories (such as Marengo and Austerlitz), that could not be mentioned. The same applied to authors of the eighteenth-century Enlightenment, such as Rousseau and Voltaire.

As a result of the revolution of 1830, which was largely fuelled by opposition to restoration repression, theatre censorship was abolished. However, in 1835 the French parliament restored it, reflecting a general drift towards reaction under King Louis-Philippe owing to rising working-class unrest over the failure of the 1830 revolution to instigate real social reforms. For brief periods after 1835 and 1840 all mention of Napoleon was once again forbidden. In February 1848, growing opposition to the regime's repressiveness helped bring about another revolution and another abolition of theatre censorship, under the Second Republic. The free stage did not last long, however, as censorship was reimposed by the legislature under Louis Napoleon (later Napoleon III) in 1850, amidst another drift towards reaction in the aftermath of the abortive workers' revolt of June 1848. In the wave of repression that followed Louis Napoleon's *coup d'état* that overthrew the Second Republic in December 1851, theatre censorship was applied with astonishing severity. In 1852, out of 628 plays examined by the censors, only 246 were accepted without change, while fifty-nine were rejected outright and 323 were accepted only with modifications. In December 1852, shortly before the legislative authority for theatre censorship was due to expire, and shortly after declaring himself Emperor, Napoleon III indefinitely extended stage censorship by imperial decree. Until 1867, all the plays of Victor Hugo were forbidden, and, when a censored version of his *Hernani* was finally allowed in that year to celebrate an international industrial exhibition in Paris, crowds greeted it with a delirious acclaim that clearly turned the performances into an anti-regime demonstration. They even responded to the omissions by shouting out the correct words.

With the collapse of Napoleon III's regime in 1870, theatre censorship was abolished for the fourth time, only to be administratively reintroduced once more in 1871 during the state of siege imposed following the Paris Commune. Censorship was ratified by the legislature in June 1874, amidst continuing fears of lower-class unrest, and was applied with great harshness throughout the 1870s, with all references to the Commune forbidden. Short plays intended for performance at the popular café-concerts were treated especially severely. Café-concerts were the inexpensive predecessors of music halls, nightclubs and cabarets, and attracted large crowds to performances, often held outdoors, that featured bands, sketches and songs. In November 1872 a governmental directive sent to café-concerts informed them that political allusions were 'absolutely forbidden'. Although, with the consolidation of the Third Republic after 1880, controls eased dramatically, as late as 1903 a censor struck out all references to the Commune in one play, declaring, 'The words Commune, communards, no longer exist.'[44] In 1906, after a period of (by French standards) long-term relative political stability, theatre censorship in France was permanently abolished (saving its temporary reintroduction in wartime). Even after 1906, however, local officials were empowered to stop stage performances deemed immoral or prejudicial to public order.

EVASION OF THEATRE REGULATIONS

On the whole, regulation of the theatre in nineteenth-century Europe was effective in achieving its aim of creating a stage that would not threaten the political supremacy or professed religious beliefs or morals of the ruling classes. None the less, most censorship regulations could be evaded by those determined and inventive enough to attempt it and willing to accept the risks involved. While such evasions were not widespread enough to change fundamentally the character of the nineteenth-century theatre or to pose a threat to the established order, during the course of the century hundreds of playwrights, theatre managers and actors across Europe actively conspired to break or skirt the rules, and hundreds of thousands of theatre patrons collaborated with them by attending performances which were either technically illegal or legal in letter but not in spirit.

Where theatre monopolies existed, they could be evaded by either of two means: performances could be illegally staged in venues that were not licensed to stage public entertainments, as was common in Russia; or what amounted to 'legitimate' drama could be thinly disguised as something else and presented in technically legal form in venues licensed for other forms of entertainment but not for 'legitimate' drama, as was common in Britain.

In Russia, where monopolies kept the number of legitimate theatres in Moscow and St Petersburg to two or three until 1882, the monopolies were quite regularly violated by private entertainments which were facilitated by large bribes or which were disguised under such code names as 'family reunions' or 'dramatic evenings'. Such gatherings were commonly sponsored in Moscow by the Circle of Lovers of Dramatic Art, established in 1861, and in St Petersburg by the Nobility Assembly and such groups as the Painters' Club and Merchant Club. It is estimated that by 1875 about twenty-five such groups were regularly putting on performances in the two cities. In a society as highly regulated as was tsarist Russia, these goings-on could not remain unknown to the authorities and their toleration no doubt reflected the fact that the sponsoring groups were regarded as politically reliable. But the very fact of their widespread existence, combined with the fact that private theatres were allowed in the provinces, undermined the legitimacy of the monopolies. It was under the pressures of nascent Russian public opinion and of some influential employees of the imperial theatres, such as the director Alexander Ostrovsky, that the government finally abolished the monopolies in 1882.[45]

In Britain, while the monopoly established in 1737 restricted the 'legitimate' theatre in London to two playhouses, the vague distinction between 'legitimate' and 'non-legitimate' theatre provided a means of evasion. In addition to the two theatres licensed for 'legitimate' drama, there were a number of places of entertainment in London licensed for 'music, dancing and public entertainments' distinct from stage plays under the Disorderly Houses Act of 1751. Such other forms of entertainment were often categorised as 'burlettas', a term which was defined as including all performances with at least five pieces of music in each act. By technically putting on a 'burletta' through some subterfuge such as rewriting *Macbeth* in doggerel verse and having a piano constantly tinkling in the background or adding a chorus of singing witches, theatres which were not licensed to put on plays were able to evade the monopoly. In other cases, British theatres used techniques similar to those in Russia. Since the 1737 law only applied to performances put on for 'hire, gain or reward' it was possible for theatres not licensed for the 'legitimate' stage to put on supposedly 'free' performances under the guise of asking patrons to 'tea at 6.30' or inviting them to share a 'dish of chocolate', on the understanding that interested persons would obtain their tickets by paying an exorbitant price at a nearby shop for tea or peppermints or would supposedly pay an admission fee only for a concert or an 'auction of pictures' with a play thrown in at no cost. Thus, a London advertisement of 1774 read, 'By the Wolverhampton Company of Comedians this present Monday July 11 a Concert of Vocal and Instrumental music: between the Several Parts of the Concert will be played [gratis] the celebrated Comedy The West Indian.' Such evasions were by no means risk-free. In September 1839, police raided the Royal Union Saloon in Shoreditch, where over 800 workers were watching an illegal play sponsored by dissident groups, and made seventy arrests. However, as in Russia, the sheer number of such illegal performances, combined in Britain with a much more developed public opinion (which forced a parliamentary investigation of theatre censorship as early as 1832), helped bring about an abolition of the monopoly. This came in 1843, after 100 years in which it had been, as theatre historian Vera Roberts has noted, often 'respected more in the breach than in the observance'.[46]

While theatre monopolies generally disappeared in Europe by the last quarter of the nineteenth century, this was not the case with theatre censorship (which typically extended beyond prose plays to include musicals, burlesques, cabarets, and so on), with the inevitable result that techniques to evade censorship continued to be practised and refined throughout the century. One widespread practice was to print and circulate censored plays, drawing special attention to the banned parts. In Britain, where press censorship had ended in 1695, and in France, where such control ended in 1830, this could be done quite legally. It was common to publish censored plays with banned material printed in italics, capital letters or enclosed in inverted commas, and this often had the effect of drawing great attention to and generating large sales of censored plays. For example, after *The Happy Land*, a play co-authored by W. S. Gilbert of Gilbert and Sullivan fame, was censored in 1873 for its mimicked portrayals of leading politicians, the enraged director published the unexpurgated text with all excisions printed in capitals. The play was accompanied by a preface which tartly noted that the reader 'who will take the trouble to compare the original text with the expurgated version as played nightly . . . will be in a position to appreciate the value of the Lord Chamberlain's alterations'.[47]

In countries where press censorship was retained for part or all of the nineteenth century, banned plays could often not be legally published either, but in some cases they were clandestinely printed or circulated in manuscript. Thus, in Italy, Giovanni Niccolini's drama *Arnoldo da Brescia* could neither be performed nor printed due to its nationalistic appeal, but it was published in France in 1843 and was subsequently 'read in secret from one end of Italy to the other and its fiery patriotic passages were everywhere committed to memory by the workers for Italian freedom and unification'.[48] Similarly, in Russia, Griboyedov's banned play *Woe from Wit* (1825) became extremely widely known as the result of clandestine circulation of handwritten copies. Polish audiences could, at least after about 1860, evade the worst excesses of the censorship in Russian-occupied Poland by crossing the frontier into Galicia (Austrian Poland), since stage censorship was by then considerably less harsh in the Hapsburg lands than it was under the tsars.[49]

A means of evading censorship that was available in all lands was improvisation on the stage or from the audience. This could take manifold forms, as explained by Victor Hugo in 1849 to a French inquiry into theatre censorship:

the offences which one can commit in the theatre are all of sorts. There are those which an author can commit voluntarily in writing in a play something against the law. . . . There are also the offences of the actor; those which he can commit in adding to words by gestures or inflections of voice a reprehensible sense not meant by the author. There are the offences of the director who arranges a display of nudity on the stage; then the offences of the decorator who exposes certain seditious or dangerous emblems mixed in with the decor; then those of the costumer, then those of the hairdresser. . . . Finally there are the offences of the public, an applause which accentuates a verse, a whistle which goes beyond what the actor or author intended.[50]

The theatre-censorship bureaucracy usually had neither the manpower nor the time to attend each performánce to ensure that their instructions were carried out or that no offences of the sort Hugo described occurred, although sometimes censors would attend a dress rehearsal or an opening performance, and on occasion additional spot checks might be made, especially if a complaint had been lodged or newspaper reviews aroused concern. This spotty enforcement opened up plenty of opportunities for evasion by actors willing to risk the consequences of improvising or restoring censored lines, and at least a sprinkling of performers did so. The great Austrian dramatist and actor Johann Nestroy frequently found himself in trouble with the authorities for his improvisations (as well as his technique of frustrating the censors through satirical plays on words). On one occasion in 1826 his contract was cancelled when he refused to promise to keep to his script, and in 1835 he was jailed for five days for launching an unscripted verbal attack on a theatre critic. Another eminent Austrian dramatist and actor, Ferdinand Raimund, was clapped in irons for three days for 'willfully transgressing the prohibition against extemporizing on stage'. His crime had taken the form of an apology to a theatre audience for thrashing his mistress, who had refused to reveal to him the name of her theatre companion.[51]

Far more common than extemporising to administer a verbal thrashing to critics or to apologise for physically thrashing mistresses was the violation of censorship rules by gradually and surreptitiously restoring forbidden material. Under Napoleon III in France

> at the dress rehearsal and for the first few performances, the passages that had been blue-pencilled would be obediently omitted; but as performance succeeded performance, the cuts would be imperceptibly restored by the players, or the author would even add new matter that the censor had never seen.[52]

This practice became so common that in 1861 a new office of

'Commissioner-Inspector of Parisian Theatres and Spectacles' was created to monitor play performances more closely. However, many performances could still not be attended by a censor, and at least one Parisian theatre, the Porte Saint-Martin, soon worked out a system whereby, when an inspector was sighted, the actors would be signalled and would revert to the approved text.[53]

Enforcement of regulations against improvisation and restoration of censored matter seems to have been especially lax in Britain. Thus, newspaper accounts of James Haynes's censored 1840 play *Mary Stuart*, which the censors apparently viewed as referring in a number of places to Queen Victoria, reported audience reactions to many passages which had been forbidden, but no action was taken. Even the notorious Examiner George Colman tacitly suggested to at least one author that what was spoken on the stage was of less concern to him than what was in the official script; he told the dramatist Samuel Beazley, who had complained that the censorship had reduced his 'full grown angels into cherubim' and 'left them neither heaven or cloud to rest upon' that the playscript 'must be printed in strict accordance with my obliterations; but if the [uncensored] parts be previously given out, it will be difficult to make the actors preach from my text'. In 1872, a British dramatist, J. R. Planche, publicly stated that censorship instructions 'were never paid the slightest attention to', and that forbidden material 'continued to be uttered and to excite the roars and plaudits of the galleries to the last night of representation'.[54]

Theatre inspectors in the German state of Bavaria were considerably stricter in enforcing the law. In Munich, inspectors regularly attended performances, routinely noted whether or not audiences were from the 'better dressed classes', and took even closer note of the dress as well as the speech of the performers. The following details about one actress's dress noted during a censor's theatre visit in Munich in March 1909 have been preserved for posterity in the German archives:

She wore a very short little skirt, much like those of ballerinas, and shoes and stockings which came only halfway up the calf. The legs were bare from the calf to far beyond the knee, approximately to the middle of the thighs. The underwear did not consist of the opaque ruffled skirts worn by ballerinas, but rather simple skirts and panties.

In another case in Bavaria, a report of an actress's highly revealing tights was signed or initialled ten times by six different officials before the 'repulsive spectacle' was finally covered up. In fairness to these zealous Bavarians, it should be noted that in the 1830s the French authorities specified how high can-can dancers could kick up their legs, that Italian authorities repeatedly expressed concern that ballet dancers were showing too much leg, and that in 1874 the British censorship instructed one play director to lengthen the skirts of his dancers and then withdrew the play's licence when the director complied but noted in the theatre programme that the costume alterations had been prescribed by the authorities.[55]

In some cases, evading the intent of censorship regulations required interpretative help from the audence. For example, despite the efforts of censors to avoid even allegorical political criticism of the ruling regimes, as in the banning of plays deemed critical of past kings, it was virtually impossible to identify every comment in which audiences might find an allusion to contemporary situations. Thus, French officials during the reign of King Louis-Philippe banned a play about the Roman Emperor Claudius when theatre audiences cheered the comments of an actor who, after slaying the tyrant, called for the restoration of 'the old, holy republic'. Stendhal's comment about Italians that, 'If you are dealing with a race which is at once dissatisfied and witty, everything soon becomes an "allusion"' was borne out by the tendency of Italian audiences before 1860 to interpret any literary reference to past French and Spanish domination of their land as a metaphor of current Austrian domination. In one instance, a French minister in Milan reportedly became indignant when the audience cheered anti-French references in Niccolini's play *Giovanni da Procida* (1830), about a thirteenth-century Sicilian revolt against French rule. Reassuring him, the Austrian minister present observed, 'Don't take it badly; the envelope is addressed to you but the contents are for me.' The play was soon suppressed as a result of French and Austrian pressure, but was clandestinely circulated.[56]

Active audience participation also enhanced the ability of silent pantomime to express political satire. Since censors could hardly blue-pencil expression that lacked language, skilful pantomime artists and imaginative audiences could sometimes collaborate to mock the establishment with gesture in a way which could not be done by words. Perhaps the leading silent dramatic political satirist was the great French pantomimist Jean Deburau in the role of Pierrot. Writing of Deburau, the theatre critic Jules Janin noted,

It's obvious that he's mocking you, but with nary a word; his sarcastic assaults on the vicious and the mighty consist of a grimace, but one so piquant that all of Beaumarchais's wit cannot match it. . . . [He is] an actor without passion, without speech, and almost without face; who says everything, expresses everything, mocks everything.

In Britain, according to David Mayer, the pantomime was constrained by fear of reprisals from engaging in 'trenchant and incisive comment on issues of political and religious importance' but was still 'the only effective means of satire to hold the stage in the first 30 years of the nineteenth century' as the 'non-verbal portions of the harlequinades provided endless opportunities for a tentative and general satire on follies and issues'.[57]

Mimicry of well-known personalities was one form of silent stage performance that was especially difficult to control in advance. Thus, Balzac's play *Vautrin*, which had been cleared by the French censorship on its fourth submission, was banned in 1840 after one performance because the actor Frédérick Lemaître had appeared on stage in a wig which called to mind King Louis-Philippe. In Britain in 1873 the censors cracked down after three characters in W. S. Gilbert and Gilbert Beckett's *The Happy Land* were made up to resemble three Cabinet members. In at least one instance, Italians used the theatre, without the aid of any stage action at all, to express their opposition to the post-1848 Austrian occupation of their land. Italian patriots in the town of Pavia boycotted the theatre there to protest against Austrian rule, so angering the Austrian commander that he declared, 'If anybody by criminal political obstinacy should persist in not frequenting the theatre, such conduct should be regarded as the silent demonstration of a criminal disposition which merited to be sought out and punished.'[58]

Perhaps the best-known system of evading stage censorship in nineteenth-century Europe was that evolved by the 'independent' or 'free' theatres that sprang up after 1885.[59] The 'free theatres' presented banned dramas at 'private clubs', which were open only to members who paid an annual subscription fee, thereby avoiding any charge at the door and technically avoiding censorship laws, which generally applied only to plays which were staged for 'gain, hire or reward' and/or were open to the general public. The most famous of these 'private clubs' was the Théâtre Libre of Paris, which flourished under the direction of André Antoine, a former clerk at the Paris Gas

Company, between 1887 and 1894, and closed for financial reasons in 1896 after presenting a total of sixty-two programmes with 184 plays (mostly one-acters). Other prominent 'free theatres' were the Freie Bühne of Berlin, which reached its peak under the direction of the literary critic Otto Brahm between 1889 and 1891 and folded in 1901; the Independent Theatre of London, established by Jacob Grein, a Dutch immigrant, in 1891, which functioned regularly until 1897; the London Stage Society; the Abbey Theatre of Dublin; the Modern Life Society of Munich; and the Ibsen Theatre of Leipzig. Similar groups appeared in Vienna, Hamburg, Hanover, Dresden and other cities.

These 'private clubs' were all founded with similar aims: to avoid the censorship and the conservative and monetary considerations which made it impossible to present the new 'realistic' dramas associated with Ibsen and his followers on the established stages of Europe. For example, the founding statement of the Berlin Freie Bühne called for a theatre 'free from conventions, censorship and commercial aims', while one of its founders declared that the Freie Bühne was 'above all' created as 'a way of rapping the nose of the police censor'.[60] The first presentation of both the Berlin Freie Bühne and the London Independent Theatre was *Ghosts*, by Ibsen, which had been banned in Britain and much of Germany. The Freie Bühne became especially associated with the drama of Gerhart Hauptmann, presenting his celebrated play *The Weavers* after the Berlin censor banned it in 1893, while the London Independent Theatre was closely associated with George Bernard Shaw, presenting as its first production of a home-grown play his *Widowers' Houses* in 1892.

In general, the authorities were willing to turn a blind eye to the activities of the 'free theatres', probably because the annual subscription fees were so high that the lower classes were kept out. In Britain, the Lord Chamberlain explicitly told the Independent Theatre that its performances did not legally exist so long as they were open only to members and their guests. However, there was a limit to tolerance. The Bavarian authorities imposed censorship on the Munich cabaret club Elf Scharfrichter (Eleven Executioners) in 1901 in reaction to the increasingly political character of its satires; the Bavarian Interior Minister told the police that the club 'seeks to create the illusion that its shows are limited to the members of a closed society' but 'the enterprise doubtless presents its performances publicly'. For months the police had tolerated the fiction that the cabaret was open only to 'inscribed members' and their 'invited guests', although widely publicised advertisements informed the public where 'invitations' could be obtained and an inflated cloakroom fee of 3 marks was charged in lieu of an admission fee. (In general, the authorities in Munich seem to have been especially sensitive to cabaret performances. Thus, within a six-week period in 1906 the Munich police rejected eleven sketches and twenty-two songs planned for performance at a single cabaret, the second-rate Intimes Theatre.)[61]

Most of the 'free theatres' had only a brief existence. The repertoire of 'realistic' plays was in some cases quickly exhausted, and some members joined only for the novelty of enjoying forbidden fruit and quickly lost interest. To some extent the theatres were also victims of their own success: Antoine and Brahm established such outstanding reputations as directors that regular theatres hired them, while many plays which the 'free theatres' pioneered became so well-regarded that censorship and commercial barriers to their performance in mainstream playhouses were broken down. The high annual subscription fees charged by 'free theatres' limited their audiences, which meant that only a few performances of each play could be staged and permanent companies could not be established. Usually theatres were hired *ad hoc* for each production, adding to the enormous financial and artistic problems under which the societies laboured. In Britain, despite the assurances of the Lord Chamberlain, theatre managers were often afraid to let the 'free theatres' use their stages for banned dramas. When the London Stage Society attempted to put on Shaw's banned play *Mrs Warren's Profession* (1894), which treated prostitution as a serious social problem, over a dozen theatres, two music halls, three hotels and two art galleries refused to host the play before a site could be found (the play was not licensed for public performance until 1925).[62]

While few of the 'free theatres' were long-lived, they played a significant role in bringing to the stage the forerunners of the modern, socially concerned drama and in helping to break down the barriers of censorship. As Roy Pascal has noted, the 'free theatres' demonstrated to their audiences 'the dramatic quality of works known only in print and often decried on theatrical grounds' and also gave authors 'whose works were banned from the stage the chance of seeing them played', thereby, helping them to 'develop their own style' and enhancing the 'self-awareness and solidarity of the new generation of writing'.[63]

One branch of the 'free theatre' movement did have a longer life –

the 'free people's theatre' movement of Germany, which developed as a proletarian offshoot of the Freie Bühne and its imitators.[64] In 1890, the Freie Volksbühne was established in Berlin under the auspices of the Social Democratic Party, following a call in the party paper for 'public performances of plays possessing a revolutionary spirit' previously excluded from commercial theatres by the 'box office or by the police censor' and 'denied to the proletariat for economic reasons' by the high cost of subscriptions to the Freie Bühne. Despite considerable harassment by the police (which forced the Freie Volksbühne to submit to drama censorship after 1910) and a factional split which led to the establishment of a rival Neue Freie Volksbühne in Berlin in 1892, by 1913 the two groups had a membership of almost 70,000 and similar groups were scattered throughout Germany and Austria. George Bernard Shaw publicly declared, 'Among all German theatres, there is none by which I would rather be produced than by the Freie Volksbühne.'[65] The free people's theatres developed a repertoire of about 100 proletarian plays by 1914, and by that date the Neue Freie Volksbühne had built a magnificent theatre for its productions which seated almost 2000, after a fund-raising drive that obtained contributions from over 14,000 people. By 1930 there were over 300 such organisations in Germany with a membership of half a million, and even today these groups remain a significant force in the German theatre.

IMPACT OF THE THEATRE CENSORSHIP

Certainly the most deleterious effects of the censorship were on playwrights or those who considered becoming playwrights. Unquestionably some highly talented writers simply did not write for the stage due to the theatre censorship, since in many countries, as the British playwright Elizabeth Inchbald put it, the novelist 'lives in a land of liberty, whilst the dramatic writer exists but under a despotic government'. H. G. Wells told a British parliamentary committee in 1909 that the censorship 'has always been one of the reasons I have not ventured into play writing', and the drama historian Marjorie Hoover notes that Pushkin and Griboyedov wrote few plays since 'who knowingly writes plays for the drawer!'[66]

Other writers censored their plays in advance or did not write on certain subjects, since as one British Examiner of Plays remarked in 1866, authors 'know pretty well what will be allowed'. Tolstoy, whose play *The Power of Darkness* was banned in Russia and Germany, declared, 'What matters is not what the censor does to what I have written, but to what I might have written.' His compatriot Griboyedov, whose masterpiece *Woe from Wit* was butchered for years by the censorship, censored much of the play himself before even submitting it. He noted,

> The first draft of this dramatic poem, as I conceived it, was much better and more significant than the present one, clad in a frivolous dress which I was compelled to put on it. The childish ambition to hear my verses in the theatre, the ambition that it meet with success there, prompted me to spoil my creation as much as possible.

Another Russian author, Nikolai Gogol, whose play *The Inspector General* escaped severe mutilation only because Tsar Nicholas I happened personally to like it, never completed an earlier play because, as he wrote to a friend,

> I stopped when I noticed that my pen kept knocking against such passages as would never be permitted by the censorship. There remains nothing else for me than to invent a most innocent plot to which even a police precinct officer will take no offence. Yet what is a comedy without truth and indignation?

The manuscripts of the Austrian playwright Johann Nestroy reveal extensive self-censorship of his dramas. For example, in the draft of *Ground Floor and First Floor* (1835), he changed the comment 'If the rich didn't just invite other rich people but poor people instead, we'd all have enough to eat' to 'They should have invited us', removing the original note of social criticism.[67]

Even when authors did not censor themselves, theatre managers often cut the most threatening material before sending plays off for approval. When the producer of Byron's play *Marino Faliero* at Drury Lane in London sent the manuscript off to the censor in 1821 he included a note stating that the drama had been 'so curtailed that I believe not a single objectionable line can be said to ["remain" deleted] exist'. The play was a failure, at least partly because it had been 'curtailed' by 45 per cent of its original length before the censor even saw it! Where authors or theatre managers did not censor plays themselves, they were often forced to comply with official edicts if they wanted to see plays performed. Lermontov rewrote his 1835 play *Masquerade* twice to try to placate the censorship, but, even though the censor found that the third version was 'completely changed' with 'all indecencies eliminated', it still was not approved for performance until 1852 (the second version was allowed in 1862).[68]

Authors whose plays were censored were filled with the greatest indignation. The great Austrian dramatist Franz Grillparzer was deeply embittered by the censorship, declaring in his autobiography and private writings that in his homeland 'invisible chains rattle on hand and foot', that any writer 'who does not completely lose heart under such conditions is truly a kind of hero', that 'there is no place for a writer in Austria under these circumstances', and that 'the system' did not 'pin crosses on genius, but nails genius to the cross'. Johann Nestroy compared the censorship to a 'mind with the root pulled out' and noted, in a play written during the temporary collapse of theatre censorship during the 1848 revolution, that 'We actually had freedom of thought, that is, we were free to keep our thoughts to ourselves.' He added,

> A censor is a pencil turned into a man, or a human turned into a pencil, a stroke across the products of genius, a crocodile lurking on the banks of the river of ideas and biting off the heads of the writers swimming in it. . . . Censorship is the younger of two ugly sisters, the name of the elder being the Inquisition. Censorship is the living admission by our rulers that they can only kick stupefied slaves, not govern free people.[69]

Victor Hugo also compared the dramatic censorship to the Inquisition, terming it 'detestable' and a 'prison' for writers, and declaring that 'like the other Holy Office' the censorship had 'its secret judges, its masked executioners, its tortures and mutilations and its death penalty'. When theatre censorship was reimposed in 1850 after a two-year period of uncensored drama, Hugo declared, 'it brought sobs to the depths of my heart.' Another French dramatist, Albert Guinon, complained in 1901,

> If I understand correctly the functioning of the censorship, its role is to forbid all work of social satire which would tend to move the audience and thus cause a certain effervescence judged dangerous. But, if a work of social satire does not affect the public, it is clearly an inferior work. . . . From which it follows, a little humiliating for the institution of the censorship, that its role is to let pass social

satires which are weak and faded and to stop those which are strong and intense.

Gerhart Hauptmann remained embittered for the rest of his life by the harassment *The Weavers* suffered. Writing fifty years later, in 1942, he recalled, 'I was treated like a criminal, like a common rogue!' For Shaw, the British censorship was 'of the most tyrannical and impossible character'.[70]

Actors and directors suffered from the censorship along with authors. When told that King Lear could not die on the Austrian stage, actor Heinrich Anschutz, who was portraying Lear, angrily declared that if he did not have to support a family he would never put up with such 'stupidity' and 'all these inanities'. The Austrian director Joseph Schreyvogel lamented, 'It is unbelievable what difficulty the censorship poses by sitting in the path of the new.' The Russian director Konstantin Stanislavsky demanded in 1905 that something be done to prevent the theatre from being 'strangled by the arbitrary action of the authorities' and his compatriot director Vsevolo Meyerhold complained bitterly that 'in Russia they always begin by saying it's forbidden'.[71]

While many dramatists complained bitterly about the censorship, a few pointed to aspects of the censorship that sometimes benefited them. First, the censorship provided an excuse for failed works or for a failure to write at all. As Nestroy wrote in a play produced during the censorship-free days of the Austrian revolution of 1848, 'Writers have lost their favorite excuse. It wasn't a bad thing after all, when you'd run out of ideas, to be able to say to people: "God, it's awful. They won't let you do a thing."' Secondly, one of the sure paths to fame was to have a play censored and, in those countries where a censored play could be printed and sold, the financial rewards often proved substantial. Texts of censored plays sold so well in Britain that one paper reported of a recent drama that it 'was received most enthusiastically and it only requires an edict [banning it] from the Lord Chamberlain to render it to the success of the season'. When Hermann Sudermann's play *Sodoms Ende* was forbidden in Berlin in 1890, he wrote to his mother that, 'if anything was still lacking regarding my popularity, it is [remedied by] this brutal police decree'. He reported receiving dozens of requests from theatres across Germany seeking to produce the banned play, and added, 'You can hardly imagine the excitement this ban has created in the theatrical world. In Vienna, Rome and London they are writing newspaper editorials about it, American journalists come to interview me, and artists come to sketch my portrait.' The ban increased interest in one of Sudermann's earlier plays, and, when it was lifted after several months, large crowds came to see *Sodoms Ende*, as was invariably the case in Germany when forbidden dramas were later allowed.[72]

Finally, some dramatists and many directors and actors were not unhappy about the censorship because it assured them that, once a play had been cleared by the authorities, the police would not close it down in the middle of a scheduled series of performances, thereby threatening a total loss of production costs as well as unemployment for the cast and crew. Thus, in hearings held by a British parliamentary committee in 1909, the Actors Association supported continuation of the censorship, as did most theatre managers. In France in 1830–5, when there was no formal prior censorship of theatre, the authorities took advantage of the fear which theatre managers had of having productions halted in midstream by forcefully suggesting that plays should be voluntarily submitted to government officials before productions were mounted. In 1834 the Minister of Fine Arts sent theatre directors a letter informing them that

> You can avoid all problems by submitting your manuscripts in advance to the Fine Arts Ministry. Plays not submitted will be stopped, purely and simply, if by their content they merit the application of the decree [of 1806 which authorised the halting of all plays found to incite public disorder] and you will only have yourself to blame for the loss resulting from the costs of staging a production which has become useless.[73]

As the nineteenth century ended, the development of the new realistic drama combined with the growing force of public opinion turned theatre censorship into a major issue across Europe for the first time. In Britain growing opposition to drama censorship forced the 1909 parliamentary inquiry (although no substantive change resulted from it), while in Germany attempts to broaden stage censorship after 1890 got nowhere and sparked massive protest demonstrations, which attracted 4000 people in Munich alone in April 1900. Among the leading opponents of censorship in Germany were the writers Thomas Mann and Arthur Schnitzler, the painter Max Liebermann and the composer Richard Strauss, while in Britain those speaking out included such eminent authors as J. M. Barrie,

Thomas Hardy, H. G. Wells, John Galsworthy, George Bernard Shaw, Oscar Wilde, Henry James and Joseph Conrad. In Austria in 1914, parliament called for the appointment of censors with a 'psychological and literary education' in the hope of avoiding the worst absurdities, and recommended an end to theatre censorship except where there were strong grounds to believe that a performance could lead to a breach of the peace or criminal proceedings.[74]

Contention over theatre censorship was strongest in France, where rising opposition forced a parliamentary inquiry in 1891, and where, virtually every year after 1880 until drama censorship was abolished by the legislature in 1906, there were furious debates over whether or not to vote further funds for censorship operations. Caricature journals such as *Le Rire*, *L'Assiette au beurre* and *Courrier français*, themselves freed from prior censorship of drawings since 1881, devoted entire issues to attacking the censorship. Increasingly, critics of the censorship complained of unfair discrimination against the theatre. Emile Zola demanded to know why the theatre alone remained subject to censorship when his play *Germinal* (based on his novel of the same name) was banned in 1885: 'Books have been freed, periodicals have been freed. Why is the theatre condemned to eternal servitude?' Similarly, Edmond de Goncourt, another censorship victim, demanded in 1892, 'Speech is free, newspapers are free, the book is free, only the theatre is not. Why this anomaly under a Republic which has liberty for its motto?' Another argument made against the censorship was that, since all theatrical presentations had to be approved by the government, inevitably everything on the stage was viewed as having government endorsement. As one observer noted, 'With the censorship, it's the government which sings smutty songs, it's the government which dances the can-can.'[75]

Despite the growing protests that theatre censorship aroused and notwithstanding the fact that it could be evaded by determined and inventive dramatists, actors and audiences, on the whole it can scarcely be doubted that the nineteenth-century European censorship generally achieved its objective of creating a socially and politically safe and sterile stage, one which rarely presented material dealing realistically with problems of contemporary life. In 1827 the Italian playwright and critic Giovanni Pindemonte lamented that 'Among the other miseries of our Italy is that it has no theatre worthy of the name', while in 1879 the British writer Matthew Arnold decried the fact that 'In England we have no modern drama at all.'[76] Such comments could be equally applied to the theatre in most European countries during the nineteenth century. Historians have concluded that the Russian stage in this period was dominated by 'cheap melodrama, farce and trivia'; that as a result of harsh censorship controls in Austria all art there 'was dominated by total political apathy and absolute indifference to public life'; and that the German stage was 'rarely inspired', as the censorship 'contributed to mediocrity by discouraging anything considered potentially offensive', while after the suppression of the 1848 revolutions 'plays presented had to be so inoffensive as to become almost mindless'.[77] Although conservative elites in nineteenth-century Europe no doubt exaggerated the political importance of the theatre, the ability of the stage to propagate ideas subversive of the existing order was largely negated by a rigorous – and often ridiculous – censorship.

5 Political Censorship of the Opera

'Musicians are lucky, they don't have to bother about the censors', wrote the Austrian dramatist Franz Grillparzer in a 'conversation book' of his friend the deaf composer Ludwig van Beethoven. Grillparzer, who had frequently been outraged by the Austrian censors' butchery of his plays, added, 'But if only the censors knew what the musicians are thinking as they compose.' One of Beethoven's would-be collaborators, Christoph Kuffner, made a similar comment in the conversation books, noting that, 'although words are subject to the censorship, the sounds that represent and give force to words are not'. Grillparzer even wrote a poem to another musician friend, the Bohemian composer Ignaz Moscheles, celebrating what he viewed as the freedom of music from the censorship imposed on the written word:

> But music speaks a loftier tone
> To tyrant and to spy unknown,
> And free as angels walks with men
> Can pass unscathed the gaoler's ken.[1]

Grillparzer and Kuffner were essentially correct in so far as they were referring to music unaccompanied by words, although there were some incidents in which even tunes without lyrics were forbidden, as in the ban imposed by the Hapsburg authorities on performances of Hector Berlioz's 'Rakoczy March', strongly associated with Hungarian nationalism, in Austrian-controlled Hungary during the 1850s.[2] Music with lyrics, however, was a different story. Authorities throughout Europe regarded music as a powerful force which had the potential to move men's emotions and stir them to action, and when music was accompanied by words it was regarded as a potentially subversive force that had to be subjected to censorship control. Thus, the present French national anthem, 'La Marseillaise', was banned during the Restoration (1815–30) and during the regime of Napoleon III (1852–70) for its obvious appeal to republicanism. An extraordi-

155

nary document from 1870 survives in which the censors recommend to Napoleon III a continuation of the ban, since, although on the surface 'La Marseillaise' was simply 'the French song par excellence' with an 'indisputable heroic and grandiose character', in practice it had 'become the symbol of revolution; it is no longer the song of national independence and of liberty but the war chant of demagogy and the most exalted hymn of the republic'. If the government lifted the ban on the song, the report warned, its repeated performance would cause 'new and dangerous excitation', especially since 'its exclusively revolutionary character is too universally known and accepted today to hope for the government's generosity to change this at all'.[3]

Although, as in the case of 'La Marseillaise' and even cabaret songs, censorship controls in most regimes of nineteenth-century Europe applied to all music with words,[4] censorship of song was most systematically and significantly applied to opera, since in the pre-radio age opera was the most important forum for the performance and dissemination of the same lyrics before large groups of people in many different locations. In order to control this powerful force, in most countries of Europe for much of the period 1815–1914 final artistic and administrative control over opera was not in the hands of composers, librettists, conductors or producers. Rather, ultimate control over whether, when and in what form an opera could be produced was held by government censors, who functioned in every major European country and most minor regimes as well.

Verdi's repeated difficulties with the Italian censors are well-known among opera buffs, but the pervasive nineteenth-century European censorship affected to at least some extent every composer. It lead to the banning or mutilation of many operas, including works by Rossini, Donizetti, Beethoven, Wagner, Schubert, Rimsky-Korsakov and Tchaikovsky, and, among the practitioners of light opera, Offenbach and Gilbert and Sullivan. Although much nineteenth-century opera censorship was ostensibly directed against alleged immorality and blasphemy on the stage, censors were primarily concerned with politically charged material that they viewed as threatening the existing socio-political order (as with drama censorship, even supposedly immoral and blasphemous material was viewed as objectionable largely because it challenged the official standards of the ruling orders). Thus, a leading scholar of nineteenth-century Italian opera notes that, while irreligious and immoral material attracted the attention of the censorship authorities,

There is no doubt however that it was on political issues that the censors were strictest. Subjects, situations, or phrases that implied disrespect toward sovereigns or established governments, expressions of patriotism [e.g. for a united Italy] or libertarianism, mention of conspiracy or assassination, were all alike regarded with distrust, and in some parts of the country . . . they might well lead to the suppression or expurgation of the libretto.[5]

The atmosphere of repressive governmental controls inevitably affected the way in which every composer thought and wrote, since, as Henry Raynor has noted, 'the only way in which a composer in the first half of the nineteenth century could establish himself financially and win a reputation was through opera', yet 'the composer's appeal to the public was not allowed to step outside narrowly drawn limits of what was politically and socially acceptable to an old regime conscious of the fundamental dangers of its position' and 'anything that questioned official established policy was to be suppressed as prejudicial to religion, morality or good order'.[6] The impact of this atmosphere upon talented composers is clearly indicated in many of Beethoven's comments. Thus, he once warned his nephew, 'Silence, the walls have ears', and complained that the Austrian repression was becoming so severe after 1815 that 'They are discussing a law about how high a bird can fly and how quickly hares may run.'[7]

THE DEVELOPMENT OF OPERA CENSORSHIP

Opera censorship was well established in Europe by 1815. It usually operated as a part of a more general stage censorship. It was therefore subject to the same regulations as governed theatre censorship and was usually administered by the same authorities. In Britain, for example, when the stage-censorship laws were modified in 1737 and 1843, the opera was specifically included as a form of theatre subject to censorship, and elsewhere opera was either explicitly mentioned in the drama-censorship regulations or in practice treated as subject to them. Thus, in Austria in 1786, Mozart's opera *The Marriage of Figaro* (based on Beaumarchais's play, which had been banned in Austria due to the scandal that its mocking of the aristocracy created when the play was eventually allowed in France) needed the personal approval of Emperor Joseph II before it could be performed, and then was only permitted after the librettist had eliminated the most cutting remarks from the text.[8]

Under the impact of the fears aroused by the French Revolution, repressive controls were sharpened everywhere, leading Beethoven to complain in 1794 from Vienna, 'One doesn't dare lift his voice here, otherwise the police find lodging for you.' Mozart's operatic masterpiece *The Magic Flute* was banned in Austria in 1795 on the grounds that its favourable depiction of a noble brotherhood based on virtue rather than birth amounted to revolutionary propaganda. Beethoven's only completed opera, *Fidelio* (which Beethoven had predicted would 'win for me a martyr's crown'), with its theme of a political prisoner unjustly jailed by a tyrant, was premiered in Vienna in 1805 only after censorship amputations. In Naples, Domenico Cimarosa was arrested in 1799 for composing a republican hymn when the Bourbon dynasty reoccupied the city after a short period of French control.[9]

Harsh controls continued in all the major European countries long after the defeat of Napoleon. Thus, in France, all operatic references to Napoleon were forbidden during the Bourbon restoration (1815–30), and in 1844 Hector Berlioz was rebuked by the French police when the audience enthusiastically applauded passages from an opera chorus about the fourteenth-century king Charles VI which he had included in a programme he had selected to celebrate a major industrial exhibition in Paris. The audience had expressed its approval of lines concerning the Hundred Years War such as 'never shall the English dog be loved in France' at a time when the French government was attempting to improve its relations with Britain, and the authorities accused Berlioz of having 'secretly added to the programme a piece of music calculated to arouse certain passions which the government is endeavouring to suppress'. In 1852 the government of Louis Napoleon Bonaparte forbade an opera about the Fronde (a rebellion of the seventeenth century) because any theme concerning an uprising was regarded as potentially dangerous, and because it was feared that the phrase 'Aux armies!' might be picked up in other theatres and on the streets.[10]

In Russia, under Nicholas I's decree of 1837, no tsar could be represented on the opera stage. Pre-Romanov tsars (only) could appear in spoken tragedies and histories, but it was explained to composer Rimsky-Korsakov that were a tsar of any dynasty 'suddenly [to] sing a ditty, well, it would be unseemly'. On the other hand, this arbitrary decree of Nicholas could occasionally be just as arbitrarily overruled by his successors, as when Alexander II personally decided in 1872 to permit performance of Mussorgsky's opera *Boris Godunov* about a medieval tsar, after being advised that it had 'special musical merits'.[11]

In Austria and Germany, censorship controls over opera between 1815 and about 1870 were extremely strict. Thus, even Franz Schubert, an entirely non-political composer (who, because of the political activities of one of his friends, was arrested and jailed overnight in a crackdown on subversives in 1820) suffered on at least three occasions from the censorship: his 1823 opera *Die Verschwörenen* (*The Conspirators*) had to be retitled *Das häusliche Krieg* (*Domestic Warfare*) because the censorship feared anything suggesting political plotting; another 1823 opera, *Fierabras*, suffered censorship deletions; and an opera he was working on towards the end of his life, *Der Graf von Gleichen* (*The Count of Gleichen* [= 'equality']) was never completed, apparently because of censorship objections to the libretto's theme of bigamy. Thus, one of Schubert's friends noted in 1826, with regard to the last-mentioned opera, that 'Schubert is delighted with the opera but we are afraid of the censor', and, later, that 'the opera libretto is forbidden by the censors'. According to Grillparzer, censorship problems also caused Beethoven to abandon an opera project in the 1820s. Beethoven planned to revise a play about ancient Greece to make it applicable to the leading liberal cause of the day, the Greek struggle for independence against the Ottoman Empire. Grillparzer recalled, 'The idea was to connect it with contemporary events in Greece, and because of this the censor banned it.' In Germany, the Saxon censorship butchered Wagner's *Rienzi*, about a fourteenth-century revolutionary in Rome, eliminating all references which might be interpreted as a call for liberalism or national unification in contemporary Italy and, by implication, in Germany also, then divided into nearly forty petty tyrannies. Thus, Rienzi's cry 'Not only Rome shall be free! All Italy shall be free. Hail to united Italy!' was changed in Dresden to 'Not only Rome is great! All Italy shall be great. Hail to the ancient greatness of Italy!'[12]

In Austria and Germany after 1815, composers, librettists and even choral societies were kept under careful surveillance and police regulation to determine if they harboured any subversive inclinations. Metternich regarded choral societies as especially suspect since they were organised along democratic lines, with members electing their directors and managers; as he put it in tones of alarm, 'everything that involves communal activities and aspirations encourages, directly or indirectly, freedom'. Elaborate dossiers on prominent musicians were compiled by the Austrian police. Thus, a document of 1821 located in the police archives in Venice (then under Austrian rule) warns, absurdly, that Rossini, 'the famous composer', was 'strongly infected by revolutionary principles' and should be subject to the 'most rigorous surveillance'. Metternich also warned his minions in Rome that Hector Berlioz, who in an intercepted letter had expressed his desire to help the 'largest and poorest class of people' and to destroy 'every kind of privilege, which, hidden like vermin in the folds of the social body, have hitherto paralysed all attempts at remedy', displayed a 'dangerous tendency towards fanaticism' and that all Austrian students in Rome should be warned 'against contact of any kind with this young man'.[13]

Even after Metternich's demise, Austrian police harassment of every activity connected with the opera remained so severe that in 1869 a Viennese satricial journal published the following imaginary memo from the police to the Ministry of Public Safety concerning the performance of Mozart's *Don Giovanni* at the opening of the new opera house:

> The people of Vienna are definitely not yet ready for the blessings of freedom. Thirty-four women and girls were handed over to the authorities for defying the strict regulations whereby the cloak-room attendants are allowed to earn 10 Kreuzer for each outer garment. They stubbornly refused to divest themselves of their coats with the flimsy excuse that they had nothing on underneath except their shifts . . . A woman who had fainted was arrested for failing to comply instantly with an order to come to her senses. Finally, 83 persons were removed from the premises for speaking their minds about people who sing out of tune, and showing every intention of not taking the customary lenient view of the first few performances.[14]

While the censorship became increasingly stringent and ponderous almost everywhere after 1789, this was especially so in Italy, probably because opera was more important there than anywhere else and also because Italy was dominated by Austria, the leading reactionary power of Europe. The importance of opera in early-nineteenth-century Italy can hardly be exaggerated. As one Italian author wrote in 1869,

'No one who has not lived in Italy before 1848 can realise what the theatre meant in those days. . . . The success of a new opera was a capital event that stirred to its depths the city lucky enough to have witnessed it, and word of it ran all over Italy.'[15]

A modern scholar comments,

A realisation of the preponderant part then played by Opera in Italian life is of importance. To all intents and purposes there was no other amusement whatever available; the attention of everybody was focussed on the theatre, which served as a kind of club where all sections of the population met to discuss their business and their private affairs.[16]

To prevent this enormously influential art form from becoming a vehicle for subversion, cumbersome censorship apparatuses were constructed throughout Italy. Although the censorship varied somewhat from state to state, with the harshest controls in Naples and Rome, and the most lax controls in Austrian-controlled Lombardy-Venetia (perhaps because the Italian-speaking censors there sympathised with the nationalist cause), one scholar has concluded that in general the Italian censorship expunged 'any political or religious comment' and forbade any 'mention of regicide, treason, suicide, adultery, the portrayal of a priest, a crucifix, or a religious service', and 'the uttering of the words God, angel, tyrant or liberty'.[17] No doubt the most complicated censorship bureaucracy was in Rome, where each script had to be inspected by an ecclesiastical censor for 'religion, moral and good manners', by a political censor for 'respect for law and persons', and by a municipal censor for 'philological matters' (the result was that forty-one copies of every proposed opera libretto had to be submitted to Roman officials!). Naples came close to Rome in the strict-censorship competition; there the censorship rules required that opera librettos be submitted a year before the proposed opening night, and the King personally decided such details as whether new seats in the opera house should be made of wood or iron. In Parma, Duchess Marie-Louise even set the time for the start of opera performances.[18]

THE AUTHORITIES' FEAR OF THE OPERA

The authorities' fear of the opera was fundamentally similar to their fear of the stage in general, but in those countries where opera was especially significant – above all Italy, and to a lesser extent Germany, Austria, Russia and France – these fears probably had much to do with perceptions of the stirring power of words set to music. The essential arguments to the effect that the stage posed a greater danger than the printed word applied to opera in the same way as to plays: productions gathered large numbers of people together; a live performance had a more powerful impact upon the individual than a private reading of the same words (one journalist in nineteenth-century Italy supported opera censorship since some expressions, 'when sung, produce an impression not to be tolerated, though they might be tolerated in reading'[19]); and a staged performance was accessible to the illiterate lower classes while print was not.

The argument that opera and songs generally were or could be an especially powerful form of communication, perhaps even more powerful than spoken drama, was frequently stated during the eighteenth and nineteenth centuries. Thus, an Englishman named Andrew Fletcher declared in 1703, 'Give me the making of the songs of a nation, and I care not who makes the laws.' In France, Beaumarchais called in 1787 for the creation of musical drama dominated by a 'great philosophical idea' to replace the sort of opera played in houses that were 'but a social meeting place where one goes on certain days, without knowing why'. A French revolutionary declared at his trial in 1832 that 'opera is a spectacle to awaken and excite the senses . . . . a vast reservoir of powerful sensual excitements'. The young German radical Arnold Ruge, in composing his opera *Spartacus* in the 1830s, declared that it was his intention to fortify his political message with the 'magic of music'.[20]

The French revolutionary regime of the 1790s put this philosophy into practice, commissioning and sponsoring opera, hymns and huge public festivals and pageants with musical accompaniment to try to whip up support for their policies. Thus, Danton called for political operas because 'exaltation is what makes the building of republics possible', and the minutes of the French constitutional assembly of 21 December 1793 state that 'every occasion should be celebrated with the singing of hymns praising the fatherland, liberty, equality and fraternity, because hymns have the power to endow the citizens with all manner of virtues'. Among the ideological operas of the revolutionary period were *The Crimes of the Ancien Régime*, *The Republican Nurse*, *The Feast of Reason* (in which a sans-culotte is crowned with a cap of liberty while a priest publicly hails the liberating effect of shedding his robes) and *Denis the Tyrant* (described as celebrating the need 'to inculcate in children . . . the sacredness of equality'). The French government even sponsored a 'Hymn of Jubilation for the Occasion of the Victorious Entry of the Art Treasures Brought from Italy'. However, this same radical French government shared the view of nineteenth-century conservative European regimes that opera could also pose a threat. Thus, after the performance of *Le Tombeau des Imposteurs et l'inauguration du Temple de la Verité*, a satirical work out of tune with the government's inclinations, the government issued the following ban on 22 December 1793, despite the formal abolition of all theatre censorship in 1791:

> The Committee of Public Safety, anxious to discourage all counter-revolutionary maneuvres designed to disturb public tranquillity . . . herewith prohibits presentation in the theatre, the opera and elsewhere of the piece entitled *Le Tombeau des Imposteurs et l'inauguration du Temple de la Verité* as well as similar pieces liable to produce the same results, under the penalties listed in the preceeding decrees aimed at those who abuse the theatre for the promotion of views inimical to the Revolution.[21]

In countries such as Britain where operas never became as important as spoken drama, the nineteenth-century censorship appears to have treated opera more leniently than plays. Thus, Alexander Dumas's play *La Dame aux camélias* was banned in Britain by the same censor who simultanously allowed the production of *La Traviata*, Verdi's opera based on the play. The censor explained, 'If there is a musical version of a piece it makes a difference, for the story is then subsidiary to the music and singing.' However, in Italy, where opera reigned supreme, opera censorship seems to have been more strict than censorship of plays. Verdi could not get the approval of the Roman authorities for an opera based on the assassination of King Gustav III of Sweden in 1792 without changing the setting to colonial Boston, even though plays on the same subject had been allowed without difficulty. He complained to a friend, 'In Rome *Gustave III* is permitted in prose, but the same subject is not permitted as an opera libretto!!! Indeed most singular!'[22]

In the same way as for spoken drama, while nineteenth-century European elites saw an unregulated and politicised opera as posing a subversive threat, they perceived a controlled and frothy opera as helping to shore up the establishment by diverting the minds of the discontented to non-political matters. Thus, in Rome in 1837 (a time of widespread unrest in Europe), an advisory committee urged the Pope to increase his support of the opera, reasoning that

> In order for a people to be more calm and content with the government to which it finds itself subjected, it is absolutely clear and confirmed by the experience of centuries that the means most fitting and conducive to this end is a suitably distracting theatre, decently entertaining and soberly diverting; and particularly at this time the distraction and entertainment of the people is the healthiest cure for the wounds that have been inflicted in almost every part of the world.

Another advantage for fostering support of the opera was noted by the chief minister of Austrian-ruled Lombardy–Venetia during the post-1815 period. He urged that the La Scala opera house in Milan be kept busy since 'it attracts to a place open to observation during the hours of darkness a large part of the educated population'.[23]

The Italian authorities were generally successful before 1840 in their aim of using the stage to divert public attention away from politics (although, as will be pointed out below, after 1840 this strategy backfired as the opera increasingly became the site of political demonstrations). Thus, the writer Massimo d'Azeglio noted that La Scala for many years after 1815 attracted 'far keener interest than the whole crowd' of Italian nationalists and confessed, 'One must pay tribute to the refinement and shrewdness of the Austrian government', since 'for years they could be said to have governed Lombardy by means of La Scala and one has to admit that for some time they succeeded well'. The French writer Stendhal commented in a similar vein that the Italian authorities fostered opera because 'it requires no activity on the part of the mind', especially as the music was generally characterised by a 'sweet sensuality', and 'sensual pleasures' were unlikely to 'trouble the government'.[24]

DISORDERS AT THE OPERA

As we have seen from the French decree of 22 December 179. warning against threats to 'public tranquillity' from the 'abuse [of the theatre for the promotion of views inimical to the Revolution' the authorities feared that subversive operas might lead to politica disorders. Such fears were not entirely unfounded, as opera audiences were even more highly excitable in the nineteeth century than they are today. Between 1820 and 1830, there were several occasions when operas were seen as contributing to successful revolutions. Thus, a briefly successful revolution in the Italian state of Piedmont in January 1821 was generally perceived as partly precipitated by an operatic performance and the emotions it had aroused. In France, during a rehearsal of Rossini's *William Tell* on 29 July 1830, the hero's cry of 'Independence or death' was taken up by everyone in the theatre, and musicians, stagehands and soldiers on guard rushed into the streets to join in the revolt that overthrew the repressive regime of Charles X.[25]

Perhaps the most inflammatory opera of the nineteenth century was Daniel-François Auber's *La Muette de Portici*, which portrayed a commoners' revolt against Spanish rule in Naples in 1647 and was widely interpreted as a general call for democracy and nationalism.[26] One opera historian notes that after its first presentation, in Paris in 1828, *Portici* 'very soon developed political overtones which threw into the foreground its scenes of riot and revolt' and, 'appearing as it did on the eve of the July [1830] Revolution, it was almost an accessory before that fact'.[27] After the 1830 revolution in Paris, *Portici* was banned by fearful authorities in Brussels and in German towns near the French border. However, the ruling Dutch authorities in Brussels (Belgium was then united with the Netherlands) subsequently revoked their ban and allowed a performance on 25 August 1830. While Belgian patriots had long resented Dutch rule, the sentiments of the audience were inflamed by passages such as the following:

> Better to die on the ramparts of danger,
> Than to live in chains, outcasts and slaves!
> Let us unite and throw out the strangers,
> With one blow, save our country's freedom!

During the performance, members of the audience began to stream into the streets, destroying symbols of Dutch rule and howling, 'Down with the Dutch!' According to one account, 'by the time the opera ended with a pyrotechnic onstage eruption of Mount Vesuvius . . . the lava of revolution was already coursing through the streets of Brussels'.[28] Thus, an opera performance is generally credited with sparking off – although by no means causing – the successful 1830 Belgian revolution against the Dutch.

In Italy, as nationalist sentiment against Austrian domination mounted after 1840, audiences throughout the peninsula repeatedly seized upon passages in Verdi's operas as excuses for patriotic outbursts.[29] If before 1840 the opera had diverted attention away from politics, afterwards the opera house became transformed into a political arena. Thus, when Verdi's *Nabucco* was performed in 1842 in Milan, the audience interpreted the references to the Hebrews under the Babylonian yoke as a metaphor for their own plight. They demanded and received an encore of the chorus of the Hebrew slaves, 'Va, pensiero', with its reference to 'my country, so lovely and lost' (despite a law which sought to head off such patriotic demonstrations by forbidding encores) and subsequently it became something of a national anthem. The response to *Nabucco* was so strong that the Milan police commissioner upbraided the conductor, Angelo Mariani, and threatened him with arrest for giving Verdi's music 'an expression too rebellious and hostile to the imperial government'.[30]

There were similar responses from Italian audiences to passages in Verdi's other operas – for example, the shouts of 'Guerra!' ('War!') in reaction to the song 'The Holy Land today will be ours' in *I Lombardi* (1843), an opera about Italian crusaders seeking to liberate Jerusalem from the Saracens; and the stormy applause and shouts of 'Italy for us!' which greeted the passage in *Attila* (1846) in which a Roman declared to the Hun chieftain during his assault on medieval Italy, 'You take the universe, leave Italy to me.' In response to the chorus 'Oh fatherland oppressed' in *Macbeth* (1847), audiences in Venice threw onto the stage bouquets in the Italian colours of red and green, and, when the police forbade this, flowers in the Austrian colours of yellow and black were thrown in the knowledge that the singers would refuse to pick them up. One Florentine censor noted dejectedly in a report that 'the perplexity of the censor is due to the public reaction' which gives performances an interpretation 'over and above their literal meaning'. Charles Dickens, after observing a rowdy opera crowd at Genoa, concluded that the Italian dictatorship had created a situation in which 'there is nothing else of a public nature at which they are allowed to express the least disapprobation' and 'perhaps they are resolved to make the most of this opportunity'.

By the 1850s, Italian audiences did not even require lyrics to stage political demonstrations at the opera. Thus, the cry 'Viva Verdi' accompanied by clenched fists, was often shouted when Austrian soldiers were spotted at the opera. The cry not only honoured the

'Maestro della rivoluzione italiana', as he became known for his patriotic choruses, but also expressed the political demand which the letters of his name spelled out – the unification of Italy under Vittorio Emmanuele, then King of Sardinia (*Vittorio Emmanuele, Re* [King] *d'Italia*). When the prominent nationalist leader Emilio Dandolo died in 1857, the people of Milan surrounded La Scala and forced it to close for three days in his honour.[32]

In France, the romantic–democratic appeal of the opera seems to have been what made it the focus of a series of assassination attempts directed against French monarchs and royalists in the name of freedom. Thus, of two plots hatched against Napoleon in 1800 (one of which killed or wounded eighty people), one was planned to occur during a climactic chorus of an operatic premiere and the other while he was *en route* to the opera. In 1820, the Duc de Berry, the heir to the throne, was assassinated in the Paris Opéra. In 1858 Napoleon III was the target of a spectacular attack which killed or wounded over 150 people when a bomb exploded outside the Paris Opéra while he was on his way there to attend a performance of Rossini's *William Tell*, an opera about resistance to repressive Austrian rule in medieval Switzerland.[33]

THE CAPRICIOUSNESS OF THE CENSORSHIP

In general, nineteenth-century opera censorship was dominated by capriciousness and inconsistency. As was the case with censorship of other media, the harshness of opera censorship usually reflected the general state of political repression in that country. Therefore the most repressive regimes, such as Russia under Nicholas I (1825–55) and Austria and most of the Italian and German states before 1860, tended to have the strictest opera censorship. Thus, while *William Tell* was allowed in France in 1829, it was mutilated by the Russian, Prussian, Austrian and Italian censors. The Austrian censors insisted that, before *William Tell* could be performed in Austrian-controlled Lombardy, the setting would have to be shifted to far-away Scotland, English oppressors would have to replace Rossini's Austrians, and William Tell would have to be transformed into William Wallace.[34]

Not only were some operas banned or censored in some countries but not others, but in a number of instances they were first forbidden and later allowed, or first allowed without change and then banned or censored, in the same country. Thus, Rimsky-Korsakov's *Christmas*

Eve (1894) originally ran into trouble with the censors because its semi-disguised portrayal of Catherine the Great was ruled a violation of the 1837 ban on any depiction of a tsar (or tsarina) in an opera. (A similar fate had earlier befallen an attempt by Tchaikovsky to base an opera entitled *Vakula the Smith* on the same Gogol story as Rimsky-Korsakov used for *Christmas Eve*.) However, by using personal connections (as he had done earlier to overcome similar objections to the portrayal of Ivan the Terrible in his 1872 opera *The Maid of Pskov*), Rimsky-Korsakov succeeded in having the opera approved. Nicholas II wrote in person to inform him that 'permission has been granted for admitting the opera *Christmas Eve* composed by you to be produced on the Imperial stage without change in the libretto'. None the less, when two influential members of the imperial household complained about the depiction of Catherine after attending a final rehearsal in November 1895, the composer was forced to change Catherine into a 'most serene highness', which reduced the central incident of the plot to nonsense. He wrote bitterly to a friend that the authorities 'forget the saying: "Don't give your word unless you intend to keep it."'[35]

Rimsky-Korsakov's final opera, *The Golden Cockerel*, an allegorical satire on the decay of the Russian autocracy, based on a well-known poem by Pushkin, was held up by the censorship for two years. In part the trouble may have resulted from the composer's staunch support for democracy during the 1905 revolution, which led to his temporary dismissal from his position at the St Petersburg Conservatory and a two-month ban on the performance of all of his works. As a result of the censorship problems, *The Golden Cockerel* was first performed, in a mutilated version, only after the composer's death in 1908 (some accounts suggest that the censorship difficulties hastened his death). The tsar of the original libretto was transformed into the 'Mighty Tsar's General', and a number of important textual changes were made; thus, near the end of the opera, where the original text had the chorus asking, 'What will the new dawn bring? the censors insisted on changing the threatening-sounding 'new dawn' to a 'white dawn'.[36]

In Milan, permission to stage Donizetti's opera *Maria Stuarda* (which had been banned in Naples) was withdrawn after six performances. In Rome, as mentioned earlier, although a play based on th assassination of the Gustav III of Sweden in 1792 was allowed in th late 1850s, Verdi's opera based on the play, *Un Ballo in Maschera* (*A Masked Ball*), had to have its setting changed to seventeenth century North America, with the assassination target transformed into 'Riccardo', the 'colonial governor' of Boston. Earlier the opera had been so severely multilated by the Naples censorship, with changes required in 297 of the 884 lines, that Verdi cancelled a planned production there. Part of the problem in Naples was that Verdi had the bad luck to complete the opera in 1858 shortly before the notorious assassination attempt on Napoleon III at the Paris Opéra, an event which set authorities throughout Europe on edge.[37]

In Britain, Gilbert and Sullivan's *Mikado* was suddenly banned in 1907 after twenty years of unmolested performance, because British officials feared it would give offence to a visiting Japanese prince; it was again permitted after his departure. In France, Eugène Scribe's *Les Huguenots*, about religious strife in that country in the seventeenth century, was allowed in the 1830s in Paris, but was banned from Protestant towns. Thirty years later, the government of Napoleon III censored a number of passages in Jacques Offenbach's operetta *La Grande-Duchesse de Gerolstein*, which gently satirised the European ruling classes, for fear of offending royalty visiting Paris for the 1867 Universal Exposition; yet many rulers and aristocrats liked the production so much that they saw it over and over. After a change in regime in France in 1870, the operetta was banned completely.[38]

Many censorship decisions produced truly ludicrous results. In Austria, *Les Huguenots* was allowed only after it was renamed *The Ghibellines of Pisa* and outfitted with a new libretto that featured thirteenth-century Italians singing a sixteenth-century hymn by Martin Luther. When the word 'Rome' was banned from the Austrian stage after the 1859 Austro-Sardinian war over the fate of Italy, the hero of Wagner's *Tannhäuser* had to be sent 'dort' ('there') for absolution by the Pope. The authorities in Parma in 1837 demanded a change of costume for the female chorus in Donizetti's *Lucia di Lammermoor*: their dresses sported red and green ribbons against a white background, inadvertently reproducing the patriotic colours of Italy. In Milan, the censors forced the heroine of Donizetti's *Maria Padilla* (1841) to die of a 'surfeit of joy' rather than commit suicide, as originally provided in the libretto. Roman censors forced the heroine in Rossini's *L'Italiana in Algeri* (*The Italian Girl in Algiers*) to substitute the nonsensical phrase 'Think of your spouse!' for the original 'Think of your country!'[39]

As in the case of *Un Ballo in Maschera*, Italian censors repeatedly forced Verdi to change the period, the setting and the names of characters in his operas, in what was usually a vain attempt to prevent audiences from reading into them any contemporary significance. Thus *I Vespri Siciliani* (*Sicilian Vespers*, 1855), concerning a thirteenth-century revolt in southern Italy against French rule, could only be performed in Italy (until independence was won in 1860) under the title *Giovanna de Guzman*, with the rebellion removed to faraway Portugal and directed against Spanish rule in the seventeenth century. After the crushing of the Italian revolutions of 1848, Verdi's opera of the same year, *La Battaglia di Legnano* (*The Battle of Legnano*), celebrating a medieval defeat of the Germans by Italian cities, could only be performed under the title *L'Assedio di Haarlem* (*The Siege of Haarlem*), but after the Austrians were ousted from most of Italy in 1859 it was retitled *La Disfatta degli Austriaci* (*The Defeat of the Austrians*).[40]

In Russia, where opera-censorship rules forbade any depiction of ecclesiastics, one Italian journalist noted in 1862 that 'monks are changed into pilgrims, or even magistrates or procurators'.[41] To gain approval for *The Maid of Pskov*, Rimsky-Korsakov had to agree to remove all references to republicanism and self-government in sixteenth-century Pskov. Tchaikovsky was forced to make drastic changes in his opera *The Oprichnik* (1873), which dealt with political abuses during the reign of Ivan the Terrible (the play upon which the opera was based had been banned for eight years before it was first performed in 1867).[42] As one historian of Russian opera notes. *The Oprichnik* was a failure partly because 'in order to comply with the demands of the censor, the central figure of the tragedy, the tyrant himself [Ivan the Terrible], had to be reduced to a mere nonentity'.[43]

One of the more absurd conditions that the French censors imposed on Offenbach's *La Grande-Duchesse de Gerolstein*, was that the heroine-ruler of an imaginary land should not wear a symbolic royal decoration in case it were seen as mocking some real decoration of a visting monarch. The star of the show, Hortense Schneider, got back at the authorities by commissioning a portrait of herself as the Grand Duchess, complete with the forbidden decoration. In another incident involving Offenbach, a duet of two gendarmes was forbidden in his operetta *Geneviève de Brabant* in 1867, because, the censor stated, 'We cannot have the gendarmerie held up to ridicule. However, the duet was approved so long as the gendarmes were given the rank of sergeant rather than corporal (the former rank did not exist in the gendarmerie) and the piece subsequently became the hit of the show. In Britain, the ban on any representation of biblical characters on stage led to bizarre renaming of many operas. Thus, Rossini's *Moses*, which was a great hit in many continental countries with generally far stricter opera-censorship controls than Britain, was presented to British audiences as *Peter the Hermit*.[44]

The frustration caused by the capriciousness of the censorship was heightened by the vague reasons (if any) offered by the censors to explain their actions. In 1850, when the Venetian authorities rejected Verdi's opera *Rigoletto* (based on a play by Victor Hugo that depicted a libertine medieval French king and had been banned in France), they simply declared that the libretto was characterised by 'revolting immorality and obscene triviality' (eventually they approved the opera after decreeing numerous changes). The Naples censorship offered Donizetti no explanation at all for banning his opera *Maria Stuarda* in 1834, leaving him fuming in a letter, '*Stuarda* was prohibited. Heaven knows why. It is enough that one must hold one's tongue, for the King commands it.'[45]

THE IMPACT OF OPERA CENSORSHIP

As a result of opera censorship, composers and librettists not only endured the banning or mutilation of their work, but also censored operas in advance or did not write at all on certain subjects. Thus, William Ashbrook, a leading historian of nineteenth-century Italian opera, writes that, since the 'ultimate authority over the plot and wording of an operatic text lay in the hands of the censors', 'the extent of their influence in Italy during the first six decades of the nineteenth century [after which censorship eased markedly] can scarcely be exaggerated'. He adds that the 'intimidation of librettists' who avoided 'potentially censorable situations' was 'undoubtedly the most insidious aspect of the whole ugly situation, as well as the most far-reaching in view of its ultimate effect upon the composer seeking his inspiration in such a compromised text'.[46] Similarly, Robert Oldani, a historian of the Russian opera, notes that 'any composer or dramatist [in Russia] had to be careful to exclude politically unacceptable material, and it was often difficult to know what would be acceptable and what would not'.[47]

Concrete examples of artistic self-censorship are not hard to find: Bellini abandoned plans to compose an opera based on Victor Hugo's play *Hernani*, since, as he put it, 'the subject would had had to undergo some modifications at the hands of the police' and his librettist did not wish 'to compromise himself'. Donizetti's librettist for *Lucrezia Borgia* assured the manager of La Scala that he could not 'go more carefully as far as the censors were concerned' (although the opera was none the less banned in Naples in 1834). Verdi termed the Naples censorship 'too strict to permit interesting subjects', although during the briefly successful 1848 revolution there he exulted that he could now 'compose absolutely any subject'.[48]

Composers whose operas were censored were filled with the greatest indignation. Verdi was the most outraged, or at least the most vocal, victim of what was his wife termed 'that gloomy thing called the censorship'. When informed in 1850 that *Rigoletto* was 'absolutely forbidden' by the Venetian censorship (it was later allowed with modifications), he wrote to a friend that 'I have almost lost my head', that the banning decree 'reduces me to desperation', and that the 'hurt and displeasure which this prohibition occasions me are so great that I do not have words to describe them'. In December 1851, Verdi wrote to a sculptor friend that his operas *Rigoletto* and *Stiffelio* had been 'ruined' by the Roman censorship, and asked, 'What would you say if a black mask were stuck on the nose of one of your fine statues?' Once, in despair, he suggested that the billboard for *Rigoletto* should read, 'Rigoletto, poetry and music by Don ——', with the censor's name inserted. In 1858 Verdi termed the changes that the Naples censorship required in *Un Ballo in Maschera* an 'artistic murder', and declared'

> The composer who respects his art and himself could not and should not incur dishonour by accepting as material for music written on an entirely different level these bizarreries, which violate the most obvious principles of dramatic art and degrade the artist's conscience. . . . What about drama, what about common sense? Bah! Trash! Trash!

Verdi declared that he was 'in a real hell' owing to the changes the Neapolitan censorship required in *Un Ballo in Maschera*, and subsequently reported that he was 'nauseated' by the Roman censors' treatment of the same opera in 1859: this, he said, was characterised by 'capriciousness, ignorance, the mania to upset everything'. *La Traviata*, too, received a mangling from the Roman censors, who wanted the character of Violetta, the courtesan heroine to be 'purified'. Verdi stormed,

The censors ruined the sense of the drama. They made *La Traviata* pure and innocent. Thanks a lot! Thus, they ruined all the situations, all the characters. A whore must remain a whore. If the sun were to shine at night, it wouldn't be night any more. In short, they don't understand anything![49]

After seeing a performance of his opera *Maria Padilla* in Naples in 1842, another victim of the Italian opera censorship, Donizetti, complained that the opera had been 'massacred unrecognisably by the censors' and 'in a horrible fashion'. Expressing concern over the fate of his *Caterina Cornaro* in the same city, he wrote to a friend, 'I have worked hard and conscientiously on this opera and wouldn't wish to see an interesting subject rendered ridiculous because of the whims of a few or because of perfidy.' After hearing reports of the opening of *Caterina* in Naples in 1844, Donizetti lamented, 'God knows what a slaughterhouse the censorship has created.'[50] Rimsky-Korsakov, responding to the censorship of his opera *Christmas Eve* (based on a story by Gogol), declared bitterly in private, 'It would be better if all of Gogol's works were banned along with my opera. Then, at least, no one would be tempted to write on his subjects.' (On the other hand, Rimsky-Korsakov also admitted privately that some music was so bad that, 'while in theory one can be vehemently opposed to all censorship, in practice you can want to preserve it'.[51])

On the whole, it can scarcely be doubted that, just as with spoken drama, the censorship generally achieved its objective of creating a socially and politically safe opera in most European countries during all or most of the period 1815-1914. While the effect of this musical emasculation upon the course of European history during the nineteenth century can scarcely be evaluated independently of the impact of political repression generally, the impact upon opera and upon composers cannot be exaggereated. Although politically attuned audiences in Italy and elsewhere were able to find contemporary political allusions even in operas set in the distant past and in far-away settings, composers and librettists could not write directly about subjects of concern to them and had to do their work with the censorship constantly in mind. Henry Raynor has noted that under these conditions most operas were 'set in a remote and largely unreal past' and focused on events that were 'romanticized out of reality' and 'which, if they had ever happened, would have happened a long time ago and preferably a long way away'. The composer or librettist had either to risk a series of headlong collisions with the authorities or to accept that his work could never be more than a pleasant decoration of the surfaces of life and to work in a vacuum where political and social realities no longer applied and the relationship of his characters were falsified by their removal from social reality.[52]

In short, political censorship in nineteenth-century Europe created an opera that not only was politically safe but also had virtually any significant connection to reality sterilised and sanitised out of existence.

6 Political Censorship of the Cinema

During the twenty years preceding the outbreak of the First World War in 1914, a new form of entertainment was born: the motion picture. Its accessibility to mass audiences far outstripped that of any previous form of entertainment, and by general consensus the movies were viewed as a far more powerful means of communication than the theatre or the press. Given this perception that the cinema was both the most wide-reaching and powerful means yet developed of communicating with a mass audience, and conservatives' well-established fears of the spread of 'dangerous' ideas through an attractive medium which could speak to all classes of the population, it is not surprising that demands for censorship of the movies developed quickly. Such demands gained widespread support among conservative elites, who generally viewed movies in much the same way as earlier authorities had perceived the theatre, as a hotbed of vice and subversion. They were especially concerned over the enormous appeal (and affordability) of the cinema to the lower classes. Thus, in 1914, a conservative Russian legislator, outraged by a newsreel depicting him in what he viewed as an 'insulting way', termed the movies 'the new plague', and warned his colleagues, 'Beware! It may be I today, but it will be another tomorrow, and the day after loftier persons – in the service of the state – who will be ridiculed by this frightful weapon of propaganda, employed towards the revolutionisation of the popular masses.'[1] Reflecting similar fears, censorship of film was imposed in virtually every European country in the years leading up to the First World War, even as controls over the theatre were coming under growing attack (leading, for example, to the end of drama censorship in France in 1906) and as Russia, the last European country to do so, abolished press censorship in 1905.

The spread of the cinema was phenomenal. The first movies, shown in 1895–96, consisted of little more than short films of everyday life, such as a train arriving at a station, or brief travelogues or comedy sketches, which were typically displayed at fairgrounds or as interludes between live performances at music halls. However, as public fascination with the movies mushroomed, longer films with plots

175

were introduced, and special buildings, known by such terms as 'picture palaces' and 'electric threatres', were constructed to show them. In Berlin alone, the number of cinemas grew from twenty to over 200 between 1905 and 1914. By the latter date, there were over 2500 cinemas throughout Germany, 4500 in Britain, and 1200 each in Russia and France.[2]

The same fantastic growth was reflected in every aspect of the movie industry. Thus, the number of companies engaged in film distribution in Britain grew from three to 464 between 1908 and 1912, and the profits of one of the leading film production companies, Pathé of France, soared from 421,000 francs in 1901–2 to 8 million francs in 1912–13. By 1914, an estimated one-and-a-half million Germans a day attended the cinema. By 1916, twelve times as many Russians went to the movies each year as attended the live theatre, and the total Russian cinema audience exceeded that for all other theatres, concerts, circuses and music halls combined.[3] One Russian observer noted around 1910,

> If you walk in the evenings along the streets of the capital, of the large provincial towns, local towns, large settlements and villages, on every street you will see the same phenomenon with the solitary, flickering kerosene lights: an entrance illuminated by lamps, and by the entrance a crowd waiting in a queue – the cinema. If you look in the auditorium the composition of the audience will amaze you. Everyone is there – students and gendarmes, writers and prostitutes, officers and cadets, all kinds of intellectuals, bearded and with pince-nez, and workers, shop assistants, tradesmen, society ladies, fashionable women, officials – in a word, everyone.[4]

Although, as this observer noted, 'everyone' seemed fascinated by the cinema, the vast majority of audience members belonged to the working class, which among other things reflected the fact that the cheap ticket prices and the highly informal atmosphere of cinemas imposed fewer barriers to the poor than did the higher prices and more refined atmosphere of the live theatre. In Britain, one observer recalled, 'Cinema in the early years of the century burst like a vision into the underman's existence and, rapidly displacing concert and theatre, become both his chief source of entertainment and one of the greatest factors in his cultural development.' Indeed, Gary Stark has concluded that, throughout Europe by 1914, 'next to sex and drink the cinema and become the entertainment medium of the masses.'[5] Much early film was the pictorial equivalent of pulp fiction, with a heavy stress on cheap melodrama, crime stories and sexual escapades and innuendo. The popular Russian name for the cinema, *Illyuziony* ('illusions'), reflected the overwhelming stress of the movies on escapist entertainment for a mass audience. The Russian poet Moravskaya wrote of the movies, 'For those whom life has cheated, open the electric paradise', while the Austrian playwright Hugo von Hofmannsthal termed the cinema 'a substitute for dreams' for the 'masses of working people'.[6]

HOPES AND FEARS FOR A NEW INDUSTRY

Although relatively few early films had major political overtones or contained serious social criticism, the potential of cinema for political propaganda, especially given the working-class domination of the audience, was immediately evident both to the authorities and opposition elements. Among the latter, the French socialist leader Jean Jaurès predicted that the cinema would become 'the theatre of the proletariat'. In 1913, the Russian realist writer Leonid Andreyev predicted that 'an enormous unimaginable socio-psychological role is destined' for what he termed the 'miraculous Kinemo [cinema]'. He exulted that the lack of spoken language in films (all films were, of course, silent at this time) merely made them 'equally comprehensible to the savages of St Petersburg and those of Calcutta'. In this way the cinema became 'the genius of international contact, brings nearer the ends of the earth and the spheres of the soul, and gathers into a single stream the whole of quivering humanity'. Similarly, in 1914, Vladimir Zelensky, a Russian opposition spokesman, called for the development of 'workers cinematographs' since the existing movies were characterised by 'bourgeois vulgarity' and 'cloying philistine morality' that made them 'a servant of capitalists'. Against this, the screen had the potential to 'tell of the life of the workers of all countries, opening the pages of international artistic and scientific book-treasuries, reflecting all the phenomena of social life in living illustrations, in order to demonstrate the advance of the working class in all countries'. Less radical forces also saw positive uses for the cinema, teachers and other professionals being quick to perceive the educational potential of film. As early as 1902, the First Russian Congress of Teachers of Natural History called for the 'cinefication' of the schools, and subsequently organisations ranging from the All-

Russian Congress of Bee-Keepers urged increased use of film for educational purposes. Similarly, a writer in the British *Times Engineering Supplement* noted in 1910 that, while the cinema was 'still in its infancy', it was not a 'mere means of amusement and recreation' but was 'destined to become a most powerful vehicle of instruction' which would 'furnish a powerful education medium in the hands of the teacher and public lecturer'.[7]

The potential of film as a vehicle of propaganda or instruction was, however, a source of trepidation to conservative European governments, which were terrified lest film be used to exert a subversive influence on the masses. Such fears were clearly an important factor behind the establishment of film-censorship mechanisms in virtually all European countries by 1914. Thus, in France before 1914, the Interior Minister periodically warned local officials to ban films that were 'susceptible of provoking demonstrations that might disturb the public order and tranquillity', while the official Bavarian film-censorship guidelines of 1912 barred any film or scene 'contrary to state institutions, public order, religion, morality or decency'. The British Board of Film Censors, a self-censorship organisation run by the film industry and heavily relied upon for guidance by local censorship authorities, declared that it would recommend the censoring of material 'calculated and possibly intended to foment social unrest and discontent', scenes 'which bring into contempt public characters acting in their capacity as such', 'stories showing any antagonistic or strained relations between white men and the coloured population of the British empire' and 'themes calculated to give an air of romance and heroism to criminal characters, the story being told in such a way as to enlist the sympathies of the audience with the criminals, while the constituted Authorities and Administrators of the Law are held up to contempt as being either unjust or harsh, incompetent or ridiculous'.[8]

In Germany, a conservative commentator writing in 1912 noted that the influence of the cinema 'on the population of our cities and in particular on the youth of our large cities is rightly of increasing concern to public opinion', and that the 'great daily papers that consider the future of our people are primarily concerned about the sociopolitical aspect of this burning issue and for this reason most of them demand the strongest possible police censorship'. Reflecting this concern, in 1910 the Berlin police chief told the Prussian Interior Minister that, since movie audiences were primarily lower-class individuals and adolescents, it was 'important that precisely among these kinds of people no film be shown that might leave a false impression about the personalities or actions of any member of our ruling dynasty or that might undermine popular loyalty toward the royal family'. In 1915, a Prussian school inspector complained that popular movies constantly depicted the upper classes as lazy elites living decadent lives of luxury and mistreating the poor. He warned other government officials that 'especially when most moviegoers come from the lower classes' it was dangerous to perpetuate in their minds such 'false perceptions and distorted images'.[9]

In Italy, the Ministry of the Interior's decree of 1914 establishing film-censorship regulations directed censors to ban all movies that could be 'injurious to the national fame and self-respect, or against the public order' as well as material that 'would lessen the name and fame of public institutions and authorities, or of the officers and agents of the law'. In Russia in 1913, Tsar Nicholas II characterised the cinema as 'complete rubbish' and 'an empty, totally useless and even harmful form of entertainment', which only an 'abnormal person' could view as art. That same year, Russian authorities directed the censors to pay the

> strictest attention to films dealing with the lives of workers and under no conditions whatever can there be allowed the exhibition of films depicting difficult forms of labour, agitational activity, nor those containing scenes that may arouse workers against their employers, films of strikes, of the lives of indentured peasants, etc.

Russian film censorship rules also banned the depiction of any 'political murders or attempts at murders' or 'political gatherings or processions except as depict scenes from the distant past of purely historical interest'.[10]

The concern of the ruling classes over the content of movies was not restricted to overtly political material, but also reflected fears that the stress of many of the early films on crime and sex would more subtly and gradually erode the morals and docility of the working classes, especially among children and adolescents, who constituted a large part of cinema audiences. Thus, the Prussian Minister of Culture warned in 1912 that popular junk films were dangerous because they

> exercise a harmful effect on the ethical sensibilities in that they portray unsuitable and ghastly scenes that excite the senses and

unfavourably stimulate the imagination. Viewing such material poisons the impressionable minds of the young just as much as reading trashy pulp fiction or looking at pornography does. Seeing such material on the screen is bound to corrupt one's sense of good and evil. . . . The unspoiled character of many a child can be pointed down the wrong path; the aesthetic sensibilities of the young are also perverted.[11]

While such an erosion of morals and sensibilities might not directly lead to political upheaval, such expressions reflected a general concern that a steady diet of films might cause the lower classes to forget or reject their 'place' in society and engage in various forms of anti-social activity that might threaten the existing order, or reject the moral standards of their social betters. As a historian of the early German cinema notes, 'the state's efforts to control the popular cinema clearly sprang from upper-class fears of the urban lower classes', since it was feared that widespread viewing of films 'by the lower classes would disorient and deprave those classes, undermine their attachment to traditionally sanctioned values, and lead to moral, perhaps even to social, anarchy'.[12]

The movies were especially blamed for inducing criminal behaviour among children. Thus, a Belgian children's court judge declared that his colleagues were 'unanimously of the opinion that the harmful influence of the cinema on Belgian youth is one of the principal causes of crime among children', and the British Home Secretary in 1916 reported that police chiefs in many British towns had declared that the 'recent increase in juvenile delinquency is, to a considerable extent, due to demoralising cinematograph films'. The King of Spain was told in 1912 by a royally sponsored council 'for the Protection of Children and the Repression of Mendacity' that children should be prevented from

frequenting alone displays like the cinematograph, where a numerous public is gathered in the dark, breathing vitiated air and, what is more lamentable, having daily reflected before them the image of lust, passion and crime, a spectacle that may exert lifelong deplorable consequences of a moral and pathological nature of the delicate organism of the child.

A German film critic, writing in 1912, warned of the impact o crime films, which 'seen simultaneously by hundreds has a far mor inflammatory effect, with its glorification of daring criminals, its blood-soaked bull-fights and its brutal executions, than the printed word which is read in private'.[13]

Films were also blamed for encouraging immoral behaviour in darkened theatres. Phrases such as 'knee flirtation' soon developed, and one American writer termed the cinemas 'favorite places for the teaching of homosexual practices'. The police chief of the German town of Bremerhaven declared in 1912 that 'cinemas are often sought out by lovers in the expectation that during the darkness they will have the chance to engage in actions that normally shun the light of day'. Even in Serbia, the Belgrade teachers' magazine *Uchitel* declared in 1913 that films were marked by 'the absolute nonexistence of any art whatever, offering only a misleading satisfaction of the basest sort, constituting a threat above all to young boys and girls'. Authorities in Madrid were so alarmed by the threat movie theatres posed to morals that it was decreed that single men had to sit in one section, single women in another and couples in a third, which had to be illuminated by a red light! Cinemas were also criticised for posing a threat to eyesight and for creating a fire hazard by crowding people together in dangerous conditions, leading one Russian critic of the cinema to term the movies a 'breeding ground of fire, blindness and moral perversion'. The state government of Württemberg in Germany warned in 1913 that movie scenes that kept viewers 'in a state of constant suspense and tension . . . can lead to severe mental agitation, high excitability and even nervous disorders, especially in children or in persons with a minimum of nervous resistence'. A historian of Danish film sums up these complaints by noting that soon 'every breach of the law was blamed on the cinema which gradually became the root of all evil'.[14]

In some cases, opposition to the cinema reflected material self-interest as well as moral and political objections. Thus, live-theatre owners, saloon proprietors and others who viewed movies as an economic threat, and ministers who feared that the movies would decrease attendance at religious services, often joined other, less disinterested opponents of the cinema. In Britain the churches and their supporters forced the closure of cinemas on Sundays for many years, and Russian economic interests who felt threatened briefly succeeded in convincing the Russian government to limit the hours during which cinemas could function.[15]

Collectively, all of these concerns virtually ensured that the cinema, like previous forms of mass communication and entertainment, would come under censorship regulations soon after its emergence. That press and theatre censorship either had been abolished or was under increasing attack mattered little, because the cinema was seen as potentially a far more powerful and threatening medium than either print or the stage, especially given the composition of the audience. Thus, the British Board of Film Censors declared it 'necessary to repudiate the idea that because a story has been published in literary form it is necessarily suitable for the screen', given the 'fundamentally different psychological impression made by the printed word in the book and the photographic representation on the film, a principle which is understood by those with only a rudimentary knowledge of human psychology'. In 1913, a French court, in upholding the legality of film censorship despite the recent abolition of theatre censorship, declared,

> In truth, film shows are not just the image or photograph of the dramatic work [on which they might be based]; they are not made for the same audience; infinitely more varied, proceeding by means different from those used by dramatic authors, they attempt rather to excite and sometimes to astonish public curiosity, rather than to awaken and develop the aesthetic feelings of the spectators.

Similarly, a contemporary German observer noted in 1913 that many considered it indisputable that,

> compared to the traditional theatre, the cinema exerts an infinitely more sustained impact upon the broad masses, that the cinema audiences are more susceptible to suggestive influences, that cinema shows have more suggestive effect on their viewers, and that the type of entertainment shown more often appeals to one's baser instincts.[16]

THE ESTABLISHMENT OF FILM CENSORSHIP

The film-censorship mechanisms established in Europe before 1914 had a haphazard, jerry-built quality reminiscent of early press and theatre censorship. In most countries, censorship of films was first imposed by local authorities under long standing laws or traditions which allowed them to license places of public entertainment. The result was that policies varied wildly from town to town, creating, as in France, a 'crazy quilt of standards and wild fluctuations in censorship practices'.[17] The difficulties that such practices created for film producers and distributors, and the obvious lack of logic evident in a system that allowed a given film to be shown in one town but not in its neighbour, led to growing pressure for more centralised and standardised film-censorship systems. Such systems were established, with varying degrees of centralisation and standardisation, in Sweden in 1911, in Spain in 1912, in Italy, Norway and Britain in 1913, in Denmark and Germany in 1914, and in France in 1916.[18]

In Russia, a haphazard and primitive national censorship was established very early, with police visiting theatres whenever a new programme was first shown. However, the costs this system imposed upon distributors and exhibitors when films already paid for were seized by the police – for example, one importer had paid for twenty prints when a French adaptation of Turgenev's *Fathers and Sons* was confiscated – were so great that distributors convinced the police to watch a preview copy of each film paid for 'on approval' before making arrangements for distribution.[19] (The Russian and German film censorships collapsed with the governments of those countries in 1917–18, but successor regimes soon established their own procedures. As if to prove the thesis that film was more feared than the stage, the Weimar Republic in Germany did not re-establish drama censorship after the fall of the imperial regime, but did re-institute film censorship. Another proof of the principle came in Britain in the 1920s, when Ibsen's *Wild Duck* was permitted on stage, but a film version of the play was forbidden.[20])

In Germany, all the major constituent states developed a standardised censorship system by 1914, and only the outbreak of the First World War sidetracked a legislative proposal by the central government to establish national standards to license and restrict the number of cinemas, on the grounds that films preyed 'on that segment of the population which lacks the education to resist the evil influences of popular films' and that the 'attraction of the cinema for youth and the undereducated classes – an attraction that is enhanced by the cheap admission prices and by the nature of the film advertisements – represents a moral threat to the nation that must absolutely be resisted'.[21] Beginning in about 1906, various German cities had independently initiated film-censorship systems under police administration. Berlin, for example, required theatre operators to submit all films to the police for screening three days before the first scheduled showing. Since each city had its own procedures and standards, this created a confusing patchwork of censorship policies, burdening often unqualified local police with an unwanted task and imposing severe practical difficulties on film distributors and exhibitors. In 1912, the Stuttgart police chief complained of the difficulties untrained police had in reaching intelligent decisions:

> If one of my constables raises an objection to this or that film he is told that it's Shakespeare and that he would be a narrow-minded philistine to object to it. What is the poor policeman to do? If the cinema house owner tells him it is one of Shakespeare's works, then he no longer has the courage to ban it. Or it sometimes happens that in the middle of a private [censorship] screening someone drops a bunch of keys and the policeman, wishing to be helpful, bends down to pick them up. Weeks later it turns out that during this little diversion with the keys one of the most ghastly murder scenes ever put on film was taking place up there on the screen.[22]

As a result of these various difficulties, most major German states, including Prussia, Bavaria, Saxony and Württemberg, gradually created a single centralised state film censors' office, whose decisions were effective throughout the state. In practice, the Berlin film-censorship office became a *de facto* national censorship agency, since film companies generally first submitted their new films to the Berlin censors and other states generally deferred to Berlin's judgement. Although in theory individual cinema owners were supposed to submit their films to the censor, in practice film production and distribution companies cleared films with the censorship before releasing them to cinemas, so that cinema owners would not be faced with last-minute cancellations of films they had already rented and advertised. In Berlin, film censorship was initially handled by the same police officials as were responsible for drama censorship, but after the centralisation of Prussian film censorship in 1912 a special Film Censorship Office (*Filmprufungsamt*) was established, with four Berlin police inspectors charged with reviewing the twenty to thirty films submitted each day for approval.

Several other European countries progressed in this way from haphazard and decentralised to more standardised film censorship. In Denmark, the film industry's demands for standardised policies, along with public criticisms of local censorship officials – as when film censors in Copenhagen and Frederiksberg were charged with being so lax that they were laying 'the foundations for a batch of new lunatic asylums and prisons'[23] led to a ministerial decree establishing a nationwide system of film censorship from January 1914. Under the Danish system, the Minister of Justice appointed a three-man board of censors; in practice one member always represented the Justice Ministry and one was always connected with the theatrical profession. Sweden also used a three-man board, but the King himself made the appointments. In Italy, film censorship was delegated to high ranking national police officials, with the Minister of the Interior entitled to demand further police review if he felt the censors were too lenient. Local authorities in Italy were empowered to supplement the national film censorship by ensuring that advertisements and posters for films were also acceptable. In Spain (under a royal decree of 1912) and in Norway (under a law of 1913), some film-censorship provisions applied nationally, but ultimate authority was delegated to local officials. Under the Norwegian law, local authorities were empowered to decide not only which films could be shown in their districts, but also how many cinemas would be allowed and to whom cinema licences would be granted. In Spain, the inevitable variation of standards from region to region became so great that one historian of Spanish films has concluded that by 1921 censorship was threatening the very existence of the cinema, since each governor and mayor felt free to meddle.

The technical procedures established in Italy and Sweden for applying for censorship clearance were typical of most countries: film companies not only had to supply one or two copies of the film for viewing, but also had to provide written descriptions of the scenes and transcripts of all film titles and sub-titles. The options available to censors were similar everywhere: they could approve a film without cuts, approve it only on condition that changes were made, or ban it completely. Films typically could be approved for both children and adults, approved for children only if accompanied by adults, or restricted to adult audiences. Those applying for censorship approval usually had to pay a fee, based on the length of the film, whether or not the movie was approved. Once approved, as the Italian regulations put it, 'the films thus exhibited must be exactly such as have been licensed', with the exhibitor 'careful not in any way to change the title, sub-titles, reading matter, nor to change the scenes and pictures, to add nothing and to leave the sequence unchanged'.[24]

In Britain, where the British Board of Film Censors had only an advisory role, film producers and exhibitors could ask local authorities to overrule the Board's recommendations (which they sometimes did). Elsewhere, where censorship decisions were reached by official bodies, usually no appeal was possible (as in Denmark until 1933) or appeals could only be addressed to other administrative officials (as in Sweden and Italy). Exceptionally, decisions of the German censors could be challenged in the courts, but such appeals were rarely successful. In one case where an appeal did succeed, a Prussian court overturned a Berlin police ban on a short comedy film of 1913 entitled *A Cheap Meal*, originally forbidden because the censors feared audiences might imitate the disgruntled diner who was shown storming out of a restaurant without paying his bill after being harassed by a surly waiter.[25]

Although in most countries film censorship was originally initiated by local authorities without any clear legislative authority (as in Germany and France) or imposed by royal decree (as in Sweden and Spain), attempts to challenge the fundamental legality of censorship systems failed everywhere. For example, in Britain local authorities were empowered under a law of 1909 to demand proper fire precautions in any cinema before granting the owners a licence to operate, and they used the law as a basis for imposing control over film content (usually, after 1913, by endorsing the recommendations of the Board of Film Censors). Although the 1909 act was clearly passed only with safety considerations in mind (it was entitled a law 'to make better provision for securing safety at Cinematograph and other exhibitions'), a court challenge in 1910 to the further conditions that the London County Council required to be satisified before granting a licence failed when the court decided that the act 'was intended to confer on the county councils discretion as to the conditions which they will impose, so long as those conditions are not unreasonable'.[26] The net result, as one historian of British film has noted, was 'censorship by a completely unofficial body [the industry-run British Board of Film Censors], enforced by the local authorities by means of an Act of Parliament which was originally intended to secure the public's safety'.[27]

In France, film censorship was based on a law of 1790 requiring local officials to license 'public spectacles' (French drama censorship, which ended in 1906, came under a different law). Officials typically granted cinema licences on condition that no films 'liable to undermine public order and morality' should be shown, and to enforce this restriction demanded to inspect films before they were shown to the public. Challenges to the application of the 1790 law to the cinema were rebuffed by the courts, which declared in one case that in banning film scenes viewed as likely 'to provoke disorder or be dangerous to public morality' the authorities were 'only using the powers' given to them.[28] In Germany, the courts had to split hairs to uphold cinema censorship in view of a national press law which barred prior censorship of 'any printed material or pictorial representations that have been reproduced mechanically or chemically for the purpose of public distribution'. The courts held that movies were not covered under the law, since what the viewer saw in the cinema was not the celluloid film itself but its incorporal projected image, which in turn was an optical illusion created by the rapid, successive projection of many individual frames. This meant, the courts held, that no tangible 'pictorial representations' were themselves displayed and thus the press law did not apply![29]

As had been the case previously with censorship of the press and the live theatre, attempts by governments or censorship bodies to explain what principles they used to decide what was permissible were extraordinarily vague, making it impossible for the film industry ever to be sure their efforts would not end up in confiscation or banning orders. Thus, in 1914 the British Board of Film Censors declared its intention to eliminate 'anything repulsive and objectionable to the good taste and better feelings of English audiences'. In Württemberg, under the law of 1914, films were forbidden if their 'subject matter, or the way the material is presented, is likely to endanger the health or morality of the viewer, offend his religious feelings, brutalise his senses, deprave or overexcite his imagination, or blunt and disorient his sense of justice and public order'. Among the guidelines for censors put forward by the 1914 Italian censorship regulations was the directive to avoid scenes 'calculated to unsettle the mind and provoke to evil', while the sole principle articulated by the royal decree of 1911 establishing film censorship in Sweden was the need to ensure that films were not 'contrary to law or morality or might otherwise have a demoralising or excitative effect, or be subversive of morality'. In like manner, the royal decree of 1912 that established film censorship in Spain simply stated that films must be 'free of all pernicious tendencies'; elsewhere it suggested that this would be secured where films presented 'pictures of normal and sane life' and scenes likely to 'stimulate to good actions, and which exalt the love of country and of home and extol the heroism of sacrifice for the welfare of humanity, instead of giving the appearance of reality to fantastic, tragic, comic, terrifying or disturbing scenes'.[30]

POLITICAL FILM CENSORSHIP IN OPERATION

The operation of film censorship in politically charged cases clearly reflected the general political situation in each European country in the years leading up to the First World War. Authoritarian states such as Germany and Russia frequently censored films on the basis of explicitly political considerations (although, curiously, the normally repressive Habsburg government rarely, if ever, imposed film censorship).[31] More democratic regimes such as those in France, Britain and Denmark concentrated more on films thought likely to damage the general moral fibre of the population (especially children) through exessive or unseemly treatment of subjects dealing with violence and sex. Thus, in 1907, the Danish Justice Ministry urged local police chiefs to ensure that nothing be shown in films 'which may be considered offensive either morally or through the way in which the carrying out of crime is shown or which by their nature are apt to corrupt their audience and especially the young people who are usually present in great numbers'. In 1913, the French Interior Ministry similarly instructed local officials to ban 'representations on the cinema screen of recent crimes', since such depictions would 'endanger good order'. The vast majority of the thirty-five films banned outright and the 314 censored in part by the British Board of Film Censors in 1913–14 (of a total of 14,119 films submitted) were found morally objectionable, through their portrayal of, for example, 'indecent dancing', 'cruelty to animals', 'gruesome murders', 'medical operations' and 'scenes suggestive of immorality'.[32]

Even in the relatively democratic lands, explicit political considerations were sometimes invoked. Thus the British Board of Film Censors forbade scenes 'tending to disparage public characters and institutions'. In France, all films dealing with the Dreyfus Affair were banned after 1899 (a restriction lifted only in 1950!) and in 1913 as international tension increased, the French authorities urged local officials to ban all films in which characters appeared in German uniform.[33] Even where films were rarely banned on explicitly political grounds before 1914, the establishment of censorship mechanisms facilitated such decisions in the future. Thus, in Britain, the Russian director Eisenstein's masterpiece *Potemkin* (1925), about the Russian revolution of 1905, was forbidden, as were many other politically touchy films. This decision, and others like it during the 1920s, led one critic of the British system, in which local authorities generally deferred to the film industry's own censorship recommendations, to complain that, given the clear signs of government influence on the Board of Film Censors, Britain was suffering,

> by means of the 'unofficial' censorship, the exercise of a far more stringent ban on politically controversial films, a far more effective indirect expression of the Government's will, than would directly be exercised by an official censorship, responsible and answerable for its acts in the Houses of Parliament.

Indeed, in 1937 the president of the Board of Film Censors triumphantly declared, 'We may take pride in observing that there is not a single film showing in London today which deals with any of the burning questions of the day.' In France, meanwhile, not only was *Potemkin* banned, but for several years, beginning in 1928, all Russian films without exception were forbidden.[34]

In Russia and Germany, explicitly political factors were repeatedly invoked to ban or censor films before the First World War. Thus, the first recorded act of political censorship of the movies occurred in Russia in 1896. Cameras and films were seized after photographers had filmed the Khodinka Field disaster, in which the incompetence of the authorities had occasioned a stampede in which hundreds of persons who had gathered to celebrate the inauguration of Nicholas II were killed (after the disaster, the new tsar danced the night away at a ball while press censorship prevented any mention of the catastrophe). The Russian authorities subsequently confiscated and destroyed all film documenting the revolution of 1905. Entire subjects, such as the French Revolution, and any depiction of the guillotine or the violent death of royalty (even the execution of the sixteenth-century Scottish Queen Mary Stuart) were forbidden by the tsarist authorities. Topics dealing with class struggle also received extremely close attention, with the result that films of Hugo's *Les Misérables* and Zola's *Germinal* were both butchered, and a film about the dangers of alcoholism was banned solely because it had the word 'strike' in the title. Newsreels were also examined with great care, with the result that film of the funeral of an opposition legislative deputy was forbidden for fear that it would spark off demonstrations, and pictures of the famous opposition writer Maxim Gorky in exile in Capri (taken despite the fact that Gorky both beat up and offered bribes to the photographer in a futile effort to secure his privacy) were banned on the specious ground that he was not celebrated enough. Restrictions on photographers were so stringent in Russia that, in order to meet foreign demands for film on such subjects as anti-Jewish pogroms and the 1905 revolution, French cinema companies resorted to such techniques as fabricating 'Russian' news-reels in Paris.[35]

Ironically, despite the severe supervision of the Russian cinema, opposition groups discovered that the darkened theatres presented an unusual opportunity for clandestine agitation. Nikolai Chaykovsky, a socialist, reported the following typical incident from the 1906 elections, during which opposition parties faced severe restrictions on their activites:

> During a film showing in one of the electric-theatres, a voice was heard from somewhere in the completely dark hall, appealing to the audience to vote for the Social-Democratic candidates. In consternation at this illegality the theatre manager ordered lights up. In a few minutes a pale and shaking police inspector entered the theatre, followed by the manager, frigid with horror. The theatre was crowded and the audience, knowing the strength of its numbers, greeted his frightened search with derision. He finally beat a hasty retreat to an accompaniment of whistling and laughter, empty-handed.[36]

In Germany, the police tried to prevent the showing of all movies deemed controversial on political, social or religious grounds. They were particularly on their guard against negative portrayals of German monarchs, past or present, believing that such material might provoke public disturbances or 'might damage patriotism'. Among the films banned in Prussia on such grounds were one about the Portuguese revolution of 1910, seen as glorifying revolution; one about the life of the mentally disturbed nineteenth-century king Ludwig II of Bavaria; and a film of 1913 which was seen as showing the German army in a bad light. As in Russia and Britain, all film portrayals of Jesus Christ were forbidden in Prussia, on the grounds that 'Christ's life would be stripped of its holy, consecrated aura if it were to become part of a show in a commercial cinema', and that such a show would offend 'public sensibilities and would likely cause disruptions of the public order'. In one bizarre decision of 1910, the Berlin police banned a science-fiction film on the grounds that children might believe the 'improbably absurd' scenes of an imaginary future war it contained, such as 'an explosive torpedo being dropped from the sky by an aircraft and burning a city to ashes' and an aircraft being 'hit by an air torpedo and crashing into the sea'. It was reasoned that children who believed 'such utterly fantastic' scenes (which were of course to be realised within a few years) would suffer 'extreme mental agitation and serious nervous disorders'. Overall, 15 per cent of the films submitted to the Prussian authorities in September and October 1911 were banned or partly censored, and the same fate befell 18 per cent of movies submitted to the Bavarian authorities over a five-month period in 1912.[37]

Although the movies' potential for political subversion was a source of enormous concern to the European ruling classes in the years leading up to the First World War, few if any early films posed any serious threat to the existing order or could be classified as political propaganda of any kind. Escapism, not political activism, was the main focus of pre-1914 cinema. And, ironically, when film was first deliberately and extensively used for political propaganda, during the First World War, it was so used not by domestic subversives but by governments themselves, to whip up support for their policies at home and abroad. Thus, General Erich Ludendorff informed the German War Ministry in 1917,

> The war has shown the overwhelming force of pictures and film as a medium for educating and influencing the masses. Unfortunately our [foreign] enemies have used the advantage they have over us in this field so completely that we have suffered considerable damage. . . . For this reason it is desirable, if the war is to be brought to a successful conclusion, to ensure that film is used to make the deepest possible impression wherever German influence is still possible.[38]

Even after the war, it was regimes such as those of Bolshevik Russia and Nazi Germany, rather than domestic opposition groups, that led the way in the use of film for propoganda. Thus, shortly after taking power in Russia, Lenin ordered the production of films 'contrasting the oppression and misery in the capitalist world – colonial rule in India, starvation in Berlin – with the progress of the new Russia'. He said that these films should be shown 'especially in villages and in the East [of Russia], where they are yet novelties and where our propaganda will thus be especially successful'. Scores of *agitki* (short propaganda films) were produced as one of the top priorities of ther new Bolshevik regime, with over 110,000 children attending such films in Moscow alone in the second half of 1918, and hundreds of thousands of others watching them in travelling propaganda trains (*agitpoezda*) and even on a propaganda steamship which brought movies to rural areas where peasants had never before seen them. Lenin quickly concluded, 'Of all the arts, for us cinema is the most important.'[39]

7 Conclusions

Political censorship in nineteenth-century Europe can be usefully perceived as a combination of political Rorschach test and barometer, reflecting with great accuracy the fears of regimes and the general political atmosphere within each country at any particular time. As a Rorschach test, censorship registered for each ruling elite the type and degree of the fears it felt with regard to its own population. Thus, the heightened fears which most European regimes had of the 'unwashed masses' were reflected in censorship provisions which were particularly designed to control the availability and content of media that were especially accessible to the poor. Because many of these fears were exaggerated and irrational, the same was often true of the political censorship that sought to allay them. And, because the intensity of these fears varied from time to time and from place to place, the harshness of political censorship in different countries and periods during the nineteenth century was high variable.

As a barometer, the varying harshness of political censorship in nineteenth-century Europe provides a measure of the general political atmosphere within each country at any particular time. As pointed out in Chapter 1, political censorship functioned within the general context of a broader network of political controls, including restrictions on the suffrage and on freedom of assembly and association, and strong restraints on the content and availability of education. The harshness of political censorship usually reflected the severity of political controls in general within each country, often with an extraordinary precision that makes it an extremely sensitive measure of the political atmosphere, at least with regard to tolerance of dissent and the extent of authoritarianism.

Thus, virtually everywhere in Europe, political censorship was tightened up in the aftermath of the French Revolution and the revolutions of 1848 as part of a more general reactionary trend. On the other hand, just as everywhere in Europe the general trend over the course of the nineteenth century as a whole was in the direction of a more-or-less reluctant yielding to pressures for greater democraticisation, so, everywhere, censorship controls were looser in 1914 than they had been in 1815. But, again reflecting the role of political censorship as a general political barometer, throughout the nineteenth century the more liberal regimes of North-western Europe generally exercised a more tolerant political censorship than did the relatively authoritarian regimes of South-western, Central and Eastern Europe.

Within each regime, changes in the legislation governing political censorship and in the way it was administered typically reflected broader political currents. Thus, historians have noted that in France 'all political changes were soon accompanied by a modification of the press laws' and that the size of the 'security bond' required to establish a newspaper fluctuated in 'inverse ratio to the liberality of the regime and also to the degree of security it felt it enjoyed'.[1] The barometrical role of censorship rules is also extraordinarily clear in relation to changes in the French laws governing the theatre and caricature. Liberal revolutions in France in 1830, 1848 and 1870 each led to the termination of prior censorship of those media, while growing conservative fears of lower-class upheavals led to the reinstitution of censorship of caricature and the theatre within a few years in each case. Thus, one observer of French politics observed that, 'One could, one day, write an exact history of the liberty which we enjoy during the era that we live through by writing a history of our caricatures.'[2] The same would be true, to varying degrees, for political censorship of other media and in other countries.

As a combined Rorschach test and barometer, political censorship provides considerable insight into the minds of the political elites of nineteenth-century Europe. Although censorship of the press, drawings, the theatre and opera started long before the nineteenth century, all these media were subjected to more detailed and systematic regulation after 1789 than ever before. This greater degree of control clearly reflected the fears generated by the French Revolution and the emergence of non-aristocratic actors onto the political stage as Europe rapidly modernised after 1789. The huge amount of money and energy and the large numbers of personnel devoted to political censorship during the nineteenth century demonstrates that the European governing classes clearly took mass public opinion seriously and feared it greatly. In short, they cared deeply about what the masses thought, because the French Revolution demonstrated that 'subversive' ideas, widely circulated and adopted, might ultimately lead to very real threats to the power, wealth and ultimately the lives of the traditional elites.

The basic guiding principle of all nineteenth-century political censorship was the suppression of the circulation of ideas that were seen as especially threatening to governments in power. As noted previously, Odile Krakovitch, the leading expert on French theatre censorship during the nineteenth century, has concluded, 'whether the censors based their actions on political, religious or moral grounds, they always acted on one and the same principle: the defence of the social class in power' and 'respect for the established order'.³ Since the particular threats to the 'established order' and the degree of fear felt by political elites differed from country to country, so did the focus and intensity of censorship policies, reflecting their function as Rorschach tests of fear. Thus, before 1860 in Italy, censors in the Austrian-dominated Italian states especially concentrated on appeals to anti-Austrian sentiment and to Italian nationalism, issues that of course were of little concern to censors elsewhere. This focus led to such absurdities as the substitution of 'Think of your spouse' for 'Think of your country' in a Rossini opera produced in Rome, a change that surely would not have been made in most (if any) other countries. The turbulent history of France led censors there to be especially watchful for references to past revolutions or rulers regarded as symbolic representatives of principles opposed to the existing regime. Therefore there was a ban on stage references to the Bourbon dynasty during the reign of Napoleon, followed by a ban on references to Napolean during the Bourbon restoration. While almost all nineteenth-century governments were fundamentally conservative and therefore directed their censorship fire exclusively to the Left, conservatives also suffered where regimes felt threatened from the Right. Thus, when a centrist republican regime gained power in France in the late 1870s, it did not hesitate to impose harsh censorship on caricatural attacks from both the republican Left and the monarchist Right.

The degree to which each regime feared its own population was generally reflected in the level of absurdity of the country's censorship policies. Probably the most fearful regimes in nineteenth-century Europe were those in Austria under Francis I (1792–1835) and Russia under Nicholas I (1825–55). Therefore, it is not surprising to find that under Francis the slogan 'liberté' was not tolerated on the sides on imported china boxes, while under Nicholas cookbooks could not refer to 'free air' in ovens. While both the Prussian and the Russian regimes were extremely fearful of their populations throughout the nineteenth century, the level of anxiety was clearly more extreme in Russia. Thus, while the Prussian regime forbade any stage representation of members of the ruling dynasty, living or dead, that might 'undermine popular loyalty toward the royal family', the

Russian regime, not taking any chances, banned all portrayals of Romanov-dynasty tsars in the theatre and opera, and even judged it 'unseemly' for pre-Romanov-dynasty rulers to sing in operas (they could, however, appear in plays).

While the intensity and focus of censorship policies varied from regime to regime and time to time, all nineteenth-century European regimes were especially fearful of the rising political interest of the poor and their increasing potential for organised political activity. Although, at the beginning of the nineteenth century, the middle class as well as the poor were viewed by the ruling elites in most countries as potential threats to their power, their worst nightmares always centred around working-class upheavals fuelled by egalitarian and socialist ideologies. Therefore, a continuing major focus of political censorship was the media most likely to appeal to the poor, particularly where this appeal was coupled with advocacy of threatening ideologies. This especially became the case after about 1850, when the traditional elites realised that the upper middle classes shared their fears of the masses and wanted not to overthrow but to join their social and political betters. Thus, the general acceptance, almost everywhere in Europe, by 1870 of freedom of the press from prior censorship, and the easing of stage censorship in the latter part of the nineteenth century, in practice often meant that the middle-class oriented press and theatre became largely free of government harassment, while plays and newspapers oriented towards the lower classes and perceived as espousing radical ideologies and/or fanning class hatred continued to be constantly threatened with severe reprisals. This discriminatory application of political-censorship rules again provides a general barometer of political change, coinciding with similar class-based discrimination after 1870 in the lack of availability of secondary education to the poor, in the biased administration of laws concerning freedom of assembly and association, and in the continued exclusion of the poor from the suffrage or the adoption of rigged suffrage systems which undervalued or counted out their votes.

The especial fear of the poor that afflicted nineteenth-century European regimes explains much of what otherwise would appear as a contradictory hodge-podge of censorship regulations. Thus, attempts to exert strict control of what was accessible to the poor explains the widespread adoption of special press taxes; the exemption, in Germany after 1819 and in Russia after 1865, of long books but not short ones from prior censorship; and the practice, in

Russia and Austria, of barring certain books from general sale but making them legally available to selected individuals. Similar considerations probably explain why in a number of countries, the largely middle-class oriented 'free theatres' were generally unmolested by the authorities when they put on plays not submitted to the censorship, and why in France and Germany dramas could sometimes be legally performed in some theatres and not others (recall that in overturning a police ban on Hauptmann's *The Weavers* a Berlin court in 1893 noted that the theatre presenting it was 'visited primarily by members of those circles of society who do not tend towards acts of violence or other disturbances of public order').[4]

Concern about the particular danger posed by media which attracted large crowds of the undesirable 'circles of society', and about their perceived persuasive powers, also explains the otherwise baffling differences between the media in the intensity and longevity of the political censorship to which they were subjected by nineteenth-century European regimes. Most governments censored pictures more harshly than print, and some governments, such as those of Russia and France, continued to censor caricatures long after press censorship had been abolished. Almost all regimes maintained theatre censorship long after abolishing press and caricature censorship. Cinema censorship was inaugurated after 1900 in seeming contradiction to the general trend towards an easing of censorship controls – a trend which led, for example, to the abolition of press censorship in Russia in 1905, the end of theatre censorship in France in 1906, and the temporary end of stage censorship in Russia and Germany in 1917–18.

These seemingly inconsistent policies were in fact quite consistent and logical from the standpoint of the fears of the European governments which administered them, since in each case the longevity and harshness of censorship controls was in proportion to the accessibility of the medium to the poor, the social context in which it was 'consumed', and its perceived power in transmitting images and ideas. Of all the media subject to censorship in nineteenth-century Europe, the press was ultimately seen as the least threatening, because many poor people were illiterate and because it was usually 'consumed' by solitary individuals or at most by small groups. Press censorship also became in many countries a highly symbolic political target of the middle-class elites, which, in view of their increasingly critical economic role, most European governments felt the need to court by mid-century. These factors, combined with the available arsenal of post-publication prosecutions and special press taxes which could be used to keep the lower-class oriented press in check, explain why press censorship toppled first. Reflecting the barometer function of political censorship, in several countries abolition of press censorship roughly coincided with the enfranchisement of the middle classes (thus, in France, the abolition of press censorship in 1830 was accompanied by an extension of the franchise to middle-class elements of the population, and there were similar developments in Prussia in 1848–9, Piedmont in 1848, Spain in 1837, and both Austria and Hungary in 1867). Similarly, it is no coincidence that censorship of the press was abolished last in Russia, which was also the generally most repressive regime in Europe and the last to implement constitutional government and to establish an elected legislature.

Although in most countries censorship of caricature was abolished at the same time as press censorship, the harsher administration of caricature censorship, together with its continuation after the end of prior censorship of the press in Russia, France and Portugal, reflected the greater accessibility of drawings to the illiterate and also the perception that drawings had a much greater impact and were therefore more to be feared than the printed word. Thus, while the authorities in France after 1830 and in Russia after 1905 felt they could take the risk of having subversive attacks appear in print, prosecuting after publication, they were not willing to run the same risk with caricatures until 1881 in France and never before 1914 in Russia (except for a few months during the 1905 revolution). Plays and operas too were accessible to the poor and perceived as more powerful than the printed word, but, unlike caricature, they were 'consumed' by large groups of people gathered together at once, and so seemed even more dangerous. Because of this, prior censorship of the stage continued in almost all European countries long after censorship of the press and caricature had been abolished. The emergence of the cinema brought new censorship controls. Like the stage, the cinema was feared as a forum of mass entertainment, but the strength of its appeal to the poor and its greater accessibility to them, owing to low ticket prices, made it seem the most dangerous medium of all. Thus, even those few countries which had abolished prior stage censorship by 1910, such as France and Sweden, inaugurated film censorship shortly after the proliferation of films had begun.

It is traditional for the author of a study such as this to conclude by arguing that the subject he has examined is clearly of immense significance. While, as will be argued below, political censorship was unquestionably of importance in shaping the course of European history in the nineteenth century, it is not possible to reach a more precise conclusion concerning its overall significance. This is so for at least three reasons.

First, this book has examined political censorship of five different media over a period of 100 years in many different countries, and has found censorship so variable by medium, time and country that any summary statement concerning its significance would be a gross oversimplification.

Secondly, as Chapter 1 sought to stress, political censorship was part of a much broader fabric of political controls in nineteenth-century Europe, and it is not possible to disentangle the impact of political censorship from these other controls. For example, if the European masses remained largely impotent politically until late in the nineteenth century, how can one prove that this was because censorship prevented the spread of dissident ideas rather than because education was politically manipulated, the suffrage was withheld from the poor, and freedom to organise was denied them?

Thirdly, to the extent that censorship succeeded in its aims, it created 'non-events' that cannot be accurately assessed and measured: it not only blocked the distribution or presentation of works that had already been created, but also prevented the creation of works that might have been produced but for fear of censorship. How can one possibly accurately assess the potential impact of works that could not be distributed, let alone newspapers and caricatures that were never created, books, plays and operas that were never written, and films that were never produced? In Tolstoy's haunting statement, 'What matters is not what the censor does to what I have written, but to what I might have written.'[5] Tolstoy was clearly not alone. As prior discussions of the impact of censorship on the various media clearly suggest, many nineteenth-century European authors and artists did not write newspaper articles, books, plays and operas that they feared would be banned, and often self-censored what they did create. Thus, recall the Russian playwright Griboyedov, who rebuked himself for 'spoiling as much as possible' his drama *Woe from Wit* in order to fulfil 'the childish ambition to hear my verses in the theatre'.[6]

Despite the impossibility of formulating a precise assessment of the overall significance of political censorship in nineteenth-century Europe, some conclusions can be drawn. Fear of the censorship unquestionably did kill many 'subversive' ideas in the crib, and the censors themselves clearly prevented or mutilated before publication or presentation tens of thousands of news articles, books, plays, caricatures, operas and films. Hundreds of newspapers and plays were suppressed, and thousands of journalists as well as many caricaturists were fined, jailed or exiled for violating censorship laws. Censorship controls largely explain the general lack of realistic drama and opera in nineteenth-century Europe, as well as the similarly anodyne quality of most works of journalism and caricature before 1870. As part of the broader network of political controls, the censorship helped to delay the emergence and hinder the organisation of opposition groups, especially from the working class, and played a particularly significant role in retarding political democratisation in those countries with the most stringent, extensive and enduring censorship systems – Austria, Italy and France before about 1880, and Hungary, Spain, Russia and Prussia throughout the nineteenth century.

Probably the best evidence that political censorship played a considerable role in blocking the dissemination of opposition thought is the rapid and extensive flowering of such ideas when censorship and other political controls collapsed amidst the 1848 revolutions in France, Austria, Germany and Italy and during the 1905 revolution in Russia, as well as when repressive restrictions were terminated by regimes under less pressing circumstances. Thus, with the end of censorship in Germany in 1848, France in 1881 and Russia in 1905, there was an explosion in the number of caricature journals. Similarly, in revolutionary Europe in 1848, hundreds of newspapers sprang up almost overnight – 400 in France alone – but they collapsed or were crushed just as quickly when repressive controls were reinstituted. There were also sudden explosions of general political organisation when restrictions on freedom of assembly and association collapsed; in 1848 and in Russia in 1905, and equally sudden contractions of activity followed when the authorities regained control.[7] The lifting of special press taxes also had an immediately invigorating impact upon the number of newspapers published and their circulations. Thus, British newspapers doubled their circulation within two years of the drastic lowering of the stamp tax there in 1836.

Censorship clearly had a drastic impact upon the circulation of ideas in nineteenth-century Europe. Yet this impact was probably less than either the authorities expected or the dissidents feared. Censorship restrictions were widely evaded by determined publishers, artists and consumers and on many occasions helped stimulate the public's interest in and craving for 'forbidden fruit', thereby actually increasing general awareness of the censored material. Readers and audiences also often collaborated with writers and artists to read into or see in works approved by the authorities an anti-regime message that the censors failed to perceive, proving Stendhal's comment (made about Italians) that, 'If you are dealing with a race which is at once dissatisfied and witty, everything becomes an "allusion".[8] Aside from the fact that political censorship was rarely evasion-proof, it was probably less significant than either regimes or dissidents believed for another reason: governments had grossly exaggerated fears and opposition elements had equally exaggerated hopes of what would happen if the press and the arts were freed from censorship controls. All of the media subjected to censorship in nineteenth-century Europe were feared by the ruling elites as threatening the overthrow of the whole social and political order. Thus, Metternich saw the press as the 'greatest' evil of the day, a French police minister in 1852 termed caricatures 'one of the most dangerous' threats to a 'well-ordered society', and the cinema was seen as a possible threat to the political order, good morals and even eyesight. On the other hand, those who advocated an end to political censorship held out the promise of heaven on earth if they had their way. A free press would inaugurate the reign of truth and justice, an uncensored stage would bring about the education of the masses and end class conflict, and the cinema would, in the words of one Russian writer, unite all humanity, as it 'brings nearer the ends of the earth and the spheres of the soul, and gathers into a single stream the whole of quivering humanity'.[9]

Where political censorship was abolished it brought about, in fact, neither the sudden toppling of governments (although sometimes the toppling of governments led to the end of censorship) nor the solution of all human ills. Ultimately the struggle over political censorship was both a practical and a symbolic part of the broader struggle over power and principles that dominated domestic politics in nineteenth-century Europe. The struggle against censorship was won by 1914 in some countries, at least in some spheres, while stalemate persisted in other spheres and other countries. However, everywhere the broader political struggles continued, much as before.

Notes

Preface

1. 'Arts in Seoul: Censors Lift Veil a Bit', *New York Times*, 20 Sep 1987; 'Seoul is Accused of Press Controls', *New York Times*, 26 Oct 1986; 'Censored: S. Korean Government Decides What's News', *Ann Arbor News*, 24 June 1986; 'Regulated: Press Curbs Still Tight in S. Korea', *Ann Arbor News*, 26 Mar 1987.

2. 'Poland's Press After the Crackdown', *Columbia Journalism Review*, Sep–Oct 1984, pp. 36–9; 'Taiwan Magazines Play "Mice" to the Censor's "Cat"', *New York Times*, 4 Feb 1985; 'A Risky Refrain in Taiwan: Calls for "Self-Determination"', *New York Times*, 14 Dec 1986; 'Indonesia vs. Press: Twain Can't Meet', *New York Times*, 1 May 1986; 'Even Tighter Press Curbs in South Africa', *Manchester Guardian Weekly*, 21 Dec 1986; 'Holding the Front Page', *Manchester Guardian Weekly*, 29 June 1986; 'The Manacles on South Africa's Media', *New York Times*, 23 June 1986; 'South Africa Bans Oscar-Nominated Film', *New York Times*, 7 Mar 1987; 'Nicaragua: Strange Workings of the Censor', *Manchester Guardian Weekly*, 1 June 1986; 'Argentine Films Thrive Anew', *Ann Arbor News*, 4 Mar 1987; 'Portrait of a Playwright as an Enemy of the State', *New York Times*, 23 Mar 1986; 'Illegal Drama in Living Rooms – and a Bit of Cultural Breathing Space', *New York Times*, 29 Mar 1987.

Chapter 1 The Context of Political Censorship in Nineteenth-Century Europe

1. J. M. Roberts, *History of the World* (New York, 1983) p. 657.

2. Theodore Hamerow, *The Birth of a New Europe: State and Society in the Nineteenth Century* (Chapel Hill, NC, 1983) p. 135.

3. Alain Plessis, *The Rise and Fall of the Second Empire, 1852–1871* (Cambridge, 1985) p. 111.

4. Eric Hobsbawm, *The Age of Revolution, 1789–1848* (New York, 1962) p. 248.

5. Hamerow [note 2] p. 119.

6. Jerome Blum, *The End of the Old Order in Rural Europe* (Princeton, NJ, 1978) p. 422.

7. Charles Ruud, *Fighting Words: Imperial Censorship and the Russian Press, 1804–1906* (Toronto, 1982) pp. 58, 69.

8. Frederick Artz, *Reaction and Revolution, 1814–1832* (New York, 1963) p. 238; Oscar Jaszi, *The Dissolution of the Habsburg Monarchy* (Chicago, 1966), p. 80; Bolton King, *A History of Italian Unity*, I (London, 1912) 39; Irene Collins, *The Age of Progress: A Survey of European History, 1789–1870* (London, 1964) p. 39; Nicholas Riasanovsky, *A Parting of*

Ways: Government and the Educated Public in Russia (Oxford, 1976) p. 131.

9. J. McClelland, *Autocrats and Academics: Education, Culture and Society in Tsarist Russia* (Chicago, 1979) pp. 116–17; Hans Rogger, *Russia in the Age of Modernisation and Revolution, 1881–1917* (London, 1983) p. 133; Andrew Janos, *The Politics of Backwardness in Hungary, 1825–1945* (Princeton, NJ, 1982) pp. 162–3.

10. W. L. Guttsman, *The German Social Democratic Party, 1875–1933* (London, 1981) p. 65; Norman Stone, *Europe Transformed, 1878–1919* (London, 1983) p. 121; Jay Bergman, *Vera Zasulich* (Stanford, Calif., 1983) p. 67.

11. Robert Gildea, *Barricades and Borders: Europe 1800–1914* (Oxford, 1987) p. 358.

12. Douglas Chalmers, *The Social Democratic Party of Germany* (New Haven, Conn., 1964) p. 7.

13. John Snell, *The Democratic Movement in Germany, 1789–1914* (Chapel Hill, NC, 1976) p. 15; B. J. Hovde, *The Scandinavian Countries, 1720–1865* (Boston, Mass., 1943) p. 600; Gerald Brenan, *The Spanish Labyrinth* (Cambridge, 1964) p. 56; Gildea [note 11] p. 36; J. N. Westwood, *Endurance and Endeavour: Russian History, 1812–1980* (Oxford, 1981) p. 16.

14. Gildea [note 11] p. 249; Mary Jo Maynes, *Schooling in Western Europe: A Social History* (Albany, NY, 1985) pp. 54, 105; Martin Clark, *Modern Italy, 1871–1982* (London, 1984) p. 37.

15. P. L. Alston, *Education and the State in Tsarist Russia* (Stanford, Calif., 1969) p. 129; Hamerow [note 2] p. 161; Roger Magraw, *France 1815–1914: The Bourgeois Century* (Oxford, 1983) p. 83.

16. C. McClelland, *State, University and Society in Germany, 1790–1914* (Cambridge, 1980) pp. 218–19; A. J. May, *The Age of Metternich, 1814–1848* (New York, 1963) p. 79; Maurice Agulhon, *The Republican Experiment, 1848–1852* (Cambridge, 1983) p. 177; Snell [note 13] p. 249.

17. William Langer, *Political and Social Upheaval, 1832–1852* (New York, 1969) p. 55; James Sheehan, *German Liberalism in the Nineteenth Century* (Chicago, 1978) p. 155; Edward Berenson, *Populist Religion and Left-Wing Politics in France, 1830–1852* (Princeton, NJ, 1984) pp. 106, 210; William Hayes, *The Background and Passage of the Third Reform Act* (New York, 1982) p. 17; Vincent Knapp, *Austrian Social Democracy, 1889–1914* (Washington, DC, 1980) p. 62.

18. Denis Mack Smith, *Italy: A Modern History* (Ann Arbor, Mich., 1959) p. 200; P. G. Eidelberg, *The Great Rumanian Peasant Revolution of 1907* (The Hague, 1968) p. 18; Brenen [note 13] pp. 5–6.

19. D. Kosary and S. Vardy, *History of the Hungarian Nation* (Astor Park, Fla., 1969) p. 174.

20. Gerald Meaker, *The Revolutionary Left in Spain, 1814–1923* (Stanford, Calif., 1974) pp. 3–4; Clark [note 14] p. 64.

21. John Moses, *Trade Unionism in Germany*, I (London, 1982) 104; Stone [note 10] p. 170.

22. Westwood [note 13] p. 190.

23. Janos [note 9] p. 153; Otto Kahn-Freund, *Labour Law and Politics in*

the Weimar Republic (Oxford, 1981) p. 23; Victoria Bonnell, *Roots of Rebellion: Workers' Politics and Organizations in St Petersburg and Moscow, 1900–1914* (Berkeley, Calif., 1983) p. 425.

24. R. Aminzade, *Class, Politics and Early Industrial Capitalism: A Study of Mid-Nineteenth-Century Toulouse* (Albany, NY, 1981) p. 74; A. J. Whyte, *The Evolution of Modern Italy* (New York, 1965) p. 48; Guttsman [note 10] p. 61; Snell [note 13] p. 203.

25. John Gooch, *Armies in Europe* (London, 1980) p. 57; Charles Tilly, 'Collective Violence in European Perspective', in Hugh Graham and Ted Gurr (eds), *Violence in America* (New York, 1969) p. 42; Peter Stearns, *Revolutionary Syndicalism and French Labor* (New Brunswick, NJ, 1971) p. 14.

Chapter 2　Political Censorship of the Press

1. Alex Hall, *Scandal, Sensation and Social Democracy: The SPD Press and Wilhelmine Germany, 1890–1914* (Cambridge, 1977) p. 13.

2. Vincent Godefroy, *The Dramatic Genius of Verdi* (New York, 1977) II, 50; J. L. Talmon, *Romanticism and Revolt: Europe 1815–1848* (New York, 1967) p. 35; Donald Emerson, *Metternich and the Political Police* (The Hague, 1968) p. 116; A. Aspinall, *Politics and the Press c. 1780–1850* (London, 1949) p. 42; A. Aspinall, 'The Social Status of Journalists at the Beginning of the Nineteenth Century', *Review of English Studies*, 21 (1945) 227.

3. Nancy Nolte, 'Government and Theater in Restoration France', *Consortium on Revolutionary Europe Proceedings 1985* (Athens, Ga., 1986), p. 435; Howard Vincent, *Daumier and his World* (Evanston, Ill., 1968), p. 52; Jeffrey Brooks, *When Russia Learned to Read: Literacy and Popular Literature, 1861–1917* (Princeton, NJ, 1985) p. 331; Harry Hearder, *Italy in the Age of the Risorgimento* (New York, 1983) p. 289; Aspinall, 'Social Status' [note 2] p. 218; Stephen Koss, *The Rise and Fall of the Political Press in Britain: The Nineteenth Century* (Chapel Hill, NC, 1981) p. 59.

4. Lenore O'Boyle, 'The Image of the Journalist in France, Germany and England, 1815–1848', *Comparative Studies in Society and History*, 10 (1968) 306; Frederick Artz, *France under the Bourbon Restoration* (Cambridge, Mass., 1931) p. 84; D. L. Rader, *The Journalists and the July Revolution in France* (The Hague, 1973) p. 222; Henri Troyat, *Divided Soul: The Life of Gogol* (New York, 1973) p. 435.

5. O'Boyle [note 4] pp. 297–8, 316; Alan Lee, *The Origins of the Popular Press in England, 1855–1914* (London, 1976) p. 24.

6. Louis Ingelhart, *Press Freedoms: A Descriptive Calendar of Concepts, Interpretations, Events and Court Actions from 4,000 B.C. to the Present* (Westport, Conn., 1987) p. 179; Kenneth Olson, *The History Makers: The Press of Europe from its Beginnings through 1965* (Baton Rouge, La., 1966) p. 156; A. Aspinall, 'The Circulation of Newspapers in the Early Nineteenth Century', *Review of English Studies*, 22 (1946) 430; O'Boyle [note 4] pp. 300, 306.

Notes						205

7. Artz [note 4] p. 84; John Hohenberg, *Free Press/Free People: The Best Cause* (New York, 1971) p. 25; Aspinall, *Politics and the Press* [note 2] p. 58; Lee [note 5] p. 42.

8. Ronald Searle, Claude Roy and Bernd Bornemann, *La Caricature: art et manifeste* (Geneva, 1974) p. 12; Raymond Carr, *Spain, 1808–1939* (Oxford, 1966) p. 240; Frederick Artz, *Reaction and Revolution, 1814–1832* (New York, 1963) p. 67.

9. Anthony Smith, *The Newspaper: An International History* (London, 1979) p. 76; Charles Ruud, 'Limits on the "Freed" Press of 18th- and 19th-Century Europe', *Journalism Quarterly*, 56 (1979) 522.

10. Lee [note 5] p. 21; Elie Halévy, *England in 1815* (New York, 1961) p. 159; Eugene N. and Pauline R. Anderson, *Political Institutions and Social Change in Continental Europe in the Nineteenth Century* (Berkeley, Calif., 1967) p. 253; Aspinall, 'Social Status' [note 2] p. 216; O'Boyle [note 4] p. 309; John Merriman, *The Agony of the Republic: The Repression of the Left in Revolutionary France, 1848–1851* (New Haven, Conn., 1978) p. 39.

11. Lee [note 5] p. 27; Raphael Samuel et al., *Theatres of the Left, 1880–1935: Workers' Theatre Movements in Britain and America* (London, 1985) p. 191; James Cuno, 'Philipon et Desloges', *Cahiers de l'Institut d'Histoire de la Presse et de l'Opinion*, 7 (1983) 152; Koss [note 3] p. 70; Peter Kenez, *Birth of the Propaganda State* (Cambridge, 1985) p. 26.

12. Joel Weiner, *The War of the Unstamped: The Movement to Repeal the British Newspaper Tax, 1830–1836* (Ithaca, NY, 1969) p. 120; Stephen Kippur, *Jules Michelet* (Albany, NY, 1981) pp. 116, 119; Saul Padover, *Karl Marx on Freedom of the Press and Censorship* (New York, 1974) p. xiv.

13. B. J. Hovde, *The Scandinavian Countries, 1720–1865* (Boston, Mass., 1943) pp. 541–2; Svend Thorsen, *Newspapers in Denmark* (Copenhagen, 1953) pp. 7–8.

14. Clara Lovett, *The Democratic Movement in Italy, 1830–1876* (Cambridge, Mass., 1982) p. 162; Werner Conze and Dieter Groh, 'Working Class Movement and National Movement in Germany between 1830 and 1871', in *Mouvements nationaux d'independence et classes populaires aux XIXe et XXE siècles* (Paris, 1971) p. 157.

15. Eugene Rice, *The Foundations of Early Modern Europe, 1460–1559* (New York, 1970) p. 10; Robert Shackleton, *Censure and Censorship: Impediments to Free Publication in the Age of Enlightenment* (Austin, Tex., 1975) p. 22.

16. David Pottinger, *The French Book Trade in the Ancien Régime* (Cambridge, Mass., 1958) pp. 56, 64; Henry Schulte, *The Spanish Press, 1470–1966* (Urbana, Ill., 1968) p. 115; Robert Darnton, *The Literary Underground of the Old Regime* (Cambridge, Mass., 1982) p. 185; Lucien Febvre and Henri-Jean Martin, *The Coming of the Book* (London, 1984) pp. 299, 305, 310; Charles Ruud, *Fighting Words: Imperial Censorship and the Russian Press, 1804–1906* (Toronto, 1982) p. 19; Albert Ward, *Book Production, Fiction and the German Reading Public, 1740–1800* (Oxford, 1974) p. 99; John Lough, *Writer and Public in France: From the Middle Ages to the Present Day* (Oxford, 1978) p. 174.

17. Ingelhart [note 6] p. 24; Febvre and Martin [note 16] p. 309; George Solovoytchik, *Switzerland in Perspective* (Oxford, 1954) p. 61; Pottinger [note 16] pp. 77–9; Isser Woloch, *Eighteenth-Century Europe* (New York, 1982) pp. 238, 241; Leon Twarog, 'Literary Censorship in Russia and the Soviet Union', in Joseph T. Fuhrmann *et al.*, *Essays on Russian Intellectual History* (Austin, Tex., 1971) p. 104.

18. Elizabeth Eisenstein, *The Printing Press as an Agent of Change* (Cambridge, 1980) pp. 406, 677; Ward [note 16] p. 102; Darnton [note 16] pp. 135, 201; Pottinger [note 16] pp. 74–5; Lough [note 16] p. 175.

19. Richard Herr, *The Eighteenth Century Revolution in Spain* (Princeton, NJ, 1958) pp. 247, 262; Ward [note 16] p. 100; W. E. Yates, 'Cultural Life in Early Nineteenth-Century Austria', *Forum for Modern Language Studies*, 13 (1977) 111; C. A. Macartney, *The Hapsburg Empire, 1790–1815* (New York, 1969) p. 163; Ruud [note 16] p. 22; Avrahm Yarmolinsky, *Road to Revolution: A Century of Russian Radicalism* (New York, 1962) p. 21; Crane Brinton, *A Decade of Revolution, 1789–1799* (New York, 1963) p. 181.

20. This paragraph as well as Table 1 and subsequent information concerning various press laws in nineteenth-century Europe is based on a large number of sources, as very little has been published which attempts to deal with freedom of the press in nineteenth-century Europe on a pan-European basis. This chapter is an expansion of a previous attempt on my own part to treat this subject; Robert J. Goldstein, 'Freedom of the Press in Europe, 1815–1914', *Journalism Monographs*, 80 (1983). Other useful sources include Ruud [note 9] pp. 521–30; and Anderson and Anderson [note 10] pp. 245–72. There is also some useful scattered information in some of the general histories of the press, such as in Hohenberg [note 7]; Smith [note 9]; Olson [note 6]; and S. H. Steinberg, *Five Hundred Years of Printing* (New York, 1977). However, for the most part, information must be dug out of books and articles dealing with individual countries, as indicated in most of the notes to this chapter. For the incidents in Sweden, Denmark and Holland, see D. W. Rustow, *The Politics of Compromise: A Study of Parties and Cabinet Government in Sweden* (Princeton, NJ, 1955) pp. 48–9; Thorsen [note 13] p. 27; Walter Kendall, *The Labour Movement in Europe* (London, 1975) p. 248.

21. Artz [note 8] pp. 134–5; J. F. Zacek, 'Metternich's Censors: The Case of Palacky', in P. Brock and H. Skillings, *The Czech Renascence of the Nineteenth Century* (Toronto, 1970) p. 99; E. Newman, *Restoration Radical: Robert Blum and the Challenge of German Democracy* (Boston, Mass., 1974) p. 46; E. B. Fetscher, 'Censorship and the Editorial: Baden's New Press Law of 1840 and the *Seeblatter* at Konstanz', *German Studies Review*, 3 (1980) 380; O'Boyle [note 4] p. 305.

22. Schulte [note 16]; Smith [note 9] p. 110; Irene Collins, *The Government and the Newspaper Press in France, 1814–1881* (London, 1959) p. 129; Kenez [note 11] p. 22.

23. Lough [note 16] p. 75.

24. Stanley Pech, *The Czech Revolution of 1848* (Chapel Hill, NC, 1969).

p. 11; Robert Waissenberger (ed.), *Vienna in the Biedermeier Era, 1815–1848* (New York, 1986) pp. 38, 82; Alice Hanson, *Musical Life in Biedermeier Vienna* (Cambridge, 1985) pp. 40–1; Stella Musulin, *Vienna in the Age of Metternich* (Boulder, Col., 1975) p. 255.

25. Ronald Hingley, *Russian Writers and Society, 1825–1904* (New York, 1967) p. 228; Helen Saltz Jacobson, *Diary of a Russian Censor: Aleksandr Nikitenko* (Amherst, Mass., 1975) p. xviii; J. N. Westwood, *Endurance and Endeavour: Russian History 1812–1980* (Oxford, 1981) p. 62; Hans Rogger, *Russia in the Age of Modernisation and Revolution, 1881–1917* (New York, 1983) p. 57; Marianna Choldin, *Russian Censorship of Western Ideas under the Tsars* (Durham, NC, 1985) p. 126; Twarog [note 17] p. 110.

26. Avrahm Yarmolinsky, 'A Note on the Censorship of Foreign Books in Russia under Nicholas I', *Bulletin of the New York Public Library*, 38 (1934) 907–10; Daniel Balmuth, *Censorship in Russia* (Washington, DC, 1979) pp. 145–6; Albert Resis, '*Das Kapital* Comes to Russia', *Slavic Review*, 29 (1970) 219–37; Choldin [note 25] pp. 3, 35, 188; Hingley [note 25] p. 233.

27. Jeffrey Sammons, *Heinrich Heine* (Princeton, NJ, 1979) p. 210; Annie Prasoloff, 'Le in-32, un format suspect', in *Histoire de l'édition française* (Paris, 1985) p. 48; Mary Lee Townsend, 'Language of the Forbidden: Popular Humor in "Vormärz" Berlin, 1819–1848' (Yale University PhD, 1984) p. 275.

28. Brooks [note 3] p. 299; Townsend [note 27] pp. 96, 261.

29. Ernest Simmons, *Leo Tolstoy* (Boston, Mass., 1946) p. 441.

30. Robert Keyserlingk, 'Bismarck and Freedom of the Press in Germany, 1866–1890', *Canadian Journal of History*, 11 (1976) 26; Jacobson [note 25] p. 25.

31. Collins [note 22] pp. 117–26; Inglehart [note 6] p. 203; F. W. J. Hemmings, *Culture and Society in France 1848–1898* (London, 1971) p. 55.

32. Jacobson [note 25] p. 298; Ruud [note 9] p. 526; Max Laserson, *The American Impact on Russia, 1784–1917* (New York, 1962) p. 313; Paul Russo, 'Golos and the Censorship, 1879–1883', *Slavonic and East European Review*, 61 (1983) 226–37; Ruud [note 16] p. 193; Kenez [note 11] p. 23.

33. Hovde [note 13] p. 524; Ruud [note 16] p. 15; Keyerslingk [note 30] p. 30; Hall [note 1] p. 14; Collins [note 22] pp. 79, 178; Ted Margadant, *French Peasants in Revolt: The Insurrection of 1851* (Princeton, NJ, 1979) p. 214; Merriman [note 10] pp. 31, 39.

34. Bruce Garver, *The Young Czech Party, 1874–1901* (New Haven, Conn., 1978) p. 48; Charles Gulick, *Austria from Habsburg to Hitler* (Berkeley, Calif., 1948) I, p. 22; R. W. Seton-Watson, *Racial Problems in Hungary* (New York, 1972) pp. 463–6; Denis Smith, *Italy: A Modern History* (Ann Arbor, Mich., 1959) p. 192; Balmuth [note 26] p. 136; Charles Ruud, 'The Printing Press as an Agent of Political Change in Early Twentieth-Century Russia', *Russian Review*, 40 (1981) 394; Hohenberg [note 7] pp. 155–6; Whitman Bassow, 'The Pre-Revolutionary *Pravda* and Tsarist Censorship', *American Slavic and East European Review*, 13 (1954) 62; Angus Roxburgh, *Pravda* (New York, 1987) pp. 16, 19.

35. Anderson and Anderson [note 10] p. 263; Robert B. Holtman, *The Napoleonic Revolution* (Philadelphia, 1967) p. 167.
36. Frederik Ohles, 'This Hated Office: Censors as Victims of Censorship' (paper presented at German Studies Association Meeting in St Louis, Oct 1987) pp. 6–7.
37. T. K. Derry, *A History of Scandinavia* (Minneapolis, 1979) p. 210; Aspinall, *Politics and the Press* [note 2] p. 38; Inglehart [note 6] p. 180; Padover [note 12] p. xi; Schulte [note 16] p. 142; Paul Beik, *Louis Philippe and the July Monarchy* (Princeton, NJ, 1965) pp. 146–7; Balmuth [note 26] p. 13; Bolton King, *A History of Italy* (London, 1912) p. 55; Hugh Seton-Watson, *The Russian Empire, 1801–1917* (Oxford, 1967) p. 251.
38. Jacobson [note 25] pp. xv–xvi, xviii–xix; Waissenberger [note 24] p. 230; S. Monas, *The Third Section: Police and Society in Russia under Nicholas I* (Cambridge, Mass., 1961) pp. 180–1.
39. Ohles [note 36] pp. 5–6, 9; Jacobson [note 25] pp. 131, 140; Choldin [note 25] pp. 39, 57, 73, 94.
40. O'Boyle [note 4] p. 292; Charles Ledre, *La Presse à l'assaut de la monarchie, 1815–1848* (Paris, 1960) p. 218.
41. Hemmings [note 31] p. 53; Collins [note 22]; Schulte [note 16] p. 192; T. Forstenzer, *French Provincial Police and the Fall of the Second Republic* (Princeton, NJ, 1981) p. 53; Stanley Kimball, *Czech Nationalism: A Study of the National Theatre Movement, 1845–83* (Urbana, Ill., 1964) p. 34; Ruud [note 9] p. 527.
42. Aspinall, *Politics and the Press* [note 2] p. 9; Lee [note 5] pp. 46, 64; Koss [note 3] p. 68; Weiner [note 12] p. 117.
43. Smith [note 9] p. 172; G. Sauvigny, *The Bourbon Restoration* (Philadelphia, 1966) p. 294; Kurt Bashwitz, 'History of the Daily Press in the Netherlands', *Bulletin of the International Committee of Historical Sciences*, 10 (1938) 108; Maarten Schneider, *Netherlands Press Today* (Leiden, 1951) p. 10; Keyserlingk [note 30] pp. 26–7; Garver [note 34] p. 47.
44. Collins [note 22]; Robert Holtman, *Napoleonic Propaganda* (Baton Rouge, La., 1950) pp. 44–81; Peter Amann, *Revolution and Mass Democracy: The Paris Club Movement in 1848* (Princeton, NJ, 1975) p. 48; Georges Dupeux, *French Society, 1789–1970* (London, 1976) p. 158.
45. T. E. Carter, 'Comments on German Book Production in the Nineteenth Century', *German Life and Letters*, 23 (1970) 115–16; Kimball [note 41] p. 46; Arnold May, *The Hapsburg Monarchy, 1867–1914* (New York, 1968) p. 509.
46. Ruud [note 16] pp. 254–7; Robert Auty, 'Russian Writing and Publishing', in Robert Auty and D. Obolensky, *An Introduction to Russian Language and Literature* (Cambridge, 1977) p. 51; Effie Ambler, *Russian Journalism and Politics, 1861–1881: The Career of Aleksei Suvorin* (Detroit, 1972) pp. 34–5.
47. Schneider [note 43] p. 10; Weiner [note 12] p. 260; Lucy Brown, *Victorian News and Newspapers* (Oxford, 1985) p. 33; A. P. Wadsworth

'Newspaper Circulation, 1800–1954', *Transactions of the Manchester Statistical Society*, 1954–5, pp. 18–20.

48. R. John Rath, *The Viennese Revolution of 1848* (Austin, Tex., 1957) p. 10; Yates [note 19] p. 108.

49. P. Spencer, 'Censorship by Imprisonment in France, 1830–1870', *Romanic Review*, 47 (1956) 27; Padover [note 12] p. xxi; Eda Sagarra, *Tradition and Revolution: German Literature and Society, 1830–1890* (New York, 1971) p. 133; Waissenberger [note 24] p. 230; Choldin [note 25] pp. 5, 172.

50. Herbert Bowman, *Viassarion Belinski* (New York, 1969) p. 50; Monas [note 38] p. 244; Hingley [note 25] p. 230; Troyat [note 4] p. 249; Nicholas Riasonovsky, *A Parting of the Ways: Government and Educated Public in Russia* (Oxford, 1976) p. 247; Ronald Hingley, *A New Life of Anton Chekhov* (New York, 1976) p. 212.

51. The material on Marx and Proudhon is based on Franz Mehring, *Karl Marx* (Ann Arbor, Mich., 1962), and George Woodcock, *Pierre-Joseph Proudhon* (New York, 1972).

52. Richard Clogg, *A Short History of Modern Greece* (Cambridge, 1979) p. 86; D. G. Kousoulas, *Modern Greece* (New York, 1974) p. 58.

53. Hovde [note 13] pp. 524–5.

54. Seton-Watson [note 37] p. 481; Bertram Wolfe, *Three Who Made a Revolution* (New York, 1964) p. 36.

55. Benjamin Rigsberg, 'Tsarist Censorship Performance, 1894–1905', *Jahrbücher Für Geschichte Osteuropas*, 17 (1969) 63; Laserson [note 32] pp. 291–2; Kenez, [note 11] p. 27; Ruud [note 16] p. 110.

56. Barbara Reinfeld, *Karel Havlíček* (New York, 1982) pp. 25–6; Michael Petrovich, *A History of Serbia* (New York, 1976) p. 488; John Cruikshank, *The Early Nineteenth Century* (Oxford, 1969) p. 102.

57. W. Lougee, *Mid-Century Revolutions, 1848* (Lexington, Mass., 1972) p. 39; Alex Hall, 'The Kaiser, the Wilhelmine State and Lèse Majesté', *German Life and Letters*, 27 (1974) 104–5; Robert C. Brooks, 'Lèse Majesté in Germany', *The Bookman*, 40 (1914) 76–81.

58. Thorsen [note 13] p. 27; Bassow [note 34] p. 60.

59. Hovde [note 13] p. 524; Jacob Walkin, 'Government Controls over the Press in Russia, 1905–1914', *Russian Review*, 13 (1954) 208.

60. Steinberg [note 20] p. 272; Sammons [note 27] p. 123; Hermann Weigand, 'How Censorship Worked in 1831', *Yale University Library Gazette*, 10 (1935) 17–22; Sauvigny [note 43] p. 169; Smith [note 9] p. 95.

61. Bassow [note 34] pp. 51–2; Walkin [note 59] p. 205.

62. John Gillis, *The Development of European Society, 1770–1870* (Boston, Mass., 1977) p. 219.

63. James Allen, *Popular French Romanticism: Authors, Readers and Books in the 19th Century* (Syracuse, NY, 1981) p. 140; Harry Whitemore, 'Readers, Writers and Literary Taste in the Early 1830s: The *Cabinet de Lecture* as Focal Point', *Journal of Library History*, 13 (1978) 119–29; Aspinall, *Politics and the Press* [note 2] pp. 26, 28.

64. André Jardin and André-Jean Tudesq, *Restoration and Reaction, 1815–*

210   *Notes*

1848 (Cambridge, 1983) p. 165; Yarmolinsky [note 26] p. 910; Choldin [note 25] p. 63.
65. Choldin [note 25] pp. 85, 174, 203; Laserson [note 32] pp. 265–6; John Lawrence, *A History of Russia* (New York, 1960) p. 194.
66. Gerhard Habermann, *Maxim Gorky* (New York, 1971) p. 51; Wolfe [note 54] p. 441.
67. Herr [note 19] p. 243; Hemmings [note 31] p. 151; Michael Packe, *The Bombs of Orsini* (London, 1957) p. 255; Roger Williams, *Henri Rochefort* (New York, 1966) pp. 37–8; Rath [note 48] p. 46; Petrovich [note 56] p. 307; L. Kochan, *The Making of Modern Russia* (New York, 1963) p. 207.
68. Vernon Lidtke, *The Outlawed Party: Social Democracy in Germany, 1878–1890* (Princeton, NJ, 1966) pp. 93–6; John Snell, *The Democratic Movement in Germany, 1789–1914* (Chapel Hill, NC, 1976) p. 199; Gary Steenson, *'Not One Man! Not One Penny!' German Social Democracy, 1863–1914* (Pittsburgh, 1981) p. 39.
69. Weiner [note 12]; G. A. Cranfield, *The Press and Society from Caxton to Northcliffe* (New York, 1978) pp. 126–41.
70. Anderson and Anderson [note 10] p. 265; Weiner [note 12] p. 116; Smith [note 9] p. 59.

Chapter 3   Political Censorship of Caricature

1. Georges Boudaille, *Gustave Courbet: Painter in Protest* (Greenwich, Conn., 1970) p. 75.
2. Peter Paret, *The Berlin Secession: Modernism and its Enemies in Imperial Germany* (Cambridge, Mass., 1980) p. 27.
3. André Blum, *La Caricature révolutionnaire (1789 à 1795)* (Paris, 1919) p. 14; André Blum, 'La Caricature politique sous la Monarchie de Juillet', *Gazette des beaux-arts*, 62 (1920) 29; Pierre Casselle, 'Le Régime legislatif', in *Histoire de l'édition Français* (Paris, 1985) p. 53. The Attorney General's comment is translated into English but mistakenly cited as part of the law itself in Oliver Larkin, *Daumier: Man of his Time* (Boston, Mass., 1968) p. 29.
4. The best general survey of nineteenth-century European caricature is Ronald Searle, Claude Roy and Bernd Bornemann, *La Caricature: art et manifeste* (Geneva, 1974). There is also much useful material in the following: Edward Lucie-Smith, *The Art of Caricature* (Ithaca, NY, 1981); William Feaver, *Masters of Caricature* (New York, 1981); James Parton, *Caricature and other Comic Art in All Times and Many Lands* (New York, 1878); Bevis Hillier, *Cartoons and Caricatures* (New York, 1970); and Arsène Alexandre, *L'Art du rire et de la caricature* (Paris, c. 1900). For France, the most important sources are John Grand-Carteret, *Les Moeurs et la caricature en France* (Paris, 1888); Philippe Jones, 'La Liberté de la caricature en France au XIXe siècle', *Synthèses*, 14 (1960) 220–30; Philippe Roberts-Jones, *De Daumier à Lautrec: essai sur l'histoire de la caricature française entre 1860 et 1890* (Paris, 1960) esp. pp. 21–61; Jacques Lethève, *La Caricature et la presse sous la IIIe*

République (Paris, 1961) pp. 5–45. On Germanic Europe, see John Grand-Carteret, *Les Moeurs et la caricature en Allemagne, en Autriche et en Suisse* (Paris, 1885); Mary Lee Townsend, 'Language of the Forbidden: Popular Humor in "Vormärz" Berlin, 1819–1848' (Yale University PhD, 1984); Robin Lenman, 'Censorship and Society in Munich, 1890–1914, with Special Reference to *Simplicissimus* and the Plays of Frank Wedekind, 1890–1914' (Oxford University PhD, 1975); Ann Allen, *Satire and Society in Wilhelmine Germany: 'Kladderadatsch' and 'Simplicissimus', 1890–1914* (Lexington, Mass., 1984); and W. A. Coupe, *German Political Satires* from the *Reformation to the Second World War*, 6 vols (White Plains, NY, 1985–). On Russia, see John Bowlt, 'Art and Violence: The Russian Caricature in the Early Nineteenth and Early Twentieth Centuries', *Twentieth Century Studies*, 13–14 (1975) 56–76; John Bowlt, 'Nineteenth Century Russian Caricature', in Theofanis Stavrou (ed.), *Art and Culture in Nineteenth-Century Russia* (Bloomington, Ind., 1983) pp. 221–35; and especially David King and Cathy Porter, *Images of Revolution: Graphic Art from 1905 Russia* (New York, 1983). On Spain, see Juan Carette Parrondo, 'Les Estampes hétérodoxes en Espagne au XVIII et au début du XIX siècle', *Gazette des beaux-arts*, 62 (1980) 169–82. On Italy, see Rosanna Maggio-Serra, 'La Naissance de la caricature de presse en Italie et le journal turinois *Il Fischietto*', *Histoire et critique des arts*, 13–14 (1980) 135–58.

5. Peter Morse, 'Daumier's Early Lithographs', *Print Review*, 11 (1980) 9; Robert C. Brooks, 'Lèse Majesté in Germany', *The Bookman*, 40 (1914) 68; King and Porter [note 4] p. 41.

6. Richard Godefrey, *English Caricature, 1620 to the Present* (London, 1984) p. 10; Hillier [note 4] p. 7; Jones [note 4] p. 225.

7. Lenman [note 4] pp. 98, 137; Allen [note 4] pp. 120, 154.

8. Townsend [note 4] pp. 277, 281; James Cuno, 'Charles Philipon and La Maison Aubert: The Business, Politics and Public of Caricature in Paris, 1820–40' (Harvard University PhD, 1985) p. 51; Jean Adhemar, *Imagerie populaire française* (Milan, 1968) p. 142; Lionel Lambourne, *An Introduction to Caricature* (London, 1983) p. 10: Moshe Carmilly-Weinberger, *Fear of Art: Censorship and Freedom of Expression in Art* (New York, 1986) p. 157.

9. C. A. Ashbee, *Caricature* (London, 1928) p. 47; Heinrich Heine, *French Affairs* (London, 1893) pp. 142, 331; Alla Sytova, *The Lubok: Russian Folk Pictures* (Leningrad, 1984) p. 13; Coupe [note 4], vol. 3, p. xii; Roger Bellet, *Presse et Journalisme sous le Second Empire* (Paris, 1967) p. 312; Raymond Bachollet, 'Satire, Censure et Propaganda', *Le Collectionneur Français*, 174 (1980) p. 15.

10. The law is quoted and translated into English in Paul Beik, *Louis Philippe and the July Monarchy* (Princeton, NJ, 1965) p. 147, and also in Aaron Scharf, *Art and Politics in France* (London, 1972) pp. 63–4.

11. For discussions of the censorship mechanics, see Roger Bellet [note 9] p. 35; Roberts-Jones [note 4] p. 35; J. Valmy-Baysse, *André Gill* (Paris, 1927) p. 71.

12. Roberts-Jones [note 4] pp. 98–102; Grand-Carteret, *Moeurs et caricature en France* [note 4], pp. 382–3; Bellet [note 11] pp. 88–9; Valmy-Baysse

[note 11] pp. 68–70; Charles Gilbert-Martin, 'Souvenirs d'un caricaturiste', *Le Don Quichotte*, 21, 28 May 1887.

13. Jones [note 4] p. 226.
14. Roberts-Jones [note 4] p. 107.
15. Grand-Carteret, *Moeurs et caricature en France* [note 4] p. 523; Adhemar [note 8] p. 142; Roberts-Jones [note 4] p. xi; Allen [note 4] p. 11; Steve Heller, '*Simplicissimus*', *Upper and Lower Case*, 8 (1981) 16.
16. Annie Renonciat, *La Vie et l'oeuvre de J. J. Grandville* (Paris, 1985) p. 76; Charles Fontane, *André Gill: un maître de la caricature* (Paris, 1927) I, 37; Allen [note 4] p. 199.
17. Carmilly-Weinberger [note 8] p. 56; Ashbee [note 9] p. 37; Christiane Andersson, 'Polemical Prints during the Reformation', in *Censorship: 500 Years of Conflict* (New York, 1984) pp. 35, 39; David Kunzle, *The Early Comic Strip: Narrative Strips and Picture Stories in the European Broadsheet from c. 1450 to 1825* (Berkeley, Calif., 1973) pp. 167, 434; Roberts-Jones [note 4] pp. 22–3; Parrondo [note 4]; John Bowlt, 'Art and Violence' [note 4] pp. 57–8; Pierre-Louis Ducharte, *L'Imagerie populaire russe* (Paris, 1961) p. 160.
18. On France, see Roberts-Jones [note 4] pp. 22–3; Michel Ragon, *Le Dessin d'humour: histoire de la caricature et du dessin humoristique en France* (Paris, 1960) p. 20; André Blum, 'L'Estampe satirique et la caricature en France au XVIII siècle', *Gazette des beaux-arts*, 52 (1910) 379–92, and 53 (1910) 69–87; A. H. Mayor, *Prints and People* (New York, 1971) text accompanying print 556; Michael Melot, 'The Image in France', in *Censorship: Five Hundred Years of Conflict* (New York, 1984) p. 82. On Germany, see John Paas, *The German Political Broadsheet, 1600–1700* (Wiesbaden, 1985) pp. 22–4; William Coupe, *The German Illustrated Broadsheet in the Seventeenth Century* (Baden-Baden, 1966) pp. 9, 16–19; Kunzle [note 17] p. 28. On Russia, see Ducharte [note 17] pp. 54, 164–8; Robert Philippe, *Political Graphics: Art as a Weapon* (New York, 1982) pp. 78–80; and Alexander and Barbara Pronin, *Russian Folk Arts* (New York, 1975) p. 34. On Spain, see Parrondo [note 4].
19. Ralph Shikes, *The Indigant Eye: The Artist as Social Critic in Prints and Drawings* (Boston, Mass., 1969) p. 57; W. A. Coupe, 'The German Cartoon and the Revolution of 1848', *Comparative Studies in History and Society*, 9 (1966–7) 139.
20. Blum [note 18] above, pp. 72, 384.
21. Herr, *The Eighteenth Century Revolution in Spain* (Princeton, NJ, 1958) p. 247; Parrondo [note 4] p. 171; Avrahm Yarmolinksy, *Road to Revolution: A Century of Russian Radicalism* (New York, 1962) p. 21; John Bowlt, 'Nineteenth Century Russian Caricature' [note 4] pp. 226–9; Coupe [note 19] p. 139; A. M. Broadley, *Napoleon in Caricature* (London, 1911).
22. On caricatures during the French Revolution, see Blum, *La Caricature révolutionnaire* [note 3]; Champfleury (Jules Fleury), *Histoire de la caricature sous la Republique, l'Empire et la Restauration* (Paris, 1874); and Grand-Carteret, *Moeurs et caricature en France* [note 4] pp. 41–62.
23. Alexandre [note 4] p. 108.

24. On caricature under Napoleon, see André Blum, 'La Caricature en France sous le Consulat et l'Empire', *Revue des études napoléoniennes*, 19 (1918) 296–312; Grand-Carteret, *Moeurs et caricature en France* [note 4] pp. 84–93.
25. Melot [note 18] pp. 82–3; Jane Clapp, *Art Censorship* (Metuchen, NJ, 1972) p. 108.
26. Robert Holtman, *Napoleonic Propaganda* (Baton Rouge, La., 1950) p. 166.
27. Coupe [note 19] p. 140.
28. On the situation in Britain, see, M. Dorothy George, *English Political Caricature to 1792* (Oxford, 1959); M. Dorothy George, *English Political Caricature, 1793–1832* (Oxford, 1959); and H. T. Dickinson, *Caricatures and the Constitution, 1760–1832* (Cambridge, 1986).
29. Ralph Shikes and Steven Heller, *The Art of Satire* (New York, 1984) p. 10; Searle *et al.* [note 4] pp. 157, 161.
30. Grand-Carteret, *Moeurs et caricature en Allemagne* [note 4] pp. 112, 153; Alexandre [note 4] p. 153; Robert Waissenberger (ed.), *Vienna in the Biedermeier Era, 1815–48* (New York, 1986) pp. 82, 177.
31. Townsend [note 4] pp. 164, 265; Grand-Carteret, *Moeurs et caricature en Allemagne* [note 4] pp. 98, 114–15; Searle *et al.* [note 4] pp. 162–3; and Michel Melot, 'Social Comment and Criticism', in Domenico Porzio (ed.), *Lithography: 200 Years of Art, History and Technique* (New York, 1983) p. 219.
32. Parton [note 4] pp. 250–1.
33. S. Frederick Starr, 'Russian Art and Society, 1800–1850', in Stavrou [note 4] p. 104.
34. Tobia Frankel, *The Russian Artist* (New York, 1972) p. 74; Jeffrey Brooks, *When Russia Learned to Read: Literacy and Popular Literature, 1861–1917* (Princeton, NJ, 1985) p. 64; Duchartre [note 17] p. 56; Pronin [note 18] pp. 32, 34, 113.
35. Grand-Carteret, *Moeurs et caricature en Allemagne* [note 4] p. 101.
36. Townsend [note 4] pp. 102, 111; Philippe [note 18] pp. 142–3; Coupe [note 19] p. 140; Dickinson [note 28] p. 86; Grand-Carteret, *Moeurs et caricature en Allemagne* [note 4] pp. 96–7.
37. On the growth of caricature in 1848, see Coupe [note 19]; Coupe [note 4] vol. 3, p. ix; Allen [note 4] p. 15; Lucie-Smith [note 4] pp. 81, 87; Arthur Maurice and Frederic Cooper, *The History of the Nineteenth Century in Caricature* (New York, 1970) p. 119; Melot [note 31] p. 219; Michel Melot, *The Art of Illustration* (New York, 1984), p. 155.
38. On French caricature during the Bourbon restoration, see Champfleury [note 22] pp. 308–57; Grand-Carteret, *Moeurs et caricature en France* [note 4] pp. 95–152; and especially André Blum, 'La Caricature politique en France sous la Restauration', *La Nouvelle Revue*, 35 (1918) 119–36.
39. Blum [note 38] p. 131.
40. Renonciat [note 16] pp. 63, 70; James Cuno, 'The Business and Politics of Caricature: Charles Philipon and La Maison Aubert', *Gazette des beaux-arts*, 106 (1985) 97.
41. Grand-Carteret, *Moeurs et caricature en France* [note 4] pp. 184–5.
42. Charles Baudelaire, *The Painter of Modern Life* (London, 1964) p. 172.

43. There is an enormous, growing and fascinating literature concerning the struggle over freedom of caricature in France between 1830 and 1835. Much is in English, including Cuno [note 4]; Cuno [note 40] James Cuno, 'Charles Philipon, La Maison Aubert and the Business of Caricature in Paris, 1829–41', *Art Journal*, 43 (1983) 347–53; Howard Vincent, *Daumier and his World* (Evanston, Ill., 1968); Edwin Bechtel, *Freedom of the Press and L'Association Mensuelle: Philipon versus Louis-Philippe* (New York, 1952); Roger Passeron, *Daumier* (New York, 1981); Scharf [note 10]; Morse [note 5] above; Larkin [note 3]; Robert Rey, *Daumier* (New York, 1965); and Judith Wechsler, *A Human Comedy: Physiognomy and Caricature in 19th Century Paris* (Chicago, 1982). See also, in French, Renonciat [note 16]; Antoinette Huon, 'Charles Philipon et la Maison Aubert', *Etudes de presse*, 9 (1957) 67–76; Charles Ledre, *La Presse à l'assaut de la monarchie, 1815–1848* (Paris, 1960); Andre Rossel, *'Le Charivari': un journal révolutionnaire* (Paris, 1971); Klaus Schrenk, 'Le Mouvement artistique au sein de l'opposition de la Monarchie de Juillet', *Histoire et critique des arts*, 13–14 (1980) 67–96; and André Blum, 'La Caricature politique' [note 3] pp. 257–77.
44. Vincent [note 43] p. 15.
45. Irene Collins, *The Government and the Newspaper Press in France, 1814–1881* (London, 1959) pp. 74–7.
46. Maurice and Cooper [note 37] p. 72; Grand-Carteret, *Moeurs et caricature en France* [note 4] p. 202; Wechsler [note 43] p. 73; Passeron [note 43] p. 47.
47. Jacques Sternberg and Henri Deuil, *Un siècle de dessins contestaires* (Paris, 1974) p. 28.
48. Renonciat [note 16] above, p. 87.
49. Sternberg and Deuil [note 47] p. 36.
50. Roger Macgraw, *France 1815–1914* (Oxford, 1983) p. 65; Wechsler [note 43] p. 85; Vincent [note 43] p. 73.
51. Lucie-Smith [note 4] p. 78; Wechsler [note 43] p. 95.
52. Vincent [note 43] p. 249; Fernand Drujon, *Catalogue des ouvrages, ecrits et dessins de toute nature poursuivis, supprimés ou condamnés depuis le 21 octobre 1814 jusqu'au 31 juillet 1879* (Paris, 1879) p. 89; Grand-Carteret, *Moeurs et caricature en France* [note 4] p. 583.
53. On caricature during the Second Republic see André Blum, 'La Caricature politique en France sous la Seconde Republique', *Revolutions de 1848*, 74 (1919) 203–14; and Grand-Carteret, *Moeurs et caricature en France* [note 4] pp. 291–333.
54. Charles Ramus, *Daumier* (New York, 1978) p. 130.
55. Grand-Carteret, *Moeurs et caricature en Allemagne* [note 4] p. 143.
56. Allen [note 4] pp. 19–20; Searle *et al.*, [note 4] pp. 158, 165; Coupe [note 19] p. 166; Lucie-Smith [note 4] p. 81; Grand-Carteret, *Moeurs et caricature en Allemagne* [note 4] p. 177; Coupe [note 4] vol. 3, p. ix.
57. Grand-Carteret, *Moeurs et caricature en Allemagne* [note 4] p. 340; Bohun Lynch, *A History of Caricature* (London, 1926) p. 88; Maggio-Serra [note 4] pp. 139–43.
58. Maggio-Serra [note 4] p. 149.

59. T. J. Clark, *Image of the People: Gustave Courbet and the Second French Republic* (Greenwich, Conn., 1973) p. 93; Anne McCauley, *Nineteenth-Century French Caricatures and Comic Illustrations* (Austin, Tex., 1985) p. 14; *Caricature-presse satirique, 1830–1918* (Paris, 1979) p. 25; Drujon [note 52] p. 89.

60. On caricature under the Second Empire, see Bellet [note 11]; Roberts-Jones [note 4] pp. 25–30; and André Blum, 'La Caricature politique en France sous le Second Empire', *Revue des études napoléoniennes*, 15 (1919) 169–83.

61. On the 1867–70 period, see Grand-Carteret, *Moeurs et caricature en France* [note 4] pp. 413–16; Roberts-Jones [note 4] pp. 26–30, 43–5; Bellet [note 11] pp. 87–92; Blum [note 60] pp. 171–2, 180–3; Valmy-Baysse [note 11] pp. 53–160; Fontane [note 16] pp. 33–65, 175–311.

62. Roberts-Jones [note 4] p. 8.

63. For details on these journals see the alphabetical lists of periodicals and discussion of them in Philippe Jones, 'La Presse illustré satirique entre 1860 et 1890', *Etudes de presse*, 8 (1956) 16–113; and Grand-Carteret, *Moeurs et caricature en France* [note 4] pp. 559–618. See also Charles Virmaitre, *Paris-canard* (Paris, 1888) pp. 105–6, 83–7. The leading studies on Gill are Valmy-Baysse [note 11] and Fontane [note 16].

64. Boudaille [note 1] p. 93; Thedore Reff, *Manet and Modern Paris* (Chicago, 1982) pp. 208–9; Anne Hanson, *Manet and the Modern Tradition* (New Haven, Conn., 1977) p. 115; Jacquelynn Baas, 'Edouard Manet and "Civil War"', *Art Journal*, 45 (1985) 36–7; Metropolitan Museum of Art, *Manet* (New York, 1983) p. 531.

65. There is a massive literature on caricature in 1870–1. For a complete catalogue of these caricatures, see Jean Berleux, *La Caricature politique en France pendant la guerre, le siège et la Commune* (Paris, 1890). Many of these caricatures are reprinted in Paul Ducatel, *Histoire de la Commune et du siège de Paris: vue à travers l'imagerie populaire* (Paris, 1973), and in Susan Lambert, *The Franco-Prussian War and the Commune in Caricature, 1870–71* (London, 1971). For narrative accounts, see Aimé Dupuy, *La Guerre, la Commune et la presse, 1870–71* (Paris, 1959); James Leith, 'The War of Images Surrounding the Commune', in James Leith (ed.), *Images of the Commune* (Montreal, 1978) pp. 101–50; André Blum, 'La Caricature politique en France pendant la guerre de 1870–71', *Revue des études napoléoniennes*, 20 (1919) 301–11. On Pilotell, see Charles Feld, *Pilotell: dessinateur et communard* (Paris, 1969) pp. 13–15. On suppression of journals by the Commune, see Virmaitre, [note 63] pp. 271–2; Michel Ragon, *Les Maîtres du dessin satirique en France de 1830 à nos jours* (Paris, 1972) p. vi.

66. Lethève [note 4] p. 30. In general, on the struggle of 1871–81, see ibid., pp. 11–43; Roberts-Jones [note 4] pp. 30–40; Jones [note 63]; Henri Avenel, *Histoire de la presse française depuis 1789 jusqu'à nos jours* (Paris, 1900) pp. 746–7; and the works on Gill cited in note 63.

67. These accounts are drawn from Jones [note 63] pp. 49–50, 75–7, 107–8.

68. Gary Stark, 'Cinema, Society and the State: Policing the Film Industry in Imperial Germany', in Gary Stark and Bede Lackner (ed.), *Essays*

on *Culture and Society in Imperial Germany* (College Station, Tex., 1982) p. 136.

69. Theda Shapiro, *Painters and Politics* (New York, 1976) p. 33.
70. Melot [note 31] pp. 219–20; Grand-Carteret, *Moeurs et caricature en Allemagne* [note 4] pp. 429–49; Randall Davies, 'Caricature', in Encyclopaedia Britannica, *Graphic Arts* (Garden City, NY, 1936) pp. 90–100; Parton [note 4] pp. 251–6; Jones [note 63] pp. 13–14; Shikes and Heller [note 29] p. 11; Coupe [note 4] vol. 3, pp. x–xi.
71. Patricia Kery, *Great Magazine Covers of the World* (New York, 1982) p. 282.
72. Brooks [note 5] p. 69; Allen [note 4] pp. 39–41, 111–12; Jones [note 63] pp. 41–2; Lethève [note 4] pp. 107, 238; Grand-Carteret, *Moeurs et caricature en Allemagne* [note 4] pp. 347–8; John Grand-Carteret, *'Lui' devant l'objectif caricatural* (Paris, 1905) pp. 73, 76; John Grand-Carteret, *Crispi, Bismarck et la Triple-Alliance en caricatures* (Paris, 1891) pp. 11–13.
73. On the *Cu-Cut!* incident, see Joaquin Romero-Maura, *The Spanish Army and Catalonia: The 'Cu-Cut! Incident' and the Law of Jurisdictions, 1905–6* (Santa Barbara, Calif., 1976).
74. See, on these regulations, for France, Elisabeth and Michel Dixmier, *L'Assiette au beurre'* (Paris, 1974) pp. 219–36; and for Germany, Lenman [note 4] pp. 89–90, 136–8.
75. On *Simplicissimuss*, see Lenman [note 4]; Allen [note 4]; Stanley Appelbaum, *'Simplicissimus': Satirical Drawings from the Famous German Weekly* (New York, 1975); Gerhard Bennecke, 'The Politics of Outrage: Social Satire in *Simplicissimus*', *Twentieth Century Studies*, 13–14 (1975) 92–109; W. A. Coupe, 'Kaiser Wilhelm II and the Cartoonists', *History Today*, 30 (1980) 16–23; Steve Heller, 'The Late, Great *Simplicissimus*', *Print*, 33 (1979) 35–43; Heller [note 15]; Fritz Arnold, *One Hundred Caricatures from 'Simplicissimus'* (Munich, 1983); Mark Rosenthal, *'Simplicissimus'* (New York, 1979); Franz Roh, *German Art in the Twentieth Century* (New York, 1957) pp. 35–43; Raymond Bacholler, *'Simplicissimus'*, *Le Collectioneur français*, Jan 1982, pp. 5–7, Feb 1982, pp. 7–9, and Mar 1982, pp. 8–11.
76. Allen [note 4] pp. 41–2, 89; Lenman [note 4] pp. 76, 89–91.
77. Coupe [note 75] p. 22; Allen [note 4] p. 55; Coupe [note 4] vol. 3, p. xii.
78. Grand-Carteret, *'Lui'* [note 72] pp. i–vii; John Grand-Carteret, *Nicholas: ange de la paix, empereur du knout* (Paris, c. 1906) pp. 9–15.
79. Frank and Dorothy Getlein, *The Bite of the Print* (New York, 1963) pp. 228–34; Herbert Bittner, *Kaethe Kollwitz: Drawings* (New York, 1959) p. 5; Mina and Arthur Klein, *Käthe Kollwitz: Life in Art* (New York, 1972) pp. 33–6; Paret [note 2] pp. 9–28; Marion Deshmukh, 'Art and Politics in Turn-of-the-Century Berlin', in Gerald Chapple and Hans Chulte (eds), *The Turn of the Century: German Literature and Art, 1890–1915* (Bonn, 1981) pp. 463–73; Maurice Rickards, *Posters of Protest and Revolution* (New York, 1970) p. 16; Renate Hinz, *Käthe Kollwitz: Graphics, Posters, Drawings* (New York, 1981) p. xxi; Maurice Rickards, *Banned Posters* (Park Ridge, NJ) pp. 32–3; Alan Weill, *The Poster: A Worldwide Survey and History* (Boston, Mass., 1985), p. 99.

80. There is a large literature on *L'Assiette au beurre*. The leading study is by Elisabeth and Michel Dixmier, [note 74]. Caricatures from this journal are reprinted in Stanley Applebaum, *French Satirical Drawings from 'L'Assiette au Beurre'* (New York, 1978); and J.-M. Royer, *Le Livre d'or de 'L'Assiette au beurre'*, 2 vols (Paris, 1977–8). See also Gisèle Lambert *'L'Assiette au beurre'*, *Les Nouvelles de l'estampe*, 23 (1975) 7–17; Raymond Bachollet, *'L'Assiette au beurre'*, *Le Collectionneur français*, 155 (1979) 7–9; Steven Heller, *'L'Assiette au beurre'*, *Upper and Lower Case*, 8 (1981) 12–15; Ralph Shikes, 'Five Artists in the Service of Politics in the Pages of *L'Assiette au beurre'*, in Henry Millon and Linda Nochlin (eds), *Art and Architecture in the Service of Politics* (Cambridge, Mass., 1978) pp. 162–81.

81. See Shikes [note 80] pp. 167, 175; Dixmier and Dixmier [note 74] pp. 284–90, 294–9; Vige Longevin, *Exhibition Jules Grandjouan* (Nantes, 1969) pp. 31–2; Henry Poulaille, *Aristide Delannoy* (Saint-Denis, 1982).

82. Daniel Balmuth, *Censorship in Russia, 1865–1905* (Washington, DC, 1979) p. 19; King and Porter [note 4] pp. 24–5; Bowlt, 'Art and Violence' [note 4] p. 64.

83. Charles Ruud, *Fighting Words: Imperial Censorship and the Russian Press, 1804–1906* (Toronto, 1982) pp. 238, 245; King and Porter [note 4] pp. 18, 25; Bowlt, 'Art and Violence' [note 4] p. 64; Ernest Simmons, *Leo Tolstoy* (Boston, Mass., 1946) p. 596; Serge Golynets, *Ivan Bilibin* (New York, 1981) p. 185.

84. The following discussion about Russia in 1905 relies most heavily upon King and Porter [note 4]. Also useful were Bowlt, 'Art and Violence' [note 4] pp. 66–72; John Bowlt, 'Russian Caricature and the 1905 Revolution', *Print Collector's Newsletter*, 9 (1978) 5–8; Robert C. Williams, *Artists in Revolution: Portraits of the Russian Avante-Garde* (Bloomington, Ind., 1977), pp. 63–71; Pronin and Pronin [note 18] p. 114.

85. Bowlt, 'Nineteenth-Century Russian Caricature' [note 4] p. 232; King and Porter [note 4] p. 31.

86. King and Porter [note 4] pp. 36, 43.

87. King and Porter [note 4] p. 43.

88. Balmuth [note 82] p. 132; Bowlt, 'Art and Violence' [note 4] pp. 71–3.

Chapter 4 Political Censorship of the Theatre

1. Donald Kimbell, *Verdi in the Age of Italian Romanticism* (Cambridge, 1981) p. 25.

2. John Allen, *A History of the Theatre in Europe* (London, 1983) pp. 256–7.

3. Odile Krakovitch, *Hugo censuré: la liberté au théâtre au XIXe siècle* (Paris, 1985) p. 83.

4. Krakovitch [note 3] Epilogue.

5. Roy Pascal, *From Naturalism to Expressionism: German Literature and Society, 1880–1918* (New York, 1973) p. 266.

6. Kenneth Macgowan, William Melnitz and Gordon Armstrong, *Golden*

Ages of the Theatre (Englewood Cliffs, NJ, 1979) pp. 87, 164, 239; Krakovitch [note 3] pp. 93–4, 116, 136, 212, 229; Victor Hallays-Dabot, *Histoire de censure théatrâle en France* (Paris, 1862) p. 116; Albéric Cahuet, *La Liberté du théâtre en France et à l'étranger* (Paris, 1902) p. 348; Albert Delpit, 'La Liberté des théâtres et les café-concerts', *Revue des deux mondes*, 1 Feb 1978, p. 623.

7. Krakovitch [note 3] pp. 101, 117, 130, 141, 159, 179, 200–1; Horst Claus, *The Theatre Director Otto Brahm* (Ann Arbor, Mich., 1981), p. 71; Richard Findlater, *Banned! A Review of Theatrical Censorship in Britain* (London, 1967) p. 99.

8. Jack Weiner, *Mantillas in Moscovy: The Spanish Golden Age Theater in Tsarist Russia, 1672–1917* (Lawrence, Kan., 1970) p. 25; John Palmer, *The Censor and the Theater* (New York, 1913) p. 189.

9. Findlater [note 7] p. 16; Cahuert [note 6] pp. 204–5.

10. Johann Huttner, 'Theater Censorship in Metternich's Vienna', *Theatre Quarterly*, 37 (1980) p. 64; L. W. Conolly, *The Censorship of English Drama, 1737–1824* (San Marino, Calif., 1976) p. 180; Hallays-Dabot [note 6] p. ix.

11. Krakovitch [note 3] pp. 150, 286; Vera Roberts, *On Stage: A History of Theatre* (New York, 1962) p. 411; Robert D. Boyer, *Realism in European Theatre and Drama, 1870–1920* (Westport, Conn., 1979) p. xvii.

12. Claus [note 7] p. 47; Gary Stark, 'Cinema, Society and the State: Policing the Film Industry in Imperial Germany', in Gary Stark and Bede Lackner (eds), *Essays on Culture and Society in Modern Germany* (College Station, Tex., 1982) p. 143; John R. Stephens, *The Censorship of English Drama, 1824–1901* (Cambridge, 1980) pp. 42–3; John and Muriel Lough, *An Introduction to Nineteenth-Century France* (London, 1978) p. 273; W. D. Howarth, *Sublime and Grotesque: A Study of French Romantic Drama* (London, 1975) p. 306; Huttner [note 10] p. 66–7; F. W. J. Hemmings, *Culture and Society in France, 1848–1898* (London, 1971) p. 51.

13. Lawson Carter, *Zola and the Theatre* (New Haven, Conn., 1963) p. 137; Marc Slonim, *Russian Theatre from the Empire to the Soviets* (Cleveland, 1961) p. 145; Stephens [note 12] p. 127.

14. Robert M. Isherwood, *Farce and Fantasy: Popular Entertainment in Eighteenth-Century Paris* (New York, 1986) p. 255; Huttner [note 10] pp. 61–2; Alice Hanson, *Musical Life in Biedermeier Vienna* (Cambridge, 1985) p. 75.

15. Krakovitch [note 3] pp. 225, 227; Herbert Marshall, *The Pictorial History of the Russian Theatre* (New York, 1976) p. 247.

16. Eda Sagarra, *Tradition and Revolution: German Literature and Society, 1830–1890* (New York, 1971) p. 79; Barbara Prohaska, *Raimund and Vienna* (Cambridge, 1970) p. 148; Marianna Choldin, *Russian Censorship of Ideas under the Tsars* (Durham, NC, 1985) p. 172; Nick Worrall, *Nikolai Gogol and Ivan Turgenev* (New York, 1983) p. 43; Gary Stark, 'La Police berlinoise et la Freie Volksbühne', *Revue d'histoire du théâtre*, 38 (1986) p. 9.

17. Krakovitch [note 3] p. 267; Edward Braun, *The Director and the Stage* (London, 1982) p. 60; Cecil W. Davies, *Theatre for the People: The*

Story of the Volksbühne (Austin, Tex., 1977) p. 2; Raphael Samuel, Ewan MacColl and Stuart Cosgrove, *Theatres of the Left: Workers' Theatre Movements in Britain and America* (London, 1985) p. 17.

18. Ann Marie Koller, *The Theatre Duke: Georg II of Saxe-Meiningen and the German Stage* (Stanford, Calif., 1984) p. 12; Stephen A. Kippur, *Jules Michelet* (Albany, NY, 1981) pp. 120, 130; Krakovitch [note 3] pp. 217, 266.

19. See generally Jonas Barish, *The Anti-theatrical Prejudice* (Berkeley, Calif., 1981) (quoted material from pp. 42, 58); and Mendel Kohansky, *The Disreputable Profession: The Actor in Society* (Westport, Conn., 1984) (quoted material from pp. 20, 22–23, 27). Other material in this paragraph is drawn from Cahuet [note 6] p. 8; and Macgowan *et al.* [note 6] p. 29.

20. Kohansky [note 19] pp. 26, 28, 81; Barish [note 19] pp. 199, 241; Cahuet [note 6] p. 43; Macgowan *et al.* [note 6] p. 29; Glynne Wickham, *A History of the Theatre* (Oxford, 1985) p. 1.

21. Macgowan *et al.* [note 6] p. 83; Ronald Harwood, *All the World's a Stage* (Boston, Mass., 1984) p. 177; Kohansky [note 19] pp. 48, 55, 66, 106; Barish [note 19] p. 261; Frederick and Lise-Lone Marker, *The Scandinavian Theatre* (Totowa, NJ, 1975) p. 69.

22. Oscar Brockett, *History of the Theatre* (Boston, Mass., 1977), pp. 168–9; Macgowan *et al.* [note 6] p. 117; Cahuet [note 6] pp. 17, 52, 67–8; Wickham [note 20] p. 11; John Lough, *Writer and Public in France: From the Middle Ages to the Present Day* (Oxford, 1978) pp. 75, 173; Frederick Brown, *Theatre and Revolution* (New York, 1980) p. 46; John Hohenberg, *Free Press/Free People* (New York, 1971) p. 72.

23. Brockett [note 22] p. 202; Margot Berthold, *A History of World Theatre* (New York, 1972) p. 536; Findlater [note 7] pp. 24–5; Albert Ward, *Book Production, Fiction and the German Reading Public, 1740–1800* (Oxford, 1974) p. 100.

24. See the discussion in Conolly [note 10] pp. 13–24.

25. Isherwood [note 14] p. 254.

26. Findlater [note 7] p. 41; Allen [note 2] p. 228; Lough [note 22] p. 339; Macgowan *et al.* [note 19] p. 190; Marvin Carlson, *The Italian Stage from Goldoni to D'Annunzio* (London, 1981) pp. 103, 130; Bernard Hewitt, *History of the Theatre from 1800 to the Present* (New York, 1970) p. 6; Simon Williams, *German Actors of the Eighteenth and Nineteenth Centuries* (Westport, Conn., 1985) p. 145; Lars Kleberg, '"People's Theatre" and the Revolution', in Nils Nilsson (ed.), *Art, Society, Revolution: Russia, 1917–1921* (Stockholm, 1979) p. 180.

27. The next few paragraphs are a distillation of information about theatre-censorship laws and administration in nineteenth-century Europe. Standard sources for Britain are Conolly [note 10], Findlater [note 7] and Stephens [note 12]. For France, major sources include Cahuet [note 6] and Krakovitch [note 3]. For Germany, there is a good discussion in Pascal [note 5] pp. 262–76. For Austria, see Huttner [note 10]; Robert Waissenberger (ed.), *Vienna in the Biedermeier Era, 1815–1848* (New York, 1986) pp. 232–43; and Hanson [note 14] pp. 41–4. For Denmark, see Neville Hunnings, *Film Censors and the Law* (London, 1967) pp. 307–

16. For Italy, a good deal of useful information is scattered through Carlson [note 26]. For Russia, see Weiner [note 8]; and M. A. S. Burgess, 'The Nineteenth and Early Twentieth Century Theatre', in Robert Auty (ed.), *An Introduction to Russian Language and Literature* (Cambridge, 1977) pp. 247–66. Additional information on some of the above countries as well as on some of the minor countries such as Belgium, Portugal and the Netherlands can be found in Cahuet [note 6] pp. 310–24; and Frank Fowell and Frank Palmer, *Censorship in England* (London, 1913) pp. 318–23.

28. Victor Hallays-Dabot, *La Censure dramatique et le théâtre 1850–1870* (Paris, 1871) p. 6.

29. Gary Stark, 'The Censorship of Literary Nationalism, 1890–1895: Prussia and Saxony', *Central European History*, 18 (1985) pp. 326–31; Claus [note 7] pp. 46, 71–2, 89; Pascal [note 5] p. 264.

30. Findlater [note 7] p. 73; Krakovitch [note 5] p. 286; Daniel Balmuth, *Censorship in Russia* (Washington, DC, 1979) pp. 42, 55; Carlson [note 26] p. 55; Tom Driver, *A History of the Modern Theatre* (New York, 1970) p. 201; Robin Lenman, 'Politics and Culture: The State and the Avant-Garde in Munich, 1886–1914', in Richard Evans (ed.), *Society and Politics in Wilhelmine Germany* (London, 1978) p. 100.

31. Driver [note 30] p. 201; Choldin [note 16] p. 16; Huttner [note 10] p. 65.

32. Marvin Carlson, *The German Stage in the Nineteenth Century* (Metuchen, NJ, 1972) pp. 3, 55–70.

33. Marjorie Hoover, *Alexander Ostrovsky* (New York, 1981) p. 27.

34. Berthold [note 23] p. 537; Findlater [note 7] p. 53; B. V. Varneke, *History of the Russian Theatre* (New York, 1951) p. 237; Nancy Nolte, 'Government and Theatre in Restoration France', *Consortium on Revolutionary Europe Proceedings 1985* (Athens, Ga., 1986) p. 436; Hemmings [note 12] p. 51; Cahuet [note 6] pp. 224–5; Krakovitch [note 3] p. 241; Charles O'Neill, 'Theatrical Censorship in France, 1844–1875: The Experience of Victor Séjour', *Harvard Library Bulletin*, 26 (1978) p. 434.

35. Carlson [note 26] pp. 101, 119.

36. Kimbell [note 1] p. 25; Stephens [note 12] p. 10; Cahuet [note 6] p. 217; Peter Jelavich, *Munich and Theatrical Modernism: Politics, Playwriting and Performance, 1890–1914* (Cambridge, Mass., 1985), p. 121; Charles Ruud, *Fighting Words: Imperial Censorship and the Russian Press, 1804–1906* (Toronto, 1982) pp. 251–2.

37. Findlater [note 7] p. 54; Stephens [note 12] pp. 168–9; W. E. Yates, *Grillparzer* (Cambridge, 1972), p. 12; Claus [note 7] p. 47; Cahuet [note 6] p. 206.

38. Stephens [note 12] pp. 27, 80; Nolte [note 34] p. 439; Kimbell [note 1] p. 28; Jeremy Commons, '*Maria Stuarda* and the Neapolitan Censorship', *Journal of the Donizetti Society*, 3 (1977) p. 164; Findlater [note 7] pp. 55, 58, 74–5.

39. Hemmings [note 12] pp. 48–9.

40. Ronald Hingley, *Russian Writers and Society, 1825–1904* (New York, 1967) p. 229; Sidney Monas, *The Third Section: Police and Society in Russia under Nicholas I* (Cambridge, Mass., 1961) p. 184; Varneke [note 34] pp. 203–7, 220–2; Slonim [note 13] p. 45; George Freedley and

John Reeves, *A History of the Theatre* (New York, 1941) p. 396; Weiner [note 8] p. 58; Christine Edwards, *The Stanislavsky Heritage* (New York, 1965) p. 13; Burgess [note 27] p. 257.
41. Oliver Saylor, *Inside the Moscow Art Theatre* (Greenwood, Conn., 1970) p. 215.
42. Nikolai Gorchakov, *The Theatre in Soviet Russia* (New York, 1957) p. 50.
43. This section is based primarily on the following sources: Krakovitch [note 3]; Cahuet [note 6]; Hemmings [note 12] pp. 43–51; Nolte [note 34]; Robert Holtman, *Napoleonic Propaganda* (Baton Rouge, La., 1950) pp. 145–57; Beatrice Hyslop, 'The Theatre During a Crisis: The Parisian Theatre During the Reign of Terror', *Journal of Modern History*, 17 (1945) pp. 332–55; O'Neill [note 34] pp. 417–41; Josette Parrain, 'Censure, théâtre et commune, 1871–1914', *Mouvement social*, 79 (1972) pp. 327–42; Delpit [note 6] pp. 601–23.
44. Perrain [note 43] pp. 330, 338; Lisa Appignanesi, *Cabaret: The First Hundred Years* (London, 1984) p. 11.
45. Slonim [note 13] p. 84.
46. Allen [note 2] p. 222; Findlater [note 7] p. 47; James Cleaver, *The Theatre through the Ages* (London, 1948) p. 103; Brockett [note 22] p. 250; Kohansky [note 19] p. 89; Robert Gildea, *Barricades and Borders: Europe 1800–1914* (Oxford, 1987) p. 113; Roberts [note 11] p. 355.
47. Stephens [note 12] p. 122.
48. Carlson [note 26] p. 73.
49. Simon Karlinsky, *Russian Drama from its Beginnings to the Age of Pushkin* (Berkeley, Calif., 1985) p. 305; Roman Szydlowski, *The Theatre in Poland* (Warsaw, 1972) p. 20; Edward Csato, *The Polish Theatre* (Warsaw, 1963) pp. 34–7.
50. Krakovitch [note 3] p. 84.
51. William M. Johnston, *The Austrian Mind: An Intellectual and Social History, 1848–1938* (Berkeley, Calif., 1983) p. 22; W. E. Yates, *Nestroy* (Cambridge, 1972) p. 150; Stella Musulin, *Vienna in the Age of Metternich* (Boulder, Col., 1975) p. 259.
52. Hemmings [note 12] p. 50.
53. Ibid.
54. Sally Vernon, 'Mary Stuart, Queen Victoria and the Censor', *Nineteenth Century Theatre Research*, 6 (1978) 35–40; Stephens [note 12] p. 24; David Mayer, *Harlequin in his Element: The English Pantomime, 1806–1836* (Cambridge, Mass., 1969) p. 246.
55. Robert Sackett, *Popular Entertainment, Class and Politics in Munich, 1900–1923* (Cambridge, Mass., 1982) p. 48; Jelavich [note 36] pp. 240–1; Robin Lenman, 'Censorship and Society in Munich, 1890–1914' (Oxford PhD, 1975) p. 242; Brown [note 22] p. 119; Findlater [note 7] p. 65.
56. Krakovitch [note 3] p. 47; George Martin, *The Red Shirt and the Cross of Savoy: The Story of Italy's Risorgimento* (New York, 1969) p. 219; Carlson [note 26] p. 72; H. Hearder and D. P. Waley, *A Short History of Italy* (Cambridge, 1963) p. 131.
57. Brown [note 22] p. 120; Judith Wechsler, *A Human Comedy: Physiog-*

nomy and Caricature in 19th-Century Paris (Chicago, 1982) pp. 42–63; Mayer [note 54] pp. 6, 50, 246.

58. Robert Baldick, *The Life and Times of Frédérick Lemaître* (Fair Lawn, NJ, 1959) pp. 178–80; Stephens [note 12] pp. 119–21; Martin [note 56] p. 394.

59. On the free theatres, see Anna Miller, *The Independent Theatre in Europe* (New York, 1931); Oscar Brockett and Robert Findlay, *Century of Innovation: A History of European and American Theatre and Drama since 1870* (Englewood Cliffs, NJ, 1973) pp. 89–111; Macgowan *et al.* [note 6] pp. 185–95; Roberts [note 11] pp. 411–21.

60. Carlson [note 32] p. 210; Stark [note 29] p. 336.

61. Jelavich [note 36] pp. 170–3, 243; Michael Patterson, *The Revolution in German Theatre* (Boston, Mass., 1981) p. 26.

62. Findlater [note 7] p. 92; Stephens [note 12] p. 143.

63. Pascal [note 5] p. 276.

64. On the free people's theatres, see Davies [note 17]; Pascal [note 5] pp. 273–5; Carlson [note 32] pp. 219–21; Vernon J. Lidtke, *The Alternative Culture: Socialist Labor in Imperial Germany* (New York, 1985) pp. 148–51; Stark [note 29] pp. 334–6; Stark [note 16].

65. Davies [note 17] p. 58.

66. Conolly [note 10] p. 111; Lamar Beman, *Selected Articles on Censorship of the Theatre and of Moving Pictures* (New York, 1931) p. 254; Hoover [note 33] p. 18.

67. Findlater [note 7] p. 91; Varneke [note 34] pp. 203–4, 302; Waissenberger [note 27] p. 213.

68. Thomas Ashton, 'The Censorship of Byron's *Marino Faliero*', *Huntington Library Quarterly*, 36 (1972–3) 28; Varneke [note 34] p. 237.

69. Yates [note 51] pp. 149–50; Yates [note 37] p. 221; Waissenberger [note 27] pp. 84, 243; Huttner [note 10] pp. 63, 65–6.

70. Barry Daniels, *Revolution in the Theatre: French Romantic Theories of Drama* (Westport, Conn., 1983) p. 193; Krakovitch [note 3] pp. 43, 69, 219; Cahuet [note 6] p. 281; John Osborne, *The Naturalist Drama in Germany* (Manchester, 1971) p. 119; Beman [note 66] p. 365.

71. W. E. Yates, 'Cultural Life in Early Nineteenth-Century Vienna', *Forum for Modern Language Studies*, 13 (1977) p. 110; Hanson [note 14] pp. 43–4; David Magarshack, *Stanislavsky* (New York, 1951, p. 276.

72. Waissenberger [note 27] p. 230; Stephens [note 12] p. 123; Stark [note 29] pp. 341–3.

73. Michael Sanderson, *From Irving to Olivier: A Social History of the Acting Profession in England* (London, 1984) pp. 104–5; Cahuet [note 6] p. 203.

74. Jelavich [note 36] pp. 253–4; Beman [note 66] p. 254; Findlater [note 7] pp. 100–10; Pascal [note 5] p. 268.

75. Carter [note 13] p. 141; Krakovitch [note 3] p. 245; Cahuet [note 6] p. 339.

76. Carlson [note 26] p. 73; Macgowan *et al.* [note 6] above, p. 172.

77. Gorchakov [note 42] p. 18; Waissenberger [note 27] pp. 162–3; Brockett [note 22] p. 369; Macgowan *et al.* [note 6] p. 178; Carlson [note 32] p. 121.

Chapter 5 Political Censorship of the Opera

1. Henry Raynor, *Music and Society since 1815* (New York, 1976) p. 6; Martin Cooper, *Beethoven: The Last Decade, 1817–1827* (London, 1970) p. 102; O. E. Deutsch, *Schubert: A Documentary Biography* (New York, 1977) p. 284.
2. Emile Heraszti, 'Berlioz, Liszt and the Rakoczy March', *Musical Quarterly*, 26 (1940) 229–30.
3. Maurice Mauron, *La Marseillaise* (Paris, 1968) pp. 161–4.
4. On censorship of song in general, see, for Austria, Deutsch [note 1] p. 610; for France, Alpert Delpit, 'La Liberté des Théâtres et les café-concerts', *Revue des deux mondes*, 133 (1878) 601–23; for Germany, Robert Sackett, *Popular Entertainment, Class and Politics in Munich, 1900–1923* (Cambridge, Mass., 1982).
5. David Kimbell, *Verdi in the Age of Italian Romanticism* (Cambridge, 1981) p. 25.
6. Raynor [note 1] pp. 4, 14.
7. Hans Fischer and Erich Kock, *Ludvig van Beethoven* (New York, 1970) p. 146.
8. L. W. Conolly, *The Censorship of English Drama, 1737–1824* (San Marino, Calif., 1976) p. 14; Richard Findlater, *Banned! A Review of Theatrical Censorship in Britain* (London, 1967) p. 61; Gerald Seaman, *History of Russian Music*, I (Oxford, 1967) 114; Edward Dent, *A History of Opera* (Baltimore, 1949) p. 53; Arnold Perris, *Music as Propaganda* (Westport, Conn., 1985) p. 17.
9. D. E. Emerson, *Metternich and the Political Police* (The Hague, 1968) p. 24; Crane Brinton, *A Decade of Revolution, 1789–1799* (New York, 1963) p. 178; Perris [note 8] pp. 9, 11; Richard Osborne, *Rossini* (London, 1986) p. 23.
10. Karin Pendle, *Eugène Scribe and French Opera of the Nineteenth Century* (Ann Arbor, Mich., 1979) p. 19; Raynor, [note 1] p. 10; Hector Berlioz, *Memoirs* (London, 1969) p. 363; Jacques Barzun, *Hector Berlioz and his Century* (New York, 1956) p. 225; T. J. Walsh, *Second Empire Opera: The Théâtre Lyrique, Paris, 1851–1870* (London, 1981) p. 21; Albert Boime, 'The Second Empire's Official Realism', in Gabriel Weisberg (ed.), *The European Realist Tradition* (Bloomington, Ind., 1982) p. 39.
11. Robert Oldani, '*Boris Godunov* and the Censor', *Nineteenth Century Music*, 2 (1978) 246, 250; Nicolai Rimsky-Korsakov, *My Musical Life* (New York, 1936) p. 108.
12. Raynor [note 1] pp. 8, 18, 130; Deutsch [note 1] pp. 128–30; Joseph Wechsberg, *Schubert* (New York, 1977) pp. 153, 178–9; Maurice Brown, *Schubert* (London, 1958) p. 130; Alice Hanson, *Musical Life in Biedermeier Vienna* (Cambridge, 1985) p. 46; Fischer and Kock [note 7] p. 146; Martin Gregor-Dellin, *Richard Wagner* (New York, 1983) p. 112; John Deathridge, *Wagner's 'Rienzi'* (Oxford, 1977) p. 50.
13. Raynor [note 1] pp. 8–9, 12; Marcel Prawy, *The Vienna Opera* (New York, 1970) pp. 17, 33; Herbert Weinstock, *Rossini* (New York, 1968) p. 107; John Crabbe, *Hector Berlioz* (London, 1980) p. 47.

14. Prawy [note 13] p. 39.
15. John Rosselli, *The Opera Industry in Italy from Cimarosa to Verdi* (Cambridge, 1984), p. 169.
16. Francis Toye, *Rossini* (London, 1954) p. 24.
17. R. J. Bosworth, 'Verdi and the Risorgimento', *Italian Quarterly*, 1971, p. 7.
18. Kimbell [note 5] p. 26; Nicholas Till, *Rossini: His Life and Times* (New York, 1983) p. 28; Rosselli [note 15] p. 85; William Ashbrook, *Donizetti* (London, 1965) p. 47; D. Rosen, 'Virtue Restored', *Opera News*, 42 (1977) 38.
19. Till [note 18] p. 35.
20. Perris [note 8] p. 3; Alexander Ringer, 'The Political uses of Opera in Revolutionary France', in *Bericht über den internationalen Musikwissenschaften* (Kassel, 1971) p. 238; James H. Billington, *Fire in the Minds of Men* (New York, 1980) pp. 152, 561.
21. Ringer [note 20] p. 240; Paul Lang, 'French Opera and the Spirit of Revolution', in Harold Pagliero (ed.), *Irrationalism in the Eighteenth Century* (Cleveland, 1972) pp. 106–8; Billington [note 20] p. 153; Walter Salmen, *The Social Status of the Professional Musician from the Middle Ages to the 19th Century* (New York, 1983), pp. 275–6.
22. John Stephens, *The Censorship of English Drama* (Cambridge, 1980) p. 83; Francis Abbiati, 'Years of *Un Ballo in Maschera*', *Verdi*, 1 (1960) 812.
23. Kimbell [note 5] p. 40; Rosselli [note 15] p. 82.
24. Kimbell [note 5] p. 22; Till [note 18] p. 24.
25. Billington [note 20] p. 155; Winton Dean, 'French Opera', in Gerald Abraham (ed.), *The Age of Beethoven, 1790–1830* (London, 1982) pp. 105, 112.
26. On *La Muette de Portici* and the Belgian revolution of 1830, see Frederick Artz, *Reaction and Revolution, 1814–1832* (New York, 1963) pp. 273–4; William Crosten, *French Grand Opera* (New York, 1948) p. 112; Billington [note 20] p. 156; Perris [note 8] p. 165.
27. Crosten [note 26] p. 112.
28. Billington [note 20] p. 156.
29. There are a great many biographies of Verdi, and most of them pay considerable attention to his problems with the censorship. The following paragraphs are, unless otherwise attributed, based on George Martin, *Verdi, His Music, Life and Times* (New York, 1963); James Budden, *Verdi* (London, 1985); Paul Hume, *Verdi: The Man and his Music* (New York, 1977); Francis Toye, *Giuseppe Verdi: His Life and Works* (New York, 1972); Joseph Wechsberg, *Verdi* (New York, 1976); Carlo Gatti, *Verdi: The Man and his Music* (New York, 1955); George Martin, 'Verdi and the Risorgimento', in William Weaver and Martin Chusid (eds), *The Verdi Companion* (New York 1979); Vincent Godefroy, *The Dramatic Genius of Verdi*, 2 vols (New York, 1975, 1977); Spike Hughes, *Verdi Operas* (Philadelphia, 1968); Charles Osborne, *The Complete Operas of Verdi* (New York, 1970); Abbiatti [note 22]; Bosworth [note 17]; Spike Hughes, 'Verdi and the Censors', *Musical Times*, 95

(1954) 651–3; Mary Matz, 'The Road to Boston', *Opera News*, 44 (1980) 12–14; Rosen [note 18] pp. 36–9.

30. Hume [note 29] p. 39.
31. Kimbell [note 5] p. 27; Till [note 18] p. 24.
32. Hume [note 29] pp. 3–4; Kimbell [note 5] p. 40.
33. Billington [note 20] pp. 54–5.
34. Dean [note 25] p. 105; Till [note 18] p. 119; Toye [note 16] pp. 148–9.
35. V. V. Yastrebtsev, *Reminiscences of Rimsky-Korsakov* (New York, 1985) pp. 102–3, 128–31; Gerald Abraham, *Rimsky-Korsakov* (London, 1945), pp. 47, 98–102; M. Montagu-Nathan, *Rimsky-Korsakov* (London, 1916) pp. 36, 57–8; Rimsky-Korsakov [note 11] pp. 107–9, 256–8; Robert Ridenous, *Nationalism, Modernism and Personal Rivalry in Nineteenth-Century Russian Music* (Ann Arbor, Mich., 1981) p. 202; Martin Cooper, *Russian Opera* (London, 1951) p. 48; Gerald Abraham, *Music of Tchaikovsky* (New York, 1946) p. 143.
36. Gerald Abraham, 'Satire and Symbol in *The Golden Cockerel*', *Music and Letters*, 52 (1971) 46–54; Montagu-Nathan [note 35] pp. 65–7; Abraham, *Rimsky-Korsakov* [note 35] pp. 115–25; Yastrebtsev, [note 35] pp. 350–477.
37. William Ashbrook, *Donizetti and his Opera* (Cambridge, 1982) p. 103; Matz [note 29] p. 14.
38. E. P. Lawrence, 'The Banned *Mikado*: A Topsy-Turvy Incident', *Centennial Review*, 18 (1974) 151–69; Alexander Faris, *Jacques Offenbach* (London, 1980) pp. 114, 144–7; James Harding, *Folies de Paris: The Rise and Fall of French Operetta* (London, 1979) p. 63.
39. Prawy [note 13] pp. 17–18; William Weaver, *The Golden Century of Italian Opera: From Rossini to Puccini* (London, 1980) pp. 58–9; Ashbrook [note 37] pp. 47, 495; Edward Dent, *The Rise of Romantic Opera* (Cambridge, 1976) p. 173.
40. See the sources cited in note 29.
41. Oldani [note 11] p. 246.
42. John Warrack, *Tchaikovsky* (New York, 1973) pp. 65–6; Herbert Weinstock, *Tchaikowsky* (New York, 1945) p. 93; Edwin Evans, *Tchaikovsky* (New York, 1967) p. 59.
43. Rosa Newmarch, *Russian Opera* (New York, n.d.) p. 338.
44. Faris [note 38] pp. 144–5, 157–8; Henry Krehbiel, *A Second Book of Operas* (Garden City, NY, 1926) p. 1; Toye [note 16] p. 80.
45. Charles Osborne, *Rigoletto* (London, 1979) p. 18; Jeremy Commons, '*Maria Stuarda* and the Neapolitan Censorship', *Donizetti Society Journal*, 3 (1977) 162.
46. Ashbrook [note 18] pp. 47–8.
47. Oldani [note 11] p. 246.
48. Herbert Weinstock, *Bellini* (New York, 1971) p. 94; Ashbrook [note 18] p. 143; Kimbell [note 5] p. 222.
49. Quotations in this paragraph are all taken from the following sources, which are cited in full in note 29 above, except where otherwise indicated: Hughes, 'Verdi and the Censors', p. 651; Toye, p. 69; Hume, p. 87; Wechsberg, p. 99; Kimbell [note 5] pp. 269, 279; Rosen, p. 39; Martin, p. 350; Abbiati [note 22] pp. 818–22.

50. Herbert Weinstock, *Donizetti and the World of Opera in Italy, Paris and Vienna in the First Half of the Nineteenth Century* (New York, 1963) pp. 202, 213; Ashbrook [note 37] p. 662.
51. Yastrebtsev [note 35] pp. 129, 391.
52. Raynor [note 1] pp. 11, 14.

Chapter 6 Political Censorship of the Cinema

1. Jay Leyda, *Kino: A History of the Russian and Soviet Film* (Princeton, NJ, 1983) pp. 72–73.
2. Gary Stark, 'Cinema, Society and the State: Policing the Film Industry in Imperial Germany', in Gary Stark and Bede Lackner, *Essays on Culture and Society in Modern Germany* (College Station, Tex., 1982) p. 124; D. J. Wenden, *The Birth of the Movies* (London, 1974) p. 90.
3. Neville Hunnings, *Film Censors and the Law* (London, 1967) p. 35; Wenden [note 2] p. 90; Stark [note 2] p. 125; Peter Kenez, *The Birth of the Propaganda State: Soviet Methods of Mass Mobilization* (Cambridge, 1985) p. 105; Richard Taylor, *The Politics of the Soviet Cinema* (Cambridge, 1979) p. 7.
4. Richard Taylor, *Film Propaganda* (London, 1979) p. 38.
5. Michael Chanan, *The Dream that Kicks: The Prehistory and Early Years of Cinema in Britain* (London, 1980) p. 255; Stark [note 2] 122.
6. Taylor [note 3] p. 4; Wenden [note 2] p. 105.
7. Wenden [note 2] p. 106; Taylor [note 4] p. 41; Taylor [note 3] pp. 8–9; Leyda [note 1] pp. 70–1; Chanan [note 5] pp. 253–4.
8. Richard Abel, *French Cinema* (Princeton, NJ, 1984) p. 38; Paul Leglise, *Histoire de la politique du cinéma français* (Paris, 1970) pp. 30–2; René Jeanne and Charles Ford, *Le Cinéma et la presse* (Paris, 1961) pp. 313–14; Leyda [note 1] p. 68; Stark [note 2] pp. 147–8; National Council of Public Morals, *The Cinema: Its Present Position and Future Possibilities* (London, 1917) pp. 314–15; Ivor Montagu, *The Political Censorship of Films* (London, 1929) pp. 30–2.
9. Taylor [note 4] p. 134; Stark [note 2] pp. 143, 156.
10. National Council of Public Morals [note 8] pp. 315–16; Taylor [note 3] p. 1; Leyda [note 1] p. 68.
11. Stark [note 2] p. 132.
12. Stark [note 2] p. 165.
13. Wenden [note 2] p. 116; John Trevelyan, *What the Censor Saw* (London, 1973) p. 26; National Council of Public Morals, [note 8] p. 319; Robin Lenman, 'Censorship and Society in Munich, 1890–1914' (Oxford PhD, 1975) p. 118.
14. Wenden [note 2] p. 116; Stark [note 2] pp. 126–7, 131; Mira Liehm, *The Most Important Art: Eastern European Film since 1945* (Berkeley, Calif., 1977) p. 12; Nicholas Powell, *The Sacred Spring: The Arts in Vienna, 1898–1918* (New York, 1974) p. 46; Peter Besas, *Behind the Spanish Lens* (Denver, 1985) p. 17; Taylor [note 3] p. 7; Hunnings [note 3] p. 311.

15. Leyda [note 1] p. 28; Wenden [note 2] p. 117; Taylor [note 3] pp. 6–7; Chanan [note 5] p. 255.
16. Montagu [note 8] p. 33; Leglise [note 8] p. 31; Stark [note 2] p. 129.
17. Abel [note 8] p. 38.
18. The texts of the Spanish, Swedish and Italian film-censorship regulations are printed in National Council of Public Morals [note 8] pp. 314–31. Norway is briefly discussed in this source at pp. 326–7, as well as in UNESCO, *The Film Industry in Six European Countries* (Paris, 1950) p. 73. There are brief mentions of Norway and Sweden in John Harley, *World-wide Influences of the Cinema: A Study of Official Censorship and the International Cultural Aspects of Motion Pictures* (Los Angeles, 1940) pp. 169, 186. Additional material on Spain is included in Besas [note 14] p. 17. Discussions of the Danish and French systems are included in Hunnings [note 3] pp. 307–12, 332–9. For France, see also Abel [note 8] pp. 38–9; and Leglise [note 8] pp. 29–33. The British system is discussed in James C. Robertson, *The British Board of Film Censors* (London, 1985); Montagu [note 8]; Hunnings [note 3] pp. 29–61; Trevelyan [note 13] pp. 23–33; Rachel Low, *The History of the British Film, 1906–1914* (London, 1949) pp. 84–91; Guy Phelps, *Film Censorship* (London, 1975); Ernest Betts, *A History of British Cinema* (London, 1973) pp. 47–9; and Dorothy Knowles, *The Censor, the Drama and the Film, 1900–1934* (London, 1934) pp. 167–276. Stark [note 2] pp. 122–66, contains a superior account of the German censorship.
19. Leyda [note 1] p. 29.
20. Paul Monaco, *Cinema and Society: France and Germany during the Twenties* (New York, 1976) pp. 52–3; Daniel Cook, *A History of Narrative Film* (New York, 1981) p. 111; M. S. Phillips, 'Nazi Control of the German Film Industry', *Journal of European Studies*, 1 (1971) 43; Montagu [note 8] 230; Kate Betz, 'As the Tycoons Die: Class-Struggle and Censorship in the Russian Cinema, 1917–1921', in Nils Nilsson (ed.), *Art, Society, Revolution: Russia, 1917–1921* (Stockholm, 1979) pp. 198–236.
21. Stark [note 2] p. 153.
22. Stark [note 2] p. 138.
23. Hunnings [note 3] p. 311.
24. National Council of Public Morals [note 8] p. 318.
25. Stark [note 2] p. 142.
26. Trevelyan [note 13] p. 25.
27. Low [note 18] p. 85.
28. Hunnings [note 3] p. 336; Leglise [note 8] p. 37.
29. Stark [note 2] p. 136.
30. Robertson [note 18] p. 7; Stark [note 2] pp. 147–8; National Council of Public Morals [note 8] pp. 316, 319, 328.
31. Michael Stoil, *Cinema beyond the Danube* (Metuchen, NJ, 1974) pp. 40–2.
32. Hunnings [note 3] pp. 310, 334; Low [note 18] pp. 90–1; Leglise [note 8] p. 30.
33. Low [note 18] pp. 90–1; Leglise [note 8] p. 32; Stephen Bottomore, 'Dreyfus and Documentary', *Sight and Sound*, 53 (1984) 292.

34. Montagu [note 8] pp. 12, 14; Knowles [note 18] pp. 197–248; Margaret Dickinson and Sarah Street, *Cinema and State: The Film Industry and the Government, 1927–84* (London, 1985) p. 8; Monaco [note 20] p. 52. See generally Nicholas Pronay, 'The Political Censorship of Films in Britain between the Wars', in Nicholas Pronay and D. W. Spring (eds), *Propaganda, Politics and Film, 1918–45* (London, 1982) pp. 98–125; Marcel Le Pierre, *Les Cent Visages du Cinema* (Paris, 1948) pp. 269–86.
35. Taylor [note 3] pp. 4, 8; Taylor [note 4] p. 37; Leyda [note 1] pp. 19–20, 29–30, 48–9.
36. Leyda [note 1] p. 27.
37. Stark [note 2] pp. 143–7.
38. David Welch, 'The Proletarian Cinema and the Weimar Republic', *Historical Journal of Film, Radio and Television*, 1 (1981) 4.
39. Wenden [note 2] p. 137; Richard Taylor, 'Agitation, Propaganda and the Cinema: The Search for New Solution', in Nilsson [note 20] pp. 237–61.

Chapter 7   Conclusions

1. Jean-Pierre Bechu, *La Belle Epoque et son envers: quand caricature écrit l'histoire* (Paris, 1980) p. 54. F. W. J. Hemmings, *Culture and Society in France, 1848–1898* (London, 1971) p. 53.
2. *L'Eclipse*, 20 Sep 1874.
3. Odile Krakovitch, *Hugo censuré: la liberté au théâtre au XIXe siècle* (Paris, 1985) pp. 150, 286; Odile Krakovitch, 'Les Romantiques et la censure au théâtre', *Revue d'histore du théâtre*, 36 (1984) 65.
4. Horst Claus, *The Theatre Director Otto Brahm* (Ann Arbor, Mich., 1981) p. 71.
5. Richard Findlater, *Banned! A Review of Theatrical Censorship in Britain* (London, 1967) p. 91.
6. B. V. Varneke, *History of the Russian Theatre* (New York, 1971) pp. 203–4.
7. See for example Peter Amann, *Revolution and Mass Democracy: The Paris Club Movement in 1848* (Princeton, NJ, 1975); P. H. Noyes, *Organization and Revolution: Working Class Associations in the German Revolutions of 1848–1849* (Princeton, NJ, 1966); and Sidney Harcave, *The Russian Revolution of 1905* (New York, 1970).
8. George Martin, *The Red Shirt and the Cross of Savoy: The Story of Italy's Risorgimento* (New York, 1969) p. 219.
9. Richard Taylor, *Film Propaganda* (London, 1979) p. 41.

Index

229